SPONSORSHIP
What it is and how to use it

Steve Sleight

McGRAW-HILL BOOK COMPANY
London · New York · St Louis · San Francisco · Auckland
Bogotá · Guatemala · Hamburg · Lisbon · Madrid · Mexico
Montreal · New Delhi · Panama · Paris · San Juan · São Paulo
Singapore · Sydney · Tokyo · Toronto

Published by
McGRAW-HILL Book Company (UK) Limited
MAIDENHEAD · BERKSHIRE · ENGLAND

British Library Cataloguing in Publication Data
Sleight, Steve
    Sponsorship.
    1. Great Britain. Sponsorship by business
    firms
    I. Title
    658.8'2

ISBN 0-07-707084-4

Library of Congress Cataloging-in-Publication Data
Sleight, Steve.
    Sponsorship : what it is and how to use it / Steve Sleight.
        p.   cm.
    Bibliography: p
    Includes index.
    ISBN 0-07-707084-4 : £17.95
    1. Sports——Economic aspects. 2. Public relations——Sports.
3. Corporate sponsorship. 4. Marketing. I. Title.
GV716.S53   1989
338.4'7796——dc19   88-39365
                                                            CIP

1234 CUP 9089

Typeset by
STYLESET LIMITED · Warminster · Wiltshire

Printed in Great Britain at the
University Press, Cambridge.

Contents

Preface

Several friends asked me during the writing of this book, 'Why a book on sponsorship?' As the project developed and became inevitably more complex so the reply grew shorter until, 'It seemed a good idea at the time' became the standard retort.

This book grew out of my experiences with sponsorship; as a seeker of funds for my own sporting projects and those of others, later as a sports journalist and television producer covering many sponsored events, and also for a time running a sponsorship agency, I found myself at one stage or another experiencing most of the frustrations that this marketing medium has to offer.

Although I have no formal training in marketing the many apparent contradictions I came across in the world of sponsorship fascinated me. Quite simply I was one of the many people feeling their way in a relatively new marketing medium that was confusing because of its diversity and because, unlike most marketing techniques, it involves a business relationship between, at best, organizations with vastly different aims and, at worst, a commercial company and an amateur organization or individual with different needs and expectations.

This book is an attempt to take a step back from the hype and hyperbole that often accompanies talk of sponsorship and to try to define the place this commercial relationship has in the context of business marketing and the funding of leisure activities. It then moves on to the practical side of making sponsorship work and examines the ways in which companies can select sponsorships and utilize them to the fullest. The final part takes a look at the problems of finding, working with and keeping a sponsor.

The most surprising discovery I made while researching this book was that few marketing people were prepared to discuss the use of sponsorship in any detailed way. Many would talk around the subject, professing to utilize the medium in a marketing-led way, but when specific questions were asked the invariable response was to the effect that such information was confidential. To a degree, of course, this was true. Some aspects of the way a company chooses, uses and researches its sponsorships need to be kept from competitors, but most of the time, especially when discussing case histories of past sponsorships, there is no need for coyness. Unless, that is, one wishes to avoid the fact that sponsorship is not used as effectively as it could be.

While the fund of corporate experience with sponsorship has now grown to a level sufficient to demonstrate the benefits and the pitfalls, it is still true that many decisions are made for the use of this particular communications medium that wouldn't bear the spotlight of disciplined marketing scrutiny. Choices are still made on the basis of senior management's personal interest rather than demonstrable marketing benefits and the effective utilization of a sponsorship project across the full range of marketing opportunities is still less common than it could be.

The situation is, however, changing as experience is shared among marketing personnel through direct experience and the growing amount of literature and seminars dealing with the industry. As the use of sponsorship has developed so marketing departments have found an increasing need to be knowledgeable in new areas. Sponsors now have to understand something of the leisure activities with which they become involved, the politics of sport and the arts, and they must develop new knowledge of the world of publicity and the changes now taking place in the media.

If this book helps add to this fund of experience it is due to the many individuals who did give freely of their time and knowledge; omissions or errors, however, are due to me alone!

While not wishing to delay the reader with a list of those who helped, special thanks are due to Mick De Haas whose help and encouragement were invaluable and whose wide-ranging experience with international sponsorships, both within major companies and while running his own consultancy, made him a most valuable source of knowledge and advice.

Finally, to Nick and Pauline who suffered the experience of living with a writer at work and who stayed smiling to the end, my very grateful thanks.

Steve Sleight
Cowes

Acknowledgements

Thanks to *Sports Marketing News* for permission to use information and statistics previously published in that periodical, and to Sports inc., *The Sports Business Weekly* for permission to reproduce statistics from the premier issue.

Thanks too to the following organizations for the use of illustrations: United Distillers, Texaco Limited, The Football League Limited, Rothmans International, Mick De Haas Sponsorship Consultants Limited, Allsport, Help the Aged.

Part One

What is sponsorship?

1

Patronage, exploitation or self-indulgence?

Sponsorship: three syllables that form what must be one of the most abused and misunderstood words in the English language! Certainly there can be few business tools that, when mentioned to level-headed, rational and normally open-minded business people, frequently cause such a tearing of hair and gnashing of teeth as to suggest that the listener has certain, not complimentary, opinions on the subject.

In order to suggest some reasons why a seemingly innocent business activity creates such misapprehension we need to start from the secure base of a widely agreed definition of the activity. But, not suprisingly, that's where the problems start since there are almost as many definitions of sponsorship as there are people involved with the subject. Turning to a dictionary is little help in explaining a marketing phenomenon that has developed from nothing to a worldwide, billion-dollar industry in a few short years.

According to the *Shorter Oxford Dictionary*, for instance, a sponsor is *one who enters into an engagement on behalf of another; a surety*; while *The Concise Oxford Dictionary* defines a sponsor as *a person who makes himself responsible for another*; and *The Penguin Pocket English Dictionary* says that a sponsor is *somebody who pays for a project or activity*. This last definition is, I'm sure, one that many corporate marketing executives will recognize with horror, for it describes exactly an attitude that recognizes only one side of the business equation and which the industry is only now beginning to eradicate.

For the purposes of this book I shall define sponsorship as follows:

> Sponsorship is a business relationship between a provider of funds, resources or services and an individual, event or organization which offers in return some rights and association that may be used for commercial advantage.

The sponsor is the provider of the funds, resources or services and is normally a corporate body rather than an individual. Throughout this book I shall refer to the beneficiary or the sponsorship as the *recipient*, whether this is an individual, event or organization, rather than use the somewhat ugly term *sponsee* that is now often found in the industry's literature. The *rights and association* referred to will be covered in detail later, but can include any connection or arrangement with the recipient which the latter is prepared to sell or assign, and which may be used by the sponsor for his or her own commercial benefit.

Although we are obliged to use the term sponsorship because it is the one most commonly used to cover this rather amorphous area of business promotion, I suggest that another term, 'lifestyle marketing', perhaps better describes the activity with which most professional 'sponsors' are involved. An explanation for this will be found in Part Two when we look in detail at the opportunities offered by this marketing activity.

The most important terms in the definition above are *business relationship* and *commercial advantage*. Sponsorship in today's commercial world has, or should have, nothing whatsoever to do with charity or patronage.

Charity and patronage

Although sponsorship should not be confused with charity or patronage that is not to say that such altruism should never be contemplated by companies, rather that the reasons for doing so are more likely to be connected with humanistic or community considerations than for any to do with the bottom-line corporate performance.

At best, a company making a sizeable charitable donation, to a museum say, may wish to publicize the fact in order to support or improve its public image and to demonstrate a 'caring', 'public-spirited' attitude. It is usually impossible to measure such an exercise in terms of the 'bottom line' but other considerations such as tax advantages may make the gift appropriate.

In comparison, the sponsorship of an exhibition in the same museum may make hard commercial sense if the company's sponsorship can be effectively publicized to the visitors the exhibition will attract. If that audience is large enough, and has the correct profile for the company's marketing needs, then the sponsorship may be commercially successful.

Patronage — which I differentiate from charitable donations only in the sense that the recipient need not be a charity — is an activity with which companies are unlikely to be involved. All definitions of patronage imply that it is the provision of funds or support to an individual or organization on a non-commercial, altruistic basis. Thus a wealthy individual may help support the activities of an artist, writer or adventurer, or contribute funds to a charity, for no other reason than personal satisfaction and belief in the 'worthiness' of the cause. Such generosity is laudable and, indeed, very important to the continuing health of sport, the arts and the encouragement of talented individuals. But since it is usually a one-way arrangement, it cannot be justified on strictly commercial grounds.

Although many patrons actively dislike any publicity surrounding their generosity, some provide support in return for public acknowledgement and the associated boost to their image. After all, if your aim is status in the community and, perhaps, the bonus of some public honour, there may not be many alternatives open to you!

Yet despite this cynicism, patronage has an illustrious history and has been instrumental in encouraging and supporting many of the world's finest artists, sportspersons, explorers and adventurers, not to mention the role it has played in the advancement of science. Patronage today appears to be declining although accurate figures to demonstrate the level of activity are difficult to obtain because of its very individual nature.

Despite the rapid increase in commercial sponsorship in the eighties this still growing source of funds for sport, the arts, recreational activities and community projects is unable to provide significant support for the types of recipient who previously may have attracted patronage.

Young athletes, artists, writers or adventurers have great difficulty in attracting sponsorship funds since they are unlikely to have much to offer commercially until success rewards them with fame and publicity. Although sponsorship funds are increasingly finding their way into the grass-roots activities of many sports and, to a lesser extent, within the arts, such funds are usually directed towards group training or competitions since few sponsors are prepared to take the risk of associating themselves with even the most promising newcomer during the time when such individuals are most in need of support and encouragement. While sports governing bodies and arts associations are beginning to allocate a proportion of sponsorship funds raised from their top-class events to provide for the needs of young talent this practice is still not widespread enough to deal with a problem that could be eased considerably by the encouragement of patronage, probably through the use of tax incentives.

There is little doubt that most sporting or arts bodies, not to mention individual sportspersons and artists, would much prefer to receive their funds through patronage or charitable donations since such funds are not only untainted with any hint of commercialism, with which many individuals feel uncomfortable, but also impose significantly fewer problems and requirements on the recipient. If a company or individual makes a charitable donation, whether on a one-off basis or by providing support over a period of time, the obligations imposed on the recipient are relatively small. At most the donation, if substantial, may be publicized depending on the wishes of the donor, and the patron may be entertained as a

VIP and provided with a few fringe benefits, but after that the recipient can get on with the job of spending the money. As we shall see, the requirements imposed on the recipient by sponsorship are, or should be, considerably greater and will demand a degree of professionalism more appropriate to a commercial enterprise than a non-profit-making institution or an individual athlete or artist.

Unfortunately, however, the number of organizations competing for a slice of the charitable cake has grown considerably in recent years. We are now all assailed, whether as individuals or companies, by requests for donations to organizations active in areas as diverse as conservation, the care of the elderly, political pressure groups, child welfare, Third World aid, and many, many more. Some of these charities exist because central governments have taken a political decision to rely on the ability of such organizations to tap the public's generosity rather than to pay for such activities out of central funds.

In response to this growing competition most charities have responded by improving their own marketing efforts, directed at both the general public and the business sector, to the point where many are now very professional with a full-time staff of managers, publicists and fund-raisers. Having made this great improvement in marketing to their traditional sources of funds, moreover, many charitable organizations are now weighing up the possible benefits of corporate sponsorship as an additional and new source of funds from companies that do not normally make sizeable charitable donations.

Exploitation or self-indulgence?

So, if sponsorship is not the same as charity or patronage, do the other common misconceptions of sponsorship — that it results in exploitation of sports and the arts, or is simply the self-indulgence of company executives — have some founding in fact?

As sponsorship has boomed in recent years more and more companies, sports and arts bodies, agencies and independent promoters have been drawn into a business relationship the complexity of which few have understood from the outset. This has led inevitably to problems as practitioners have experienced varying degrees of success. Few would deny that many companies first became involved with sponsorship in ways that would be quite unacceptable in any other area of business marketing. Although there has generally been a feeling among marketing executives that sponsorship has something to offer in the marketing mix, many individuals drawn into sponsorship have been uncertain what these supposed advantages really are, or how to make maximum use of individual sponsorships.

It is not uncommon, when discussing sponsorship with individuals from all sides of the business, to hear nearly as many horror stories as examples of a well-run activity. While this is almost certainly because the failures are intrinsically more interesting than the success stories, and do not reflect the true situation, there have certainly been enough problems in a number of sponsorships to cause some observers to accuse corporate sponsors of false motives in their dealing with sport and the arts.

Accusations of exploitation arise most often when the benefits to a sponsor can be seen without equivalent benefits seemingly accruing to the activity being sponsored, or to the general public. This most commonly happens when a governing body or other organization arranges a major sponsorship to support one of its high-profile events or activities. Unless the governing body demonstrates that the sponsorship also benefits the sport as a whole, and in particular grass-roots participants, the sponsorship may be perceived as divisive or irrelevant to the sport and the sponsor charged, fairly or unfairly, with exploitation for his own commercial ends.

While sponsorship will always suffer the taint of exploitation because of its necessary commercial nature, it is not inevitably exploitative. More and more sponsors now appreciate the often complicated relationship in which they have become a partner, and take great pains to provide far more than simple financial support to the recipient in order to make the deal work. We are also seeing more and more sponsorships aimed at grass-roots participants, especially the young, as sponsors recognize the marketing opportunities offered by such an audience and the long-term benefits that can accrue from being involved with an activity at both top and grass-roots levels.

The other common charge aimed at corporate sponsors is one of self-indulgence. This arises when a sponsorship is perceived to be undertaken on the whim of a senior executive, usually the chairman or managing director, rather than for genuine commercial reasons. There is no doubt that some companies have entered, and, I'm afraid to say, still do enter, into sponsorships for exactly this reason, but it is becoming less common as an understanding of the commercial nature of sponsorship becomes more wide-spread. Three years ago I was horrified to hear a senior marketing executive of the world's best-known computer manufacturer explain that, while they always analysed their sponsorship requirements and the opportunities offered to them in some detail, it was not unusual for the key decision-maker to become enthusiastic about a sponsorship opportunity which in reality had little to offer the company. When that happened the chairman often approved the deal leaving the sponsorship department to invent all the reasons why the decision was based on sound commercial sense!

Anyone in the sponsorship business will have many similar stories to tell, and few would disagree that there is no more frus-trating an approach for the seller of a sponsorship, or a company's own specialists, to deal with. Although the attitude has all but dis-appeared within major companies with a history of sponsorship behind them, it can still be found among new sponsors and will continue to frustrate all who encounter it.

The cost of leisure

A key reason why sponsorship has seen such tremendous growth in the last ten years or so can be traced back to the changing social and political climate that has affected most of Europe and North

America. And the most significant factor in this changing environ-ment has been the greatly increased amount of leisure time individuals now enjoy. Advances in technology have reduced the need for armies of manual workers and shortened the length of the average working week; while unemployment has forced many to adapt to an enforced non-working environment. For those in work a steady increase in their standard of living has resulted in less need for overtime working and a consequent increase in the time, and money, available for leisure pursuits. Add to these factors the increase in life expectancy due to improved health care and the lowering of the age of retirement, and we find a growing number of people with time to spend on non-work activities.

This rapid growth in the time and resources available for leisure has resulted in a booming industry that has become an increasingly important economic feature in the developed countries over the last forty years or so. Unfortunately, the provision of leisure facilities tends to be a very expensive exercise. Not only are the capital costs of facilities large and increasing, but the leisure industry also tends to be very labour-intensive with consequently high wage bills. Most leisure facilities require considerable numbers of staff either directly employed in the provision of the service, or indirectly employed in support roles. Thus a sports stadium housing a football club requires not only a team of players, coaches and an administrative staff, but will also need groundspeople, maintenance staff, cleaners, ticket staff, medical support, and many more specialized personnel on a full- or part-time basis.

The situation is no different when one looks at the provision of resources in the arts or community life. Most have high capital costs due to the need to provide specialist facilities, and also carry the burden of high labour requirements and consequent costs.

In many countries the demand for leisure services not only exceeds supply and is still growing, but the cost of providing services is also increasing rapidly. In the past the problem has been partly obscured by the role played by wealthy individuals who could afford to subsidize facilities for the less well off, and were

prepared to do so in order to have the benefit of the facilities themselves. Whether as individual patrons of sport or the arts, or as
members of clubs and organizations that relied on their wealth
and generosity, such 'pragmatic altruism' helped finance leisure
for a wider range of people. But as the real cost of providing leisure
resources has risen steeply, the number of individuals who can
afford such generosity has rapidly decreased.

If the situation were governed by simple economic laws of
demand and supply, one would expect the consumer to be
prepared to meet the costs if he or she really wanted to take advantage
of leisure-time activities. This is not the case, however, for three
main reasons. First, the real cost of providing new facilities is often
prohibitively high. Secondly, many people cannot afford to
increase their spending on leisure, especially the unemployed who
have long periods of enforced leisure time to fill. And thirdly, there
is a widespread public belief that leisure facilities are of such social
importance that their provision should be a matter, at least in part,
for local and central governments.

The role of the state

The view that leisure resources should be subsidized by the state is
based on the belief that the opportunity to participate in sport and
the arts is a fundamental right in a modern society; is necessary for
the well-being of individuals; and should be available to all irrespec-
tive of an individual's ability to pay. Thus proponents argue from
the same position as supporters of a 'free' health or education
service.

The amount of support given by individual governments to their
native sports and arts institutions varies considerably, as do the
funds available at local government or state level. Governmental
attitudes to leisure range considerably. The Eastern European
states provide extensive central support for sports and the arts.
Countries like Great Britain have government ministers for sport
and the arts, and provide some central funds through such
organizations as the Sports and Arts Councils, with further significant

sums coming from local authorities. While in the USA the view is that leisure facilities are, principally, the responsibility of the private sector, whether through commercial funding, patronage and charity, or sponsorship.

But whatever the amount of government support, in times of economic recession the funds available from all public sources tend to evaporate first since they are rarely regarded as essential areas of expenditure. Add to this the changing attitudes in the last ten to fifteen years to the role of central government in the provision of public services and it is clear that sport and the arts cannot rely on government for their existence. When governments reduce even health and education to a strictly economic cost-benefit analysis, without including difficult-to-measure social benefits in the equation, it comes as no surprise to find an increasing insistence on the need for private enterprise to find a way to balance the demand and supply equation.

This economistic view can be demonstrated to be extremely simplistic even when one ignores the social factors and considers only the purely economic benefits offered by healthy industries surrounding sports and the arts. And industries they are. Figures published by Sports inc., *The Sports Business Weekly*, show that in 1986 the American Gross National Sports Product — the economic input to the US economy from sports-related activity — was a staggering $47.2 billion, up 7 per cent from $44 billion in 1985. This places the sports industry 25th in the top 50 US industries, well ahead of the motion picture industry at $8.5 billion, or the tobacco industry at $12.7 billion. In Britain, in 1986, the sports industry accounted for a £6.85 billion boost to the economy and provided a government revenue of £2.4 billion, almost five times the level of public expenditure on sport.

All this money comes from the huge infrastructure that surrounds sport, as it does the arts. If people are attracted to an event they become consumers, not just of the event itself, but all the extras that surround it. Hence the growth of merchandising and the value of concessions at major venues. The golf supporter who visits the British or US Open is also a consumer of golf equipment, magazines, refreshments, club memberships, coaching, golf books, clothing, videos, tickets to events, etc. Beyond the obvious areas of ticket sales, concessions and sporting goods, the net extends even further to take in advertising, television fees, gambling and a hundred and one other activities that have grown up to service the spectator and participant. Sport and the arts are also significant earners of foreign currency since both are truly international industries and attract considerable levels of tourism and the import/export of goods and services. One does not need to use the argument that healthy sporting and artistic resources are good for national prestige, aid international relations and have numerous other intangible benefits to suggest that these industries will continue to grow in social and economic importance. The only argument will be over the role central and local governments should play in the provision of basic funding.

In many countries this role is steadily shrinking and sports and arts communities have had to adjust to finding alternative funds from a variety of sources. The very fact that many organizations have by and large succeeded in doing so does, of course, weaken the case for government intervention but also serves to highlight the hidden costs that have to be paid. Forced to become commercial in order to survive, sports and, to a lesser but increasing degree, the arts have had to change their attitudes and practices at every level of their operations — sometimes to such an extent that the very nature of the activity changes almost beyond recognition. So, sports and the arts are changing to suit the climate of the societies in which they exist, may be suffering in some cases from the need to be 'commercial' and 'professional', and are occasionally in danger of being accused of existing to fulfil commercial requirements rather than the needs of the consumer.

2

The business of sport

Before we turn to examine the business of sponsorship in detail we should take a look at the huge industry that sport has become in order to put sponsorship in perspective and to see what influences sports today. We shall concentrate on sport here because the arts industry, although not insignificant, is well behind sport in its commercial self-exploitation.

In Chapter 1 I introduced the fact that sport is now big business on both sides of the Atlantic. That will probably come as little surprise if you have taken note recently of the huge sums now earned by top sportsmen, be they golfers, racing drivers, boxers or athletes, but the actual scale of the business will probably stagger you.

For instance, a report on the economic impact of sport in the United Kingdom prepared for the Sports Council by the Henley Centre of Forecasting demonstrated that consumer spending on sport, excluding gambling, is well above public spending on other leisure activities such as DIY, books and magazines, audio equipment, records and tapes, pets, gardening, photography and home computing. Include just over one billion pounds from sports-related gambling and consumer spending on sports amounts to £4.36 billion. This includes £700 million on clothing, a similar amount for goods and equipment, and £500 million for fees and participation. As the Director General of the Sports Council told an American sports marketing audience, UK citizens spend more on sport then they do on bread!

The value added to the British economy by sport is greater than that from the manufacture of motor vehicles, drink, tobacco and textiles. Sports also account for some 376 000 jobs in Britain, about the same as the chemical industry but greater than are employed in agriculture, electricity, gas and other energy sources, and the motor vehicle industry.

As one would expect, the figures for the United States are even more impressive. While the first British study suggests a conservative total of £6.85 billion, those from an equally conservative and also first-time US study show an industry generating, in 1986, an awesome $47.2 billion, up 7 per cent from 1985. And, although historic figures do not exist in Britain or the USA, rising attendance and participation in sports suggest that the sports economy is growing faster than the overall economy and will continue to increase in economic importance.

One of the most interesting facts to emerge from this survey and that conducted on behalf of the British Sports Council is the relative economic importance of spectator and participant sports. According to the British Minister for Sport, Colin Moynihan, himself a keen sportsman and rowing medallist, for every hour of professional sport there are another 1000 hours of amateur participation. This is reflected in the fact that, although spectator sports capture the media headlines and account for most revenue from sponsorship, endorsements and television rights fees, it is the participant sports that are far more important in the total economic sporting picture thanks to the power of the consumer in purchasing sports-related goods and services.

Consider yachting, for instance. Despite the recent success of the America's Cup in capturing the world's sporting headlines, a large number of international quality competitive events and many millions of dollars of corporate sponsorship, the top-class competitive side of sailing (along with powerboating and windsurfing) is dwarfed in economic importance by the vast army of casual competitors and leisure sailors. Their spending on equipment and associated services added up to an industry turnover in Britain of some £500 million in 1986 (up from £394 million in 1985), while

Table 2.1   The breakdown of the US sporting dollar

Category		$ millions 1986
Participant/leisure sports		16 230
Sporting goods		15 100
Advertising:		3 612
magazines	512	
newspapers	2 700	
stadium signage	400	
Spectator sports (gate receipts)		3 100
Legal gambling (net take)		2 681
Concessions, souvenirs and novelties		1 920
Television rights		1 080
Corporate sponsorships		800
Endorsement fees		500
License fees for retail sports properties		487.5
Sports magazines purchases		412
Golf course construction		400
Sports book purchases		270
Stadium construction		236
Trading cards		200
Sports insurance		155
Olympic budgets		23
US Olympic team		44
Halls of fame		1.8
		47 252.3

spending in the US on pleasure boats and accessories alone amounted to some £7.4 billion (up from $6.7 billion in 1985).

Yachting is by no means the only large participant sport that, at its international, competitive end, is trying to achieve some of the status, and income, of the major spectator and television sports. Sports aiming at this sort of growth and development often assume commercial sponsorship is the first or only source of new funds, so it is worth looking at some other areas from which income is generated by the major sports.

Gate receipts

The most obvious source of income for any spectator sport, be it American football, soccer, cricket or basketball, is gate receipts. Indeed, gate receipts formed virtually the exclusive source of income for many sports until the advent of television and the phenomenon of sports marketing. Spectators wanted to see their favourite team perform and were prepared to pay for the privilege, thus providing the revenue to cover team expenses and overheads. In the days of amateur sport this source of income was by far the most important, and often the only one available to meet the costs of providing the entertainment to the public.

The size of receipts from ticket sales is predictably staggering, as seem to be all the figures associated with the marketing of modern sports. And for sheer scale, where else to turn for examples than US sport. In 1988 73 500 spectators packed into the Super Bowl XXII in San Diego bringing a ticket sale revenue of $7.26 million and helping contribute to an NFL single-event profit of $14 million. And that doesn't include the profit made by ticket touts who sold $100 tickets for up to $3000 for the best seats in the stadium.

Although gate receipts account for only one-fifteenth of the total US sports industry they still amounted to a $3.1 billion input in 1986. Of this total, college football provided $436 million, professional football another $241 million, $361 million from baseball and $179 million from professional basketball. And, as with most aspects of sports marketing, there is nothing like team success or competitive action to boost ticket sales. An increase in average attendance for Syracuse University basketball games from 35 000 to 50 000 meant an increase in ticket revenue of up to $225 000 per game. That is a lot of money in anybody's terms and highlights the pressures on the players, managers and promoters of modern sport, especially when one realizes that the multiplier effect of increased revenues from merchandising, concessions, television deals and endorsements means that all aspects of sports marketing thrive on winners and cannot be manufactured by even the most creative marketer without the important element of success in competition.

As the costs of providing sport to the public have increased, not only because of the rise in the cost of facilities but also through the increasing complexity of sport and the development of professionalism, ticket revenues have been insufficient to meet the total costs of events. The providers of sport have thus discovered the price resistance factor — or that there is a limit to what the viewing public will pay for admittance to a game.

Fortunately for sports enthusiasts — and the industry surrounding them — the development and growth of televised sports coverage has not only provided increased access to sport for armchair spectators, but it has also helped bring an increased sophistication to the marketing of sport. From extra revenues through television rights deals, the creation of an enlarged audience for the merchandising of consumer goods, the attraction of in-stadium advertising signage, the image boost for major events and the attraction of corporate sponsorship, television is intrinsically linked with most aspects of modern sports marketing. Compared with the enormous television audiences enjoyed by some sports, the live audiences are relatively insignificant, although their spend per head on associated merchandising is probably higher, but their importance to the 'feel' and 'atmosphere' of an event is of paramount importance. What, for instance, would the Super Bowl, the FA Cup Final, the US Open or Wimbledon be without their live audiences? It is certain that any of these events would not be the valuable television properties they are if tens or hundreds of thousands of people did not compete for tickets to see the events live.

And it's not a one-way street, despite the fears of some sports administrators that over-exposure by television can damage attendance at live events. Television raises the awareness of its audience for sport and helps present a new variety to the public. If the product is attractive the chances are that some armchair spectators will be converted to live attendance, especially if the sport is sensitive to the opportunities offered by television exposure. Even if they can't, the television viewer is still a potential customer for a team's or sport's merchandising or a sponsor's message.

Concessions and merchandising

One of the advantages of attracting a large audience to an event is the revenue that can be earned from the sale of concessions for the right to market consumer goods to the spectators. Each spectator is a potential customer for drinks, food, snacks, memorabilia, programmes and a variety of other goods that are limited only by the imagination of the supplier. According to Sports inc., a typical New York Rangers game at Madison Square Garden will see the concessionaire sell 20 000 hot dogs, 15 000 beers, 10 000 sodas, 2500 programmes, 500 year books, and 10 000 pennants, flags and T-shirts. Gross revenue from concessions for each game is about $80 000. The US market for sports concessions is estimated to be a $1.9 billion business, although many believe this to be a very conservative figure!

Whether a team or stadium management choose to operate on-site retail outlets themselves or to lease the concession to an independent operator will depend on individual circumstances and preferences, but merchandising designed to be sold on the back of the team's or event's image is usually contracted out via a licensing arrangement in return for a fee plus a percentage of sales. And, once again, a successful team or event can attract an enormous extra revenue by attaching its name and/or logo to a variety of consumer products. The logo of Super Bowl XXII was licensed to 90 products and earned a reported $20 million for the NFL, almost three times the income from ticket sales to the game.

Licensing is a booming area of the sports business with player, team and event names and logos appearing on a fast-expanding range of products, from T-shirts, sweat-shirts, caps, shorts, track-suits, jewellery, pins and badges, and just about anything else you can imagine a customer will buy. As spectators and television viewers come to identify ever more closely with their favourite team or player their willingness to purchase goods that display that identification has helped fuel a huge growth in licensing and merchandising. It is not only sport that has benefited from this relatively recent phenomenon, although it has led the way and accounts for the major share. The music business has also caught on to the opportunities offered by licensing and promises to be a fast-growing area in the future.

Endorsements

Endorsements are another area of modern sports marketing that feed on the general public's interest in, and identification with, their favourite sports and sporting personalities. An endorsement usually consists of a business deal between an individual sports star and a company that believes that the star's name and implied approval will directly increase sales of a product with which the star can be clearly associated. The potential of endorsements is amply demonstrated by the $110 million of sales Nike achieved when basketball player Michael Jordan endorsed the Air Jordan line of basketball sneakers during his first successful season in 1984/85 with the Chicago Bulls. When Jordan missed most of the following season through injury, sales revenue from the sneakers dropped to a mere $5 million.

Although continuing and public success is usually regarded as the key to any player's ability to command large endorsement fees, the world's top earner in the endorsement business, the golfer Arnold Palmer earned a reported $8 million in 1987 despite not having won a PGA Tour title for fourteen years. Palmer's success comes from his perceived public image as the most trusted American sports personality. Companies such as Hertz, United Airlines and Sears employ Palmer to provide the positive image associations of integrity, loyalty and credibility.

Number two in the endorsement league is another American golfer, Jack Nicklaus, along with the German tennis player Boris Becker, both with reported earnings of about $6 million. Another golfer, Greg Norman, follows with $4.5 million after his win in the British Open. While the first team player in the top ten, Michael Jordan, holds fifth place with $4 million.

Individual sports stars have the potential to earn more from endorsements than team players since they tend to be more visible to the public, and are solely responsible for their own success or failure. Individuals can often do more equipment deals than team players and can also market the advertising space on their clothing for corporate exposure.

Yachting star Dennis Conner's inclusion in the list of top money earners at number nine, with reported endorsement earnings of about $2 million from companies such as Pepsi-Cola, Ford and Rayban, comes from his rise to fame as the first US skipper to lose the America's Cup, and then to regain it in 1987. Conner's problem will be in retaining his superstar status for his exposure in the media is not guaranteed. Although he is undoubtedly one of the best yachtsmen in the world, yachting does not attract a great deal of media attention outside of the America's Cup. Conner's earnings are therefore likely to take a sharp drop unless his agents can find a way to keep him in the public eye.

One former star who has managed to retain his status with the public is the Scottish ex-racing driver Jackie Stewart. Through very careful management and organized television appearances he has maintained his commercial value and continues to enjoy a $2 million endorsement income despite having retired from competitive motor racing many years ago.

Television rights fees

Without doubt the most important influence on the marketing of
modern sport has been the worldwide growth in televised sports
coverage. A growth of 42 per cent in television household penetration
in the last ten years has been accompanied by a growth in
worldwide sports coverage from 8 per cent of total television time
ten years ago to 12 per cent today.

As we have already seen, television has influenced sport in many
ways other than through a direct financial input to its favourite
sports, however important that may be. Without television
exposure the huge growth in interest in sport would not have taken
place and the various industries surrounding it, that we have
already explored, would not have developed.

But most attention is, inevitably, focused on the often enormous
sums that television networks are prepared to pay to screen the
major sporting events. The 1988 Summer Olympics in Seoul,
South Korea, commanded television rights fees totalling some
$400 million, (up from $225 million for the Los Angeles Games) of
which 75 per cent was provided by NBC in return for North
American rights to 179 hours of programming, 135 of them live.
Add the $309 million ABC paid for the rights to the Calgary Winter
Olympics (up from $90.5 million for the Sarajevo Games) and the
fees paid by US television alone for just the Olympic events total
over $600 million.

Even when one spreads Olympic-related payments over four
years the total income to sports from television in the US
amounted to over $1 billion in 1987. This included $183 million to
baseball from ABC and NBC and $455 million to the NFL from all
three major networks. The NFL is in fact the undisputed leader in
US sports television with the highest income from rights fees, more
advertising revenue and more televised hours than any other
sport.

Despite the scale of these figures, the generally held belief that
television is the goose that lays the golden egg should not be
allowed to create the impression that TV companies will continue
to increase their expenditure on sport. Indeed, the opposite is now

the case. The trend of ever-increasing television rights fees is almost certainly over. After years of increasing expenditure on sport the prevailing attitude among television executives is now against increased spending. This is partly a gut reaction to the perceived greed of some sporting authorities, but it also reflects the increasing difficulty of the networks in making a profit from advertising in and around sports programmes. After all, rights fees are only part of the cost of screening sports. Although sport provides relatively cheap airtime in terms of production costs, advertisers are beginning to resist the ever-increasing costs of airtime, especially since research shows that the television audiences for some sports are currently falling.

Television is now entering a period of major changes as the long-established networks in every country face up to changes in viewing habits, increasing costs of production, the promise of vastly increased competition from Cable and Direct Broadcasting by Satellite (DBS) and the creation of new, commercial channels where often only non-commercial, state broadcasters existed before. Within this changing environment sports authorities may well discover that revenues from television cannot be relied upon to grow, and that the challenge of the 1990s is how to achieve television airtime against increasing competition from other sports, both old and new.

Sports marketing

The term 'sports marketing' is sometimes used to describe the sponsorship activity in which major companies are now involved, that is, it is meant to describe the marketing of a company's image or product message through the vehicle of sport. But it is a confusing use of the term, which will be used here to describe the marketing of *sport* or, in other words, the means that sports authorities, event organizers, managers and promoters use to bring money into sport.

Sports marketing encompasses all the revenue sources discussed above plus other opportunities for income, such as the growing business of hospitality at top-class events, on-site advertising and, of course, the business of corporate sponsorship. The growth of sports marketing from nothing twenty years ago to the global business it is today was a process in which two businessmen were central figures. Horst Dassler, who died in 1987, was the all-powerful head of the giant Adidas company who saw the business potential locked up in international sport and who manipulated sports federations and individual administrators to realize his vision of the future. Dassler became the most powerful, and feared, man in world sport as he used his company's influence to determine who ran the major sports, where top events were staged and how they were marketed.

The other leading figure in the development of sports marketing is American entrepreneur Mark McCormack whose International Management Group did for international golf and tennis what Dassler did for the Olympics and world soccer. As a young lawyer who had played golf at college, McCormack began his rise to international recognition when he started managing the business interests of a then unknown golfer, Arnold Palmer. His success with Palmer soon led many more sports stars to join IMG's client list and the company expanded into areas as diverse as corporate sponsorship, the creation of events, television programming and distribution, and the management of financial affairs for successful sports stars and celebrities. Thanks mainly to the influence — not always regarded as a positive one — of Dassler and McCormack the sports marketing business today has come of age and, as we shall see, is for the main part highly professional.

The effect that one person can have on an international sport, especially if he is autocratic and entrepreneurial, is amply demonstrated by the godfather of Grand Prix motor racing, Bernie Ecclestone. As president of FOCA (the Formula One Constructors Association) and vice-president of FISA (the international motor racing regulatory body) he controls virtually all aspects of the Grand Prix circus. This control extends to all television rights for a sport which can attract audiences of 300 million or more in sixty or so countries. Through his control of FOCA Ecclestone controls every nuance of the sport and can dictate his own terms to racetrack owners. In addition to commanding a large fee for bringing the 'circus' to town, FOCA takes a percentage of all revenue generated, while Ecclestone receives a reported 8 per cent for running the operation. And the money generated by just one Grand Prix can be enormous. The Monaco Grand Prix alone brings in an extra $250 million for the principality.

Ecclestone created the modern business of Grand Prix racing virtually singlehanded by taking the sport from the amateur world into one dominated by sponsorship and television, and by creating a travelling sporting circus that has all the elements of showbusiness. When, in 1981, a bitter row broke out with FISA which saw their control of the sport being eroded, it was Ecclestone who emerged the victor and who now also runs the commercial development of FISA.

Today more and more sports and events are learning of the potential for income and expansion. Take the world-renowned Tour de France for instance. This famous French bicycle race was for years run by a group of French sports journalists and ex-cyclists. After a major row following problems with a Tour of America, the owners appointed a marketing expert to run the $18 million Tour de France. Part of the new marketing plans calls for raising the fees demanded of sponsors and television, extending the race outside France, and selling the Tour's expertise for the creation of new Tours around the world. With an army of 600 media representatives following the Tour de France, $1.8 million from Coca-Cola for the main sponsorship, plus further income from a vast array of co-sponsors and towns wishing to be on the race's route, the commercial success and continuation of the event should be assured. Above all, the new director apparently recognizes the need to protect the event's sporting credibility and resist undue commercial pressures, despite his declared intention of boosting its income in coming years.

It is this balance between commercialism and sporting credibility that is at the heart of sports marketing. Sports authorities trying to take their sport into the 'big time' need to remember that they do have a choice and should not blindly accept the first offer that comes along. At the same time they should recognize that once the decision is taken to enter the world of commercial sport, the primary need is for professionalism on their part in dealing with the pressures and demands that accompany the commercial relationship.

3

The fourth medium

In the previous two chapters we have explored the differences between sponsorship, patronage and charity and have suggested a working definition of the commercial nature of sponsorship. We have also investigated the international business of sport with the intention of discovering the varied sources of revenue now tapped by the major sports.

In the context of total revenue sources available to sport the income from sponsorship is a relatively small proportion, yet it is also a vital source of funds that is steadily becoming more important.

Latest figures available at the time of writing suggest that in 1987/88 the US spend on sports sponsorship was in the region of $1.3 billion (including endorsement fees); that the spend in the UK was £165 million, with another £20–40 million going to the arts and community projects; while the best estimates suggest global sponsorship spend was in excess of $2.5 billion. Figures for other European countries support the conclusion that sponsorship is still a rapidly growing industry with a 10 per cent growth in the last year being the lowest estimated rate of expansion among European sponsorship industries.

One thing that does come as a surprise from the UK study mentioned earlier is the relative expenditure by companies on sports sponsorship compared with the provision of sporting facilities and welfare clubs for employees. The highly publicized field of sponsorship actually accounts for less than half that spent by companies on facilities. It may be that in the future companies will look for ways

to make the latter expenditure work for them by applying the
support and marketing techniques to this expenditure as if it were
direct sponsorship.

The other thing to bear in mind is that sponsorship spend
figures invariably only cover the *direct* sponsorship costs. As we
shall see, any sponsorship project needs to be supported by a
marketing budget. This will typically double the cost of the sponsorship. From the point of view of the sponsor the only cost that
matters is the *real cost*, i.e. what it will cost the company to achieve
the objectives set for the sponsorship campaign. Many recipients
and seekers of sponsorship forget this vital point and try to
convince the potential buyer of the sponsorship's value based only
on the direct cost.

Indirect costs are hard for the observer or the seller of sponsorship to estimate since they will be determined by the sponsor's objectives and hence the level of support activity he wishes to undertake,
but typical ratios are 1:1 or 1:1.5 for direct to indirect costs.

Sponsorship of sport may be a relatively small proportion of
sports' income from all sources yet it is a vitally important factor in
the health of modern sport. Its role in the arts, community and
other leisure activities may be even more important since these
activities are more difficult to finance via consumer spending, are
more diverse and do not receive equivalent levels of media
exposure. Although sport has led the way in developing sponsorship the increasing clutter in sport means that many new and
existing sponsors are looking for alternatives. As we shall see, the
arts, charities, community and leisure projects are learning from
sport and will almost certainly increase their share of the sponsorship cake quite dramatically.

We have talked at length about sport sponsorship and it is
appropriate, if we quickly dip back into the history of the subject,
to find that sport has always figured large in sponsorship's
development.

Sponsorship of sport and the arts has its roots in the ancient
practice of patronage — done for both purely altruistic reasons
and for more pragmatic image reasons. Only the communications

tools of the modern world have made the utilization of commercial sponsorship a practical marketing proposition; but some companies saw the opportunity long before others. In 1861 Spiers and Pond, an Australian firm, sponsored the first England Tour of Australia. They must have done a good job because they are reputed to have made a profit of £11 000! And in 1863 another cricket-linked sponsorship by the British sports outfitter John Wisden provided what was probably the first book sponsorship, by underwriting the now famous publication *The Wisden Cricketers' Almanac.*

Coca-Cola's first Olympic sponsorship came in 1928; while the Gillette Company is now devoting 65 per cent of its advertising and promotional budget to sport 77 years after starting with baseball in 1910 and developing its Cavalcade of Sports theme in 1939. Testimonial advertising and endorsements have also been around since the turn of the century and, like other facets of sponsorship, have developed as the techniques for benefiting from such promotions have been learnt and the communications industry has expanded to open up new opportunities and possibilities.

The title of this chapter is 'The Fourth Medium' which is a name increasingly given to the business of sponsorship. But what does it mean? The fourth medium of what, and what are the first three? Is there a fifth? What is the reason for sponsorship?

The answer, for those who have not encountered the term before, is COMMUNICATION!

Corporate communication

The central, dominant feature of business marketing is the need to communicate. In every aspect of corporate life the need to communicate a range of messages to a variety of different audiences is of paramount importance. Theories of communication within business are being given increasing prominence in company strategies as the complexities of the problem and possible solutions are becoming more understood.

Any discussion on sponsorship which omits this central feature of marketing is only scratching the surface — looking at effects without understanding the reasons. Without a cohesive *approach* to *communication* no company can successfully integrate sponsorship with its other marketing activities. Indeed, this is not a problem unique to sponsorship. Unless a company's executives understand the fundamental reasons for communicating, the techniques available to them, and the ultimate benefits, it will be impossible fully to integrate even two communications methods with each other.

The first and most obvious technique available to a company is advertising — a long-established and now conventional method using *paid-for communication intended to inform and influence a public.* Second comes public relations, commonly referred to as PR and, along with sponsorship, a system of communicating that has suffered from a lack of understanding within company management. A common definition of PR is that it is *a planned effort to establish and maintain mutual understanding between an organization and its public with the main object of acquiring and keeping a good reputation.* PR differs from advertising by the fact that it involves two-way communication between the organization and its public. It achieves this communication by disseminating information in slightly more subtle ways than the paid-for messages of advertising.

It has been said many times that the PR industry itself is most in need of public relations and I suggest that one reason for this, and the similar level of misunderstanding about sponsorship, stems mainly from a lack of understanding of the needs and reasons for corporate communication.

In the seventies, in the UK at least, the public relations sector was a very poor relation indeed to its big brother the advertising industry. It was common for agencies and staff public relations officers to feel that they were fighting their own battle of communication — trying to explain to company executives the scope of methods of communication available, beyond straight-forward advertising. The difficulties lay not just in the lack of readiness of executives to try new techniques; they often wanted a formal demonstration of the value of PR without committing to a corporate communications strategy within which PR could work effectively. On the other side of the coin, the PR practitioners also struggled against the problem of a new industry without sufficient depth of talent and experience. Hence individual practitioners and whole consultancies developed the theory of PR and corporate communications as they went along, often with a hungry intensity as they competed for accounts with rival agencies, and fought off the animosity of some advertising agencies.

The scepticism of the advertising agencies towards the increasingly important role of public relations was based on two very different factors. First, their own desire to protect their fee-earning ability from clients which they saw being eroded as PR budgets grew larger led them to defend advertising against this perceived threat. The second factor was the arguments they often used to dissuade clients from embarking on PR campaigns. A typical argument ran thus. The industry/agency/practitioner is inexperienced, naive and unprofessional. Advertising, on the other hand, is a formal communications technique based on numbers, on statistics that define the audience and the reach of an advertisement. 'We are experienced with this technique,' they said. 'We can define what you want to achieve and we can measure the results. PR is imprecise, fuzzy, often based on impressions, so how can you measure its results? How do you know that you're getting value for money?' In light of the famous remark about knowing half of the advertising budget is working, but not knowing which half, such claims from the advertising industry could perhaps be taken as the pot calling the kettle black!

But do you recognize these arguments? They have been applied to sponsorship in exactly the same way, somewhat ironically, by public relations practitioners, as well as those from advertising and marketing itself. And the arguments have some basis in fact. The PR industry is only now becoming truly accepted, formalized and professional as it has bred a depth of talent and discovered what PR can and cannot do. It has adopted more formal methods, often borrowed from advertising, of working with clients and measuring results, and has helped develop a more integrated approach to a company's communication requirements. Lucky, however, is the in-house PR executive or the external consultancy that can claim to be in a position to have integrated communications strategy to the point where their advice on the effect of corporate actions is treated as serious input at the highest levels of decision-making. More usually the PRO is in the business of day-to-day communications requirements or, at the other end of the scale, has to handle crisis management and trouble-shooting rather than being involved in advising on the future effects of corporate actions.

Today, PR is a recognized marketing tool that has found its place alongside advertising and the third medium of communications, sales promotions. In fact, the situation today is that advertising companies have expanded into the market by acquiring or setting up their own PR consultancies, as they have into sales promotion and more recently sponsorship, in order to provide their clients with a full range of communications services.

Sales promotion, the third medium, has more in common with advertising than PR in the sense that sales promotion techniques are basically a direct, one-way communication with the consumer and/or retailer of a product or service rather than the often indirect methods of PR and sponsorship that may be used for a wider range of corporate audiences. Most sales promotions are short-term campaigns designed to provide tangible added value to a product at the point of sale in order to convince you or me to buy it. Thus advertising provides the impressions designed to enhance the consumer's perception of the product; public relations responds to and attempts to influence the environment in which the company operates; and sales promotions provide direct incentives to the consumer to buy. In order to see the relative strengths of the four main communications media it is worth looking at the range of audiences with which a typical company may wish to communicate and the suitability of the options that are available.

The need to communicate
A typical company will have a range of audiences with which it

needs to communicate on a more or less regular basis. These will include:

- Product consumers
- Company staff
- The Salesforce
- Shareholders
- Distributors and retailers
- Suppliers
- Financial institutions
- Industry and government decision-makers
- The media
- Pressure groups
- The local community

The fundamental communication requirement, whichever particular audience is considered, is the creation and maintenance of:

- Awareness
- Image
- Action

In other words, a company wishes to communicate in order to make its audience aware of the company, feel good about it, and act on the information and their feelings to achieve a particular end result.

Thus product consumers must be told about a product and its advantages compared to rivals. The perceived image of the product and company must give customers 'warm feelings' — intangible added-value reasons why they should purchase that product instead of another. And the combined effect of the communications used should be to create consumer action, i.e. they should buy the product.

Take any of the possible target audiences listed above and you will see that the communication requirements are the same — all need to be made aware, to have positive images of the company or product, and their actions are of interest to the company.

PRODUCT CONSUMERS The consumer audience is the obvious one with which a company needs to communicate. A large company with many product lines will have different audiences for each product, some of which may overlap. Product advertising in all its many forms, along with sales promotions, will be the main weapon to the marketer since advertising not only creates name awareness and a product image but can also provide extensive reasons why the consumer should purchase the product. In some cases corporate image advertising may also be used to provide further intangible reasons why consumers should prefer that company's products. The one-way communication of advertising and sales promotion will be supplemented by market research to get product opinion messages from consumers.

COMPANY STAFF The company's internal audience is often the most ignored yet it is easily as important as the more obvious consumer audience. As Thomas J. Peters and Robert H. Waterman Jr point out in their study of America's best-run companies *In Search of Excellence*, top-performing companies consider internal communication as important as consumer communication in their quest for market dominance. Consumer advertising will obviously impinge on the internal audience but most internal communication will depend on public relations activities using formal and informal information dissemination techniques. Peters and Waterman point out that top-performing companies frequently encourage very informal methods of communicating information throughout all levels of the organization. In other words, the organization actively works to dismantle barriers to communication and to create an environment where ideas and suggestions can be taken from any level of the workforce. Additionally, the system works to inform the workforce of company and product objectives and the strategies to be used for securing these objectives. Such companies use systems of internal communication to create an atmosphere for product development, staff motivation and loyalty. Contrast this with the vast majority of companies which appear fearful of talking to their staff and relaxing the often impenetrable barriers that prevent internal cooperation.

THE SALESFORCE   Although the salesforce may be part of the company staff this audience will usually have specific requirements which are different from the rest of the workforce since the salesforce is a conduit to another audience of either consumers or retailers. The salesforce will need to know the plans for product advertising, sales promotion and public relations, and will also provide a channel of information back to the company on consumer and retailer attitudes to the product, the company, and its advertising and promotions. Communication with the salesforce will be a mix of formal and informal presentations and meetings, with additional PR input coming from sales literature, internal publications, incentives and motivation.

SHAREHOLDERS   As with all the different audiences, shareholders will receive impressions of their company through corporate and product advertising as well as through general public relations activity, but they are an important audience who sometimes needs to be reached directly with specific messages. This can be done through targeted advertising using relevant media and direct mail as well as through shareholder meetings, hospitality opportunities and company reports.

DISTRIBUTORS AND RETAILERS   Companies distributing products to the public through agents and retailers consider these audiences as vital to their success and will take great pains to provide tangible and intangible reasons why the distributors and retailers should give preference to their products. The difference effective communications can make lies between a product being ordered in small quantities and being poorly displayed, and large sales with prominent displays supported by point-of-sale promotions. Like the salesforce, this audience will want to know about planned product advertising and sales promotions, can be influenced by intangible factors such as the company's general PR image, and can be motivated by various incentive schemes.

SUPPLIERS   A company should consider the ease and cost of supply of its raw materials as an important factor to its profitability and will want to build a special relationship with its suppliers. Advertising tie-ins can be arranged to encourage a supplier to work closely with its client, and PR techniques can be used to build and develop a firm relationship between company workforces.

FINANCIAL INSTITUTIONS   Since the late seventies there has been a tremendous explosion in corporate advertising and public relations activity aimed at financial institutions, most especially with the increase in corporate takeovers and mergers. The attitudes of the world's stock markets and potential investors are now so important to companies that more and more effort is being expended on influencing this vital audience. As with most of the smaller-sized audiences communications techniques are increasingly aimed at producing a one-to-one relationship between key decision-makers and the company. Both formal and informal communication techniques can be used to reach these types of audience, but there is a growing use of hospitality events to stimulate involvement and personal interest.

INDUSTRY AND GOVERNMENT DECISION-MAKERS   The comments above apply to this audience too. A company's need to talk to this audience will depend on its size and area of business. A large company, or one operating in a sensitive market, may need to keep open a line of regular communication, while others will only need to respond to specific events. Once again, public relations activity will play a leading role in talking to this audience.

THE MEDIA   The media are a category of audience different from most others because it is rarely a final audience — rather it is usually a conduit to other target audiences. Advertising uses the media to deliver paid-for communication to other audiences, while public relations attempts to influence media attitudes and to provide them with positive stories in order to influence public opinion and to create awareness. The importance of the media and their role in relation to corporate sponsorship will be discussed later.

PRESSURE GROUPS   Some companies operate in industries that attract criticism from outside pressure groups. Examples are the nuclear industry, tobacco and alcohol, mineral exploration, arms manufacture, etc. Where this is the case a sensitive PR situation exists with the problem being not only to attempt to influence opinion among the critical group but how to minimize the damage of adverse publicity on the company's other target audiences.

THE LOCAL COMMUNITY   The importance of good relations with the company's local community is often undervalued, but one has only to look at the efforts many medium to large companies, especially those whose operations are based in one sizeable location, put into creating a good local environment to realize that a positive relationship helps the communication with many other audiences, not least the workforce and local consumers, but local government decision-makers and the media.

The marketing mix

The term 'marketing mix' is sometimes, wrongly, used to mean the mix of communications media available to the marketer, i.e. the combined use of advertising, public relations, sales promotions and sponsorship to reach the consumer. It must be understood that other factors influence purchasers' decisions and the media of communications cannot be expected to solve problems associated with the other factors of product, price and availability. If the product is not what consumers want, if it is offered at an uncompetitive price, or if it is not readily available, they are unlikely to buy, whatever messages they receive through whatever media. Communication can, however, help solve these problems by providing ways to identify them and to implement corrective strategies.

Which media?

The crucial point about using any of the communication media is to start from a point of knowing what messages you wish to send to which audiences. Sounds simple, I know, but it is the fundamental question that should be asked — yet often isn't — before any activity is undertaken. The first questions that must be asked are: What is the current situation? What changes do we want to make or what reinforcement can we give? And what are the options open to us?

The use of sponsorship provides added opportunities for communication to a very wide range of audiences but it should only be considered on its merits to deal with a particular objective alongside advertising, public relations and sales promotion. In order to view sponsorship in this way it is important to understand its relative performance in particular applications compared with the other three media, the range of audiences it can reach and the way it operates to communicate messages.

Table 3.1   Relative use of the four media

Audience	Advertising	PR	Sales promotions	Sponsorship
Product consumers	+++	++	+++	++
Company staff	+	+++		++
The salesforce	+	+++	++	++
Shareholders	++	+++		++
Distributors/retailers	+	+++	++	++
Suppliers	+	+++		++
Financial institutions	++	+++		++
Decision-makers	++	+++		++
The media	+	+++		++
Pressure groups	+	++		+
The local community	+	+++		++

Table 3.1 is intended to give a feeling for the relative uses of the four media in reaching particular audiences. The real values will differ depending on the type of company and the size and type of its particular audiences, but it demonstrates that sponsorship matches PR in its range of uses.

One of the problems of trying to differentiate between the uses of the four techniques is the way they overlap. Sponsorship, for instance, often lives happily under the definition of PR we gave earlier (*a planned effort to establish and maintain mutual understanding between an organization and its public with the main object of acquiring and keeping a good reputation*) but can also fit in with that of advertising (*paid-for communication intended to inform and influence a public*), yet it is clearly different in approach. Sales promotions and advertising are very closely related while all the media make use of design and market research as tools of their trade. The practice of paid-for endorsements by sporting stars is often classed as sponsorship yet it is also clearly advertising. While the PR weapons of hospitality and entertainment are often central features of sponsorship as is the PR use of the media audience.

One of the great advantages of sponsorship that guarantees it a continuing place within the marketing armoury is its ability to act as a theme that can be incorporated into advertising, public relations and sales promotion in a way that makes the combined effect far more powerful than any one individual campaign. Sponsorship works in this way, to create a 'hook' for other communications activity by relating to its audience in a different way from the other media. Sponsorship targets its audience through their *interests* and *lifestyle activities*. Thus sponsorship is distanced from the commercial nature of a company's relationship with most of its audiences by approaching them through activities in which they are personally interested. Advertising does this too in the sense that media buyers book space within television programmes and magazines that provide the target audience for a particular product, but sponsorship is generally intended, not at giving a direct sales message, but at the dissemination of a range of supportive messages to the audience in a less obvious way.

3.1a

3.1b

Figure 3.1a, b, c, d   Sponsorship helps companies reach audiences through their lifestyle interests. Every sport or activity has its own type of audience that will be useful for the right sponsor.

3.1c

3.1d

Sponsorship works because it fulfils the most important criterion of a communications medium — it allows a particular audience to be targeted with a particular set of messages. Once a company has determined the profiles of the audiences it wishes to reach these audiences can be researched to find out what leisure activities they may have in common. Alternatively, audiences for particular leisure activities can be analysed to find a correlation with a company's target audiences. Given a common theme, sponsorship can then be used to talk to specific audiences in a relatively non-commercial way, usually in a social and relaxed environment. Hence my preference, stated earlier, for the term 'lifestyle marketing' instead of sponsorship. Sponsorship today is a very varied medium that encompasses a wide range of activities that generally only have one thing in common — they typically target an audience through a leisure or lifestyle activity, thus approaching that audience from an indirect, seemingly less commercial route.

Sponsorship is such a flexible medium that it can be used for a wide range of purposes. These include:

- Name awareness
- Image reinforcement
- Media exposure
- Hospitality
- New market development
- Sales promotion and incentives
- Workforce communication and motivation
- Access to decision-makers
- Community relations
- Sampling

But sponsorship cannot work alone or be used in isolation from the other communications media. The most successful sponsorship activities make strong use of advertising, sales promotion and PR techniques to provide a *total* promotion around the theme set by the sponsorship.

Messages v. reality

Whatever the way a message is to be transmitted to an audience it is essential that the message is not only understandable but accurate. Initiating an advertising, PR or sponsorship campaign to alter perceptions, repair a tarnished image or boost flagging sales will be a pointless exercise unless the realities behind the problems are analysed and corrected before the communication campaign is undertaken. An image campaign designed to convince the public of the efficiency of a railway network, for instance, will fail to convince any user who continues to experience the faults in the service you *say* have been eradicated.

The public are not as gullible as many communicators would seem to imagine. They know they are being sold to and are increasingly sophisticated in their self-screening systems to edit out or ridicule messages that clearly differ from the reality of that product or company as they, as consumers, experience it. Sponsorship can be a very powerful communications tool because of the complex way in which it delivers its messages, but neither sponsorship, advertising nor PR can permanently influence an audience if the messages that are transmitted do not relate to the reality that audience experiences.

The sponsor/recipient relationship

We can now see that the relationship between the sponsor and recipient is almost bound to be complicated since it is built on an opportunity for both parties to satisfy very different requirements.

The recipient wishes to:

- Use the relationship to fund an individual, event or project
- Utilize the communications and management expertise many sponsors provide to add value to the event
- Balance the sponsor's requirements compared with his contribution with other sources of funding available

The sponsor wishes to:

- Use the relationship for commercial communications reasons
- Be able to analyse the sponsorship against corporate requirements
- And to allow sponsorship to compete with the other available communications media for its place in the package

Sponsorship is a complicated medium but its strengths can make it very powerful. Having attempted to put sponsorship into perspective alongside patronage and charity, and looking at how it fits into the contexts of sports marketing and corporate communications methods, Part 2 will look at the specific commercial considerations that must be given to using sponsorship in a communications strategy.

Part Two

Sponsorship –
the fundamentals

4

A marketing policy

The most sensible way for a company to start using sponsorship in its communications mix for the first time is to take time to learn about the subject and to analyse what changes, if any, will be required within its own organization in order to use the medium most effectively. This luxury was not available to most companies starting in sponsorship over the last twenty years. Very little in the way of hard commercial information existed on the subject, and most practitioners, whether sponsors, promoters, agents or recipients, have had to learn the rights and wrongs of various approaches as they went along.

Now, however, there is enough experience and information available that there is no excuse for a company (or recipient) new to the game to continue to repeat mistakes that have been made many times before.

The starting point to the use of sponsorship should most definitely not be when a company, that probably already regularly receives and rejects requests for sponsorship by the sackload, suddenly decides to buy one for no harder reason than that it appeals to the chief executive, or looks as if it just might have some relevance to the company. If you think that this statement is obvious, unnecessary or ridicules corporate management let me state quite clearly that many sponsorships are bought by companies for very 'soft' reasons. The personal preferences of CEOs still interfere with what should be hard commercial decisions in a way that would be totally unacceptable if the medium were advertising, public relations or sales promotions. Can you imagine a

CEO of a company manufacturing heavy earth-moving equipment, say, insisting that product ads are placed in tennis magazines just because he is a keen tennis player? No, neither can I, but it is far less unlikely, unfortunately, that the same CEO would happily buy a tennis sponsorship for his company, often to the horror of his marketing specialists who then have to make the sponsorship work.

Sponsorship is the one major area of corporate activity that is often still influenced by the lifestyle interests of top decision-makers. It is somewhat ironic that it is the power of sponsorship to target and communicate with selected audiences through their lifestyle interests that makes it such an effective communications medium but which can also create the confusion that often surrounds the subject, both within companies, their audiences and the recipient, unless great care is taken to understand the medium before beginning to use it professionally.

For a company that is new to the game but which is serious in its desire to add this powerful weapon to its armoury, it is essential that no decision to pursue sponsorship should be made on the basis of individual sponsorship proposals. Instead, the important decisions should be made well in advance of analysing specific sponsorship opportunities, should establish requirements in the abstract, and should be a matter of *corporate marketing policy*.

Corporate policy

Sponsorship is such a broad-based, multi-faceted medium that it is essential to spend some time setting out a corporate policy for the use of the medium and to create an internal environment in which sponsorship can be effectively utilized. Such a policy should include guidelines as to the perceived role of sponsorship relative to advertising, public relations and sales promotion, what sort of budget relationship, if any, the company expects between the use of the four media, how the activity will be split between the corporate, divisional and brand levels, and the criteria for selecting appropriate sponsorship activities. The policy should also make clear who will be the responsible decision-makers, who, or which department, has day-to-day responsibility for running sponsorship projects, how potential projects will be evaluated to ensure their fit with corporate expectations, and how the effects of individual projects will be measured.

The secret, if there is just one, to making a success out of sponsorship is quite simple. If you can put together a corporate policy that covers your expectations, i.e. what you want sponsorship to do for you; how you will evaluate sponsorship proposals to ensure they fit your requirements; and how projects will be managed and executed, you will be well on your way to creating a structure that minimizes the chances of making serious errors while making it probable that the medium will work for you.

If this sounds daunting because of the formal way in which I suggest you approach the subject, then bear with me. The formal tasks of defining your aims and methods of execution are essential precursors for successful implementation, are quite simple matters of common-sense, and should be a straightforward job for any marketing department that already integrates the other tools of corporate communication. If, on the other hand, you use advertising, public relations and sales promotions on an *ad hoc* basis with little integration between the disciplines I suggest that you take a step back and examine your corporate communications philosophy before taking on sponsorship. Unless sponsorship can be easily integrated with your other communications activities you will never achieve the best from the medium and may become yet another example of a company that starts sponsorship only to pull out of their activity all together after one or two experiments.

Having sounded a note of gloom about formalism let me reassure you; sponsorship can be the most rewarding of marketing activities. Do it well and it will not only benefit your bottom line but will also benefit the activity you are involved with, the audiences, participants, the community and your own workforce. It is a business deal in which no one needs or should, lose. What is more, it can be great fun! It offers so many ways to expand your relationships with your publics, allows you to communicate in a very personal manner, and gives your staff the opportunity to expand their skills by using a medium that demands a creative approach and rewards brilliant, off-beat ideas in a most public way.

Finally, before looking at the question of policy in more detail, the would-be sponsor should remember that sponsorship is a two-way business. It is impossible to buy a successful sponsorship; you can only earn it by putting considerable effort as well as money into the activity. To succeed with your aims you must be able to give and take, and not just pay lip-service to this principle. Sponsorship allows you to communicate with a wide range of audiences but it is essential that you are seen to be willing to participate fully in the activity.

The role of sponsorship

The role of sponsorship within your communications mix and the relative effort you are going to commit compared with advertising, public relations and sales promotion is the first thing to consider. Some companies, notably those in the tobacco or alcohol industries, are limited in the way they are allowed to advertise in many countries. Once restrictions are placed on advertising, especially television advertising, the use of sponsorship shoots up in importance. One has only to look at the high level of activity undertaken by most companies selling cigarettes and alcohol to realize two things: first, that any doubts you may have had about the effectiveness of sponsorship can be laid aside — sponsorship must work for these companies or they wouldn't continue doing it, even with their limited choice of media; and second, sponsorship works best when it is done over the long term and tied in with the use of other media to present a cohesive communications package. The outstanding examples of cigarette branding of sponsorship programmes and the high level of exposure they have achieved over long time-periods clearly demonstrate that sponsorship can be a very effective use of marketing funds.

Legislative restrictions are not the only reason why a company may be unable, or choose not to use advertising as the principal vehicle of communication. Some professions, in some countries, are not allowed to advertise in certain media, sometimes traditional advertising is inappropriate or lacks credibility, and increasingly advertising is being found to be less cost-effective than other opportunities.

While advertising still accounts for the vast majority of all communications budgets the relative sizes of budgets allocated to the other media are increasing. This is inevitable as companies take a more complete look at their communication needs and as experience is gained in the use of the other media. Another factor in the likely decline in the simple use of conventional advertising is the fragmentation of audiences and the increasing amount of media outlets offering advertising opportunities. Rapidly increasing numbers of television channels, commercial radio stations, magazines and newspapers mean that the number of advertising messages vying for attention make it difficult to be seen and heard, or to put a clear message across. When taken together with the ever-increasing costs faced by advertisers, it is not surprising that more and more companies are ready to look for alternatives.

When advertising becomes difficult or inappropriate, or just plain expensive, it is to public relations programmes that companies usually first turn for alternatives. Although a well-designed public relations programme can be a very effective marketing tool, and has a wide range of audiences that it can target, it is not a medium that is ideal for achieving high exposure in the short term. Also, most PR programmes aimed at the consumer audience need a 'hook' on which they can be hung and which will help create the media exposure for the campaign. Sponsorship works well as this catalyst and provides a very flexible tool for the PR department. Because of this versatility sponsorship has a place in the mix, whether one is targeting a large, consumer audience, or a small but important group of decision-makers. In the latter case advertising would probably be inappropriate but sponsorship's flexibility as a tactical weapon means that a programme can be found to target virtually any type or size of audience.

When writing your policy statement I suggest that you exercise this flexibility by allowing the use of all the appropriate media depending on the particular communication requirement that is to be fulfilled. By explicitly allowing for the use of all appropriate media for the particular circumstances you remove the arguments over which is the 'best' medium and allow your decision-makers to concentrate on analysing the requirements and selecting the appropriate response.

It may be informative to look back over the company's history of advertising and public relations. Go back twenty years and you will probably find that advertising totally dominated your activity. As you come up to date the growth in the variety of media used will be clear. Sponsorship is just the latest weapon to be available to you, and you must avoid trying to quantify in advance the way it should be used in specific terms relative to advertising. Create a situation in which it can be used whenever it is appropriate to the objectives and you will find that it quickly becomes accepted as a normal tool throughout the company and your agencies.

Corporate v. brand

The question of whether sponsorship should be a brand, divisional or corporate activity often arises. The point here is that sponsorship policy, and in particular the philosophical willingness to utilize sponsorship when it is appropriate, must be set at corporate level, and indeed the decision would normally be one for those at director level, with both the marketing director and the CEO taking an active role. Once a corporate philosophy on the use of sponsorship has been decided the strategic decisions about its use in particular circumstances can be taken at corporate, divisional or brand levels.

Brand managers must be given the freedom to use sponsorship in their marketing activities in exactly the same way in which they have the freedom to use the other communication tools. Brand managers who handle brand advertising decisions should have the same freedom to use sponsorship within the policy limits set down for its use.

On the other hand, sponsorship may have a role to play within a corporate PR strategy and here the decision may be one for the head of public relations or the marketing director. Equally, other departments such as sales or personnel may have communication requirements that sponsorship could help to solve. All need to be aware of its availability for use and where to find the appropriate skills and services within the organization. Therefore, the corporate views on the use of all the communication media must be known by all those who may have a need to communicate, and this can only be done by setting the policy at top level and informing the organization of the policy, the resources that are available, and areas of responsibility that are entailed.

Budgets

Provisional figures at the time of writing suggest that the money spent on buying sponsorships in the UK (not including the extra funds companies spent on supporting their sponsorships), amounted to about 5 per cent of the UK advertising spend. If total spend on sponsorship is considered, the percentage probably doubles. No hard-and-fast rules for the relative levels of spend between advertising and sponsorship can be given, however, since this will vary considerably between different industries and between companies in the same industry. Indeed, I doubt whether there is any merit in trying to set relative budgets for the predetermined use of advertising, sponsorship and public relations. Such fixed expenditure budgets reduce flexibility — the most important requirement of effective communication in the long term — and focus attention on the independent rather than combined use of the media.

If a budget is set for advertising, with another for PR and yet another for sponsorship, it becomes impossible to focus on true needs or appropriate activities. The advertising department will defend their budget allocation to the bitter end, as will the PR department and any others with vested budget interests. Nothing could be worse for encouraging the combined use of the media or the development of new strategies for flexible response to communication needs.

A far better approach is to allocate discretionary communication budgets for brand, divisional and corporate purposes that allow, and indeed encourage, the competitive use of media to find the most cost-effective solutions. Such budgets can still be based on historical expenditure in the individual media but should not specify restrictive expenditure allowances for each medium. If necessary — and it will only be so if you do not trust the effectiveness of your own communications policy — you can set guidelines for the relative levels of expected expenditure, but these should never be so rigid as to discourage the research and implementation of effective communication programmes.

Give your divisional and brand managers the flexibility to choose combinations of communication tools for specific requirements and you will create an atmosphere conducive to experimentation based on real requirements. You will also find that research is used more consistently and that data become useful for the analysis of all tactical tools as each medium has to compete on a cost-effective basis for its use in any specific role.

You will still need to create budgets specific to each medium to cover the specialist services you retain in-house or for which you use the services of outside agencies. Thus you will need advertising support services, a public relations facility, a sponsorship or special events department and market research facilities each of which will require funding through its own budget, but these should not restrict or inhibit the mix of media that is available to those who need to communicate.

One other point to consider on the matter of budgets is how you expect to react to sponsorship proposals that are attractive but which do not fit within your expenditure plans. Careful planning of overall policy and the expectations of corporate, divisional and brand use of sponsorship will help you to analyse in advance what you expect from sponsorship projects. This allows you to plan ahead for the type of sponsorships you wish to buy or to create and to make plans and purchasing arrangements within a marketing timetable. You will still find, however, that suddenly changing requirements can force you into unplanned expenditure or you may simply be offered an unexpected opportunity needing a quick decision that is too good to turn down if you are to beat the opposition, or which is more appropriate for your needs than the programme you had planned. In either case you will be better prepared to handle the problem if you have gone through the formalizing procedure described here.

Who runs it?

The question of who is responsible for running sponsorship programmes is essential to the way in which sponsorship is structured within a company. In companies that undertake sponsorship on a casual basis it is not unusual to find that it resides as the responsibility of the sales, advertising or marketing departments or it may have found a home within the public relations department. In such cases sponsorship is just one of the responsibilities of the department which cannot devote itself full-time to analysing sponsorship requirements, evaluating proposals and running campaigns.

In companies that have fully embraced the concept and use of sponsorship one usually finds that the discipline is the responsibility of a specialist executive or a full-scale department. The American brewing company, Adolph Coors, is an example of a company that utilizes sponsorship as a major part of its marketing activity. Despite being a regional company, with its products not available on a fully national basis, Coors has used sponsorship to help make it the country's fifth largest brewer. Coors doesn't have just one sponsorship department, it has three, each a full-service, in-house operation devoted to specific areas of sponsorship. This approach is common among those companies that have fully embraced sponsorship. Gillette, Anheuser-Busch, American Express, etc., all have extensive resources devoted to their sponsorship requirements.

A company that plans to utilize sponsorship in any serious way must have specialist expertise available, whether this comes from an in-house executive or department, or from an external agency. Even if an agency is retained to provide the major expertise and back-up facilities (we shall look at the role of agencies later) it is still essential to have an in-house executive to advise on policy and to set the structure and oversee campaigns based on this policy. Without such coordination sponsorship can easily degenerate into an unstructured activity that will not benefit the marketing aims that should be the sole purpose for any communication campaign.

The minimum requirement for a company just starting to use sponsorship should be an executive experienced in the medium, who will plan and coordinate activity in conjunction with the other departments whose input is necessary. Thus the executive will need to have full access to marketing information, should be available to regional, division and brand managers to help with their specific requirements, and will need to coordinate activity with the public relations department and the in-house and external advertising specialists. It is likely that this executive will report to the marketing director, but he should also be given the freedom to explore sponsorship opportunities with every department in the company.

One of the first tasks to be undertaken when embarking on the planned use of sponsorship involves the training of other staff within the company who are likely to become involved with sponsorship activities. It is essential to conduct an awareness programme within the company if the best is to be got from your campaigns. Staff need to have the theory of sponsorship explained, to know what, if any, their roles within campaigns will be, and what advantages the medium can offer to help with their specific marketing or communication responsibilities. Initial resistance may come from advertising or public relations staff who see sponsorship as reducing their budgets or encroaching on their territory, brand marketing staff may prove reluctant to experiment with the medium, and your external agencies may have their own axes to grind!

The point here is that, as we have seen, sponsorship is still often misunderstood and there is no reason why your staff should be any more aware of it than the general population unless they have already enjoyed extensive experience with the medium. If you are to ensure a readiness to experiment with sponsorship you should take the time to explain it to your staff through formal training and informal discussion sessions and to explain the specific details of the policy you expect to follow, bearing in mind that this policy should not be carved in stone. Use these sessions to encourage the various departments to suggest their own ideas on how they could use sponsorship and feed this back into your policy document.

Of key importance is the relationship between sponsorship, advertising and public relations within the company. The worst scenario is for the different departments to be jealous of each other, to create difficulties where none should exist over their mutual roles, and to be protective of their own projects. As we said earlier, no communication strategy can work effectively unless all the tactical tools of communication can be used together.

Once you have gone through the stages of evaluating your requirements, and specific sponsorship opportunities — in that order — you will be ready to begin to undertake a campaign. This process, by the way, may take several months so don't expect your new sponsorship executive to have projects underway as soon as he gets his feet under the desk. Having selected a sponsorship campaign you will need to start putting some resources in place. For companies without specialist departments that do not wish to use an outside agency to take care of the nuts and bolts of a campaign the most effective way is to build a project team around the sponsorship executive. This can easily be done on a project-by-project basis by defining the jobs that have to be done, the roles that will need filling, and then asking for volunteers from the various departments within the company that have the necessary skills. If, for example, you are planning a campaign on behalf of one of your consumer brands you should consider forming a small team, headed by the sponsorship executive, that includes a brand representative, perhaps an assistant brand manager, plus people from the in-house advertising and public relations departments. Always define your requirements and then ask for volunteers from the respective departments to form a project team who will be responsible for the campaign. Back-up resources and facilities, such as design, media targeting, buying of ad space, etc., can remain within the respective departments which the project team will call on as and when required.

Creating a project team like this is the best way of ensuring internal acceptance, provides the degree of flexibility that is required and can provide a real level of staff motivation. Each member of the project team will be working in what is likely to be a new environment in which their own specialist skills can be seen to be essential but which must be coordinated with many other skill areas to produce a one-off communication campaign. Each sponsorship project is always a unique campaign, and offers all members of the team an opportunity to expand their own skill level and experience.

As a company's level of involvement with sponsorship expands it is becoming normal to create an in-house department responsible for all aspects of using the medium. Such departments often run several campaigns at any one time and usually require a high level of resources on a dedicated basis. Thus major sponsors usually have full-service sponsorship departments handling sponsorship evaluation and selection, execution, design, public relations, promotions, advertising, merchandising, hospitality and measurement. Because of the specialized nature of sponsorship it is usually best to fund the in-house facility at corporate level with its resources and expertise made available to divisions and brands within the company. It is not normally practical to run separate sponsorship resources at divisional or brand level since this would result in considerable overlap of resources and would make it more difficult to maintain a consistent corporate policy towards the medium.

Even within a large company operating across international markets a sponsorship services or special events department can be organized to provide centralized services and expertise that allows campaigns to be coordinated on a multinational or regional basis using, if necessary, budgets from several different sources. This department should be set up to allow it to act as a central clearing-house for sponsorship proposals and as a corporate database on sponsorship information.

When this corporate facility exists, individual divisions or brands have a central source for evaluation advice, legal and taxation expertise when contracting individual sponsorship agreements, a research and measurement facility, and staff resources to support brand personnel in the management of special events. Since the necessary skills to utilize corporate sponsorship activities effectively are relatively scarce, the provision of a central resource enables companies to share expertise internally, create an atmosphere conducive to innovation and ensure that lessons learnt within any part of the company can be shared among all other brands and divisions.

The actual strategic control of sponsorship projects must, however, be left to individual brands or other market operating groups who call on the central department for the support services they require to implement the desired strategy. Although the running of projects will often be primarily in the hands of the central department, the brand or division for which the sponsorship is being run should also take an active role, both at project management level and within the different disciplines that must be used to make any sponsorship effective.

Evaluation and measurement

As the pool of experience of using sponsorship has grown so too has the realization that sponsorship projects cannot be selected on an *ad hoc* basis from the hundreds that come pouring into most companies who are seen as potential sponsors.

One of the most important parts of setting a corporate sponsorship policy is addressing the questions of evaluation and measurement. Unless this aspect is handled effectively there is little chance of your sponsorship projects really working for you.

Evaluation covers two aspects; the first is to take a long hard look at your expectations of sponsorship — what part you want it to play in your overall communications strategy, which audiences you expect to target with what messages.

Once this internal expectations evaluation is in place the second aspect is the critical evaluation of each and every sponsorship opportunity, whether this is an existing property on offer to the company or an event that you are considering creating. A system can be designed to 'score' all the relevant aspects of each project against the 'ideal' targets of the company's expectations. Putting such a system in place is the most important step in the effective selection of projects that match the company's needs. Without it you will find yourself relying on subjective assessments of the project or figures supplied by the seller. Either way is unsatisfactory, especially when sizeable funds may have to be committed to the sponsorship.

The final part of the objective measurement of sponsorship projects is the research you put in place to provide you with information on the success, or otherwise, of chosen projects. The way success is measured depends on the criteria you set during the pre-planning evaluation and all post-project measurement must be conducted on the basis of your original expectations.

Many users of sponsorship still assume that there is no way of accurately measuring the effectiveness of the medium in specific projects. This is not the case if a formal evaluation and identification process has been followed. If you know what you want to achieve, it is then possible to measure how effectively your sponsorship has achieved its goals. It is obviously not normally possible to identify a direct effect of any sponsorship project on increasing bottom-line sales — the ultimate desire of many sponsors — since too many other variables have to be taken into account. Only if all possible factors are held constant, i.e. all other communications activities *and* the other elements of the marketing mix — product price, quality and availability — can a direct influence be measured, but it is still possible to measure changes and trends that will allow fairly accurate assessments of the value of particular sponsorship activities to be made.

Gillette, for instance, which has been using sports sponsorship as a central feature of its communications strategy since 1910, has evolved a sophisticated use of sponsorship that puts it in the front rank of corporate sponsors. All activities are constantly measured and evaluated and the company is prepared to say, quite categorically, that sponsorship contributes to their bottom line. Indeed, some Gillette brands do as much of a third of their annual sales around major sporting sponsorships that last for up to two months.

There are very few successful sponsors that do not strictly evaluate possible projects against corporate requirements and then measure the effects during and after each campaign. Such research cannot provide all the answers, but without it you will be fumbling in the dark with projects that you can only hope will be successful. The different areas of evaluation and measurement will be looked at in more detail in subsequent chapters but it is raised here in order to demonstrate how important it is to include reference to these formal approaches within the corporate policy document.

Corporate policy — an example

In order to put the factors discussed in this chapter in context, what follows is a hypothetical example of a corporate sponsorship policy for a large company operating in the manufacture and sale of alcoholic drinks on a multinational basis. Such a company will have many different brands, some of which may compete with each other in the marketplace, and will have a structure that includes divisional, regional and brand managements.

INTRODUCTION Sponsorship is a communication tool that has a place in the company's marketing plans. Effectively run sponsorship can add value to corporate and brand image and awareness with a variety of our audiences and can be used as a central feature of promotional activity aimed at building sales volume in all our markets.

This policy document is aimed at focusing attention on corporate philosophy and will set out basic principles for the selection, implementation and measurement of sponsorship projects run by brands, divisions or regional managements. It is intended that these guidelines allow for lessons learnt from the use of the medium to be easily transferred within the company.

The company will only become involved with sponsorship on a *commercial* basis and specific projects will only be selected or created when they can help towards the achievement of specific corporate or brand objectives. Requests for patronage or charitable donations will be dealt with by the community affairs department.

The company will not become involved in sponsorships that may encourage anti-social activity or which may cause offence. The company will also not become involved with sponsorship projects on the basis of political or social pressures external to our marketing aims.

Different divisions, regions and brands within the company are expected to cooperate where practical to ensure successful exploitation of all opportunities.

The existing approval procedures used for other communication projects are expected to be followed for all sponsorship activities.

ROLE OF SPONSORSHIP   It is expected that sponsorship will be an integral part of brand marketing activity. Corporate marketing executives must consider sponsorship as a medium of communication for the product range. Sponsorship is made especially appropriate because of the restrictions placed on the conventional use of media advertising.

Brand and corporate communications requirements must be analysed before the choice of communications media is made on the basis of the most cost-effective solution in any particular set of circumstances.

Sponsorship should not be used in isolation but should form part of an integrated programme that makes use of all other communication tools. Every attempt must be made to lever sponsorship activities into all forms of communication.

Sponsorship projects should be considered in the context of achieving brand or corporate objectives. These include:

- Building or reinforcing corporate awareness
- Building or reinforcing brand awareness
- Reinforcing or adjusting corporate image
- Reinforcing or adjusting brand values
- Positioning a brand in a new market sector
- Targeting specific brand or corporate audiences
- Building sales or distribution opportunities
- Supporting brand advertising campaigns

Brands, divisions and regions should cooperate in the exploitation of sponsorship opportunities where spin-off benefits can be identified. In particular, brands should try to ensure that competitors of our other brands are excluded from involvement in events in which they have a major sponsorship involvement.

RESOURCES   A special events department has been formed to fulfil specific sponsorship functions that will be available to all brand, divisional and regional managers. This unit will be centrally funded and will be responsible for:

- Provide training in the use of sponsorship
- Providing feedback on developments in the sponsorship business
- Helping corporate, brand, divisional and regional managers to evaluate their communications requirements with respect to sponsorship
- Evaluating specific sponsorship opportunities
- Providing contract and legal advice
- Providing support services for implementation and project management
- Measuring the effectiveness of projects

Funding of specific sponsorship projects will be the responsibility of brand, divisional or regional managements. No central funds will be available. Projects must be funded from discretionary marketing budgets.

The special events department provides a mechanism to allow the use of a variety of budget sources for specific projects but the use of each budget must be justified against established criteria for that budget.

As experience of the medium increases it is expected that resources will be devoted to fewer, but larger, projects that can be better exploited in all our markets and through the use of all available communication tools.

SELECTION The selection of sponsorships must be done against established requirements for communication. Sponsorships will be evaluated by the special events department for their effectiveness in meeting these criteria.

No specific restrictions will be placed on the types of sponsorship that may be considered but it is expected that no sponsorship will be undertaken that involves the abuse of alcohol or which may provide ammunition for action groups opposed to our industry.

As internal experience with the use of the medium develops it is expected that more projects will be developed in-house and less emphasis placed on buying projects 'off-the-shelf'.

The organizers of events selected for sponsorship must be able to demonstrate they have the ability and resources to run the event as described. Independent verification of these claims must be obtained before commitment to expenditure is made.

Any risks associated with the event not taking place as planned or of the event/sponsor receiving adverse publicity must be evaluated in advance.

All sponsorship activity should be capable of achieving major exposure for the sponsoring brand. Minor or sub-sponsorship involvements which allow little brand exposure should not be undertaken.

Major sponsorship expenditure should allow the sponsoring brand to have a level of control over the development of the project and should also offer the opportunity of a long-term relationship.

All sponsorship payments should be made in stages against specified performance objectives to ensure the programme is executed as planned.

IMPLEMENTATION   The implementation of specific sponsorship projects must be planned into a timetable that allows sufficient lead-time for resources to be allocated and objectives to be met.

All contractual and legal documentation will be the responsibility of the special events department in conjunction with other relevant legal and contractual executives.

The implementation of specific projects will be the responsibility of the special events department.

It is expected that sponsorships will be run by an accountable project manager leading a project team with representatives from all relevant disciplines who will run the project for the duration of the campaign.

The special events department will be responsible for liaising with all relevant brands, divisions and regions to ensure maximum cross-utilization of the opportunities offered.

Monitoring and evaluation of the performance of the sponsorship will be the responsibility of the special events department.

Quantifiable measurement techniques must be used on all sponsorships to evaluate performance against initial expectations.

Writing your own corporate policy statement will help focus your attention on the role you expect sponsorship to play in your company and is really essential if you hope to use sponsorship as a mainstream activity. Before turning to the major elements of messages and audiences here are a few do's and don'ts.
Do:
remember that you are in the business of shifting product or services — you are not in the event business. Many sponsors or their executives get so carried away with special events that they forget the real purpose of the exercise.

spend time determining your real expectations — you may be surprised that they eventually turn out to be different from those you assumed at the start.

share your exploration of the benefits and disadvantages throughout your company. Allow time for training and feedback.

remember that once you start on serious sponsorship you increase your social responsibility by becoming involved with outside events and organizations who don't share the same commercial aims as you.

Don't:

expect sponsorship to be a cure-all for every marketing problem.

forget the other elements of the marketing mix that may play a far more important role in affecting your bottom line than any element of communication.

expect results overnight. Sponsorship needs time if it is to work successfully.

think money buys successful sponsorship — it doesn't. Matching the right sponsorship to your needs and working hard are the secrets of success.

5

What messages?

Once a specific corporate policy for the use of sponsorship has been put in place the second step towards successful exploitation of the sponsorship medium is to ensure consistency between the brand or corporate objectives, the messages to be portrayed, the desired audience for these messages and the characteristics of events that are to be sponsored.

Like all the communication tools the purpose of sponsorship is to transmit certain desired messages to various targeted audiences. Because of its flexibility, however, sponsorship allows such a variety of audiences to be targeted that it can be used to expand awareness, affect image, provide a platform for hospitality, consumer contact, sampling, staff relations, product sales promotions, merchandising, point-of-sale reinforcements, sales incentives, community influence and media exposure.

Central to all these different ways of exploiting and targeting a sponsorship campaign are, however, two fundamental features that are intrinsic to the way in which any audience perceives your company or brand. These features are awareness and image. Virtually any objective for communication can be boiled down to these two fundamentals. Unless your audience is aware of you or your product they cannot make any of the decisions, purchasing or otherwise, that you would like them to make. Equally, without awareness there can be no perception of image, so these two messages are inextricably linked despite the fact that they are usually considered separately when discussing communication requirements.

Awareness

One of the strongest advantages usually claimed for the use of sponsorship is its supposed strength in creating or reinforcing a public's awareness of a company or product. While I have no wish to suggest that sponsorship does not have a significant role to play in fulfilling this requirement it is important to realize that the claims made for sponsorship's effectiveness in this role are often simplistic in their assumptions.

The majority of companies who are international sponsors, most of whom have company or product awareness high on their list of objectives, start out from the position of already having high international awareness from years of operating in the market-place. In these cases the awareness of the company or product is almost certainly based mainly on extensive consumer experience of the product or company, reinforced by continuous advertising and sales promotion activities. The role of sponsorship in these cases, and indeed of the other peripheral communication tools, is limited to, at best, marginally affecting general awareness or achieving increased awareness within relatively small or specialist target groups.

Even in the case of products such as cigarettes, where media advertising is severely limited, the awareness, by consumers and non-consumers, of specific products is determined mainly by their extensive presence in the marketplace. Even non-consumers will be able readily to identify many different brands of cigarettes simply because they see them regularly in shops, in use and in the product advertising that is allowed.

While sponsorship may be used to help increase the awareness of new brands, its role in supporting this objective is bound to be far less important than achieving high penetration in the market-place. If tobacconists, for instance, can be encouraged to stock the new product (and here it is possible to conceive of sponsorship having a role to play), and if product advertising and sales promotions are used to support the product launch, the effect of sponsorship on product awareness may not be significant unless a very large-scale sponsorship can be justified.

Major sponsors who already have a high profile in their market-place tend to use sponsorship as a means for *continuing and reinforcing* their already high awareness with their audiences and as a means of preventing competitors from achieving gains at their expense. When aiming at a large consumer audience sponsorship for the objective of awareness tends to be used by major sponsors as a facilitator of a general theme of communication. In other words, sponsorship can act as a 'hook' on which theme advertising, sales promotion and other awareness-building aids can be built.

Because sponsorship's role in supporting or creating awareness works best when used as part of a communications package, I would be very doubtful of finding any justification in using a stand-alone sponsorship, without the back-up of the other tools, when the main aim is to influence awareness.

When considering sponsorship's effect on company or product awareness the key factor in evaluating a project is the degree of visibility you can achieve with the target audience. (Although we are dealing with awareness in isolation here, the quality of that visibility and of the event will also be important considerations when measured against the image you wish to project.) Hence the level of media exposure expected to be generated by the event is an important consideration as is the availability of perimeter signage, shirt advertising and the opportunities for levering the sponsor-ship into media advertising and sales promotions.

Despite my reservations about the role of sponsorship in affecting the awareness of most established companies and products, the medium can certainly offer strong benefits when companies or products start from a low awareness level.

A classic example of this is the Cornhill Insurance sponsorship of English Test Cricket. In 1977 research showed that unprompted awareness of Cornhill was less than 2 per cent. Interestingly, the research demonstrated that the general level of name awareness of virtually all the major insurance companies was also surprisingly low. The company identified the reasons for this as due to the fact that insurance is sold via third-party brokers, agents or salesmen and hence the companies are relatively distanced from their consumers. At that time most companies' promotional activities were directed at insurance brokers rather than the consumers in order to influence brokers to place business with a particular company. Therefore consumers lacked any direct association with the particular company which held their business. In addition to this problem was the fact that insurance is not a 'glamour' product; rather it is a purely passive one that is purchased out of a reluctantly perceived necessity rather than desire.

Another influence on Cornhill's management at that time was the bad publicity generated by the collapse of a number of insurance companies. This led Cornhill to conclude that the public would be increasingly reluctant to purchase insurance from an unknown company.

These factors would normally lead a company into a full-scale analysis of the problem followed by the design of an awareness campaign built on a full understanding of the requirements. In those days the chances of an insurance company choosing sponsorship as its main medium of communication to solve its awareness problem were probably very low, but in this case there occurred one of those fortunate set of circumstances that pitched Cornhill, in the course of only a few days, into what was to turn out to be a prime example of how sponsorship, of the right event at the right time, can deliver very significant benefits.

At the same time as Cornhill were identifying their awareness problems the international cricket world was being shaken by Kerry Packer and his World Series Cricket. In the middle of the 1977 Test matches between England and Australia the future of English cricket was under threat because the Test and County Cricket Board (TCCB) could not match the money being offered by Packer. As several key English players signed for Packer the TCCB were desperate to find a sponsor to help meet the earning requirements of players whom they wanted to keep in English cricket.

A temporary reprieve was granted by a businessman and cricket fanatic who agreed to sponsor the English team with £1000 per player for the remainder of the Test series while hoping that a major sponsor could be found to help guarantee the game's long-term security.

Within a few days Cornhill had made contact with the TCCB and a £1 million sponsorship fee, over the next five years, had been agreed. So serious did the cricket establishment and the sporting press take the threat of Packer's World Series Cricket that the announcement of the Cornhill sponsorship at the Oval on the Saturday of the final Test in the 1977 series created a tremendous amount of interest, especially since rain stopped play and the media were delighted to concentrate on the topical story!

An intuitive feeling that sponsorship of the Test series could help solve their awareness problem plus an ability to make a million pound investment decision in a few days and a large slice of luck helped Cornhill to start their awareness campaign on a high note. But, because the company had no experience of sponsorship, or of Test cricket, a lot of hard work had to go into making the campaign work over the full sponsorship period.

The effect of the sponsorship on unprompted name awareness was readily measured through six monthly market research surveys and could be directly associated with the sponsorship since that, and its associated advertising, was the only promotional activity undertaken by the company. From its starting point of 2 per cent awareness, it jumped to 8 per cent in November 1977, to 13 per cent by September 1978 and 16 per cent by September 1979. An interesting point to emerge from the regular surveying of market awareness was that the level of awareness fell quite substantially in the periods between Test series. Thus in the winter of 1978/79 awareness fell by 6 per cent — a substantial fall that demonstrates that the effects on awareness of sponsorship campaigns are not long-lasting and need constant reinforcement.

Cornhill's sponsorship was especially successful because it chose to become involved with an event that was not only topical, was creating heated arguments within the public at large, but which was perceived as far more than a sports sponsorship — it was seen as commercial sponsorship coming to the aid of a national institution and, in that sense, became a cause-related sponsorship.

Image

Turning to the other most common objective ascribed to sponsorship campaigns, the creation, reinforcement or alteration of a corporate or brand image, we can see that some of the reservations I mentioned earlier concerning awareness will also apply.

When compared with product experience any of the communication media have a relatively small part to play in the creation of a lasting product image. Even beyond the actual consumer experience of an individual product the total experience of all similar products in the marketplace will have an effect on image perception of the individual product. Thus, it is very difficult to divorce the image of one soap powder from the total experience of all soap powders.

Once again, many of the products supported by major international sponsorship campaigns are already extremely well known and have stable images that may only be influenced in a small way by sponsorship campaigns that are supported by a mix of the other communication media. If sponsorship is used in isolation without being tied into a combined communication campaign the effect it can have on image must be severely limited and is highly unlikely to be cost-effective or lasting.

It is likely that sponsorship, when used as a reinforcer of product image or as a facilitator for a combined communications programme, has more effect on existing product users by giving them 'warm feelings' about their ownership or use of the product and confirming their purchasing decision. In this situation sponsorship may also prove beneficial by helping to make the audience more sensitive to the other media of communications used to transmit product information.

From the above it will be clear that the use of sponsorship to reposition a product image carries the highest degree of risk, even when sponsorship forms only a part of a combined communications exercise. Altering image perceptions of a product is a very tough task that can only be achieved in the long term and which is doomed to failure unless it is consistent with the experiences gained by consumers using the product.

In the case of new products, however, sponsorship can be effective in helping to create the image the marketers are looking for. By choosing to sponsor an event that has an image consistent with that you would like to achieve for the product, and supporting the sponsorship by considerable activity in the other media, an image can be transferred to the product. However, the image must be consistent with the experiences of the consumers and must be supported by long-term promotional activity.

One of the biggest growth areas in image promotion is in the corporate area. Over the last few years there has been an explosion in the promotion of corporate awareness and image. This started with the desire by companies to raise their profile with financial institutions and other key decision-makers and has devolved to the public audience as companies perceived a need to change the often anonymous nature of their businesses. Multi-product companies and conglomerates made up of dozens of individual companies and hundreds or thousands of brands felt the need to communicate their role in the market to a far wider audience, using promotional activities to promote both the company and its products with a combined image theme.

As with the development of a different and discernible image for a new product sponsorship has proved to have a role to play in the creation of a corporate image, especially when the audience for the messages is a relatively small target group, or sub-set of the larger consumer audience. Thus sponsorship is used to target a company's workforce, its shareholders, bankers, distributors, etc., in an effort to improve these audiences' image of the company as well as to create a situation that allows a two-way flow of information.

So, sponsorship does have a role to play in the creation or reinforcement of awareness and image, of both products and companies, but its role and attributes are rarely as simple as many sellers of sponsorship would have us believe. Once again this realization should emphasize the importance of having very clear objectives and the need to analyse carefully the expected benefits of all sponsorship opportunities.

An example of the use of sponsorship to affect both the awareness and image of a company and its brands is the sponsorship campaign undertaken by the wine and spirit company Seagram Distillers.

Seagram, led by its chairman, Ivan Straker, had the long-term aim of building the awareness and image of the company; then, as the campaign progressed, transferring this awareness into brand awareness and loyalty. These objectives were based on the fact that few consumers of brands such as Champagne Mumm, Sandemann port and sherry, Glenlivet, Glen Grant, Chivas Regal, Paul Masson wines and Captain Morgan rum realized they were all Seagram brands.

In order to support the achievement of these objectives Seagram entered into sponsorship of a national institution — the Grand National. Like the Cornhill example given earlier, Seagram, by luck or design, hit on the powerful effect of a cause-related sponsorship. At the time the future of the Aintree racecourse, the home of the Grand National, was in doubt. Seagram's sponsorship of £750 000 over five years helped purchase the racecourse for the nation and saved the Grand National. Like Cornhill's experience with the Test series Seagram's sponsorship of the Grand National carried the danger of being unable to link the sponsor's name with an event that was internationally known as the Grand National. The sponsorship fee did, of course, buy name rights to the event which became the Seagram Grand National, but all sponsors will know the difficulty of persuading the media to use a commercial name of an existing and famous event. As with Cornhill's sponsorship, however, the fact that the sponsorship was clearly perceived by the media, and hence the public, as 'worthwhile' and of benefit to a wide audience meant the sponsorship deal attracted considerable publicity and the full name of the event was used by many in the media and achieved prominence on site. After the first event a survey showed that 25 per cent of the audience sampled correctly recalled the event as the Seagram Grand National.

Sponsorship of the event was just part of the communication campaign that included event-related advertising, hospitality and other activities targeting a wide range of audiences and aimed at promoting the company's brands as well as its overall image.

A second sponsorship campaign was also used to target a different audience but to continue the same theme as the overall promotion. This sponsorship involved supporting the fireworks concert at the annual Edinburgh International Festival. The rationale behind this sponsorship, which was used to promote the name of Seagram's Glenlivet brand of Scotch whisky, was that the brand is seen as being synonymous with quality in its product area, and it allowed the company to be seen as supportive to the Scottish community and Edinburgh, the capital of Scotland, in particular. The Glenlivet Fireworks Concert is held against the backdrop of Edinburgh Castle and attracted 40 000 people in its first year, 100 000 in its second, and 150 000 in the third year.

Strength of messages

One of the factors about sponsorship's role in transmitting messages that is not often mentioned is the medium's inability, in most cases, to provide *explicit* messages about a product or company. Unlike advertising which can portray a range of direct messages with considerable information content, or sales promotions which provide a consumer with very definite reasons why he or she should buy a particular product, sponsorship operates by, at best, providing implicit messages generated by the linkage between a company or product and an event. Even on-site advertising at your event, such as perimeter boards, shirt advertising, banners, flags, etc. is usually limited to name exposure since space doesn't allow for any further messages.

Thus, Cornhill's sponsorship of Test cricket, or Seagram's sponsorship of the Grand National, provides opportunities for name awareness by the inclusion of the company name in the event title, and via ancillary on-site advertising, but says nothing whatsoever about who or what the company is. A member of the audience for either sponsorship who had never heard the company name before should leave the event aware of the name but, unless other information is available, will still have no idea of what the company does. Off-site event-related advertising, sales promotion and public relations activity built on the sponsorship must be brought in, before, during and after the event to convey hard information. If not the campaign will end up like that used to promote name awareness of the brandy Metaxa. Major television exposure gained from a linkage with international soccer tournaments left millions of people around the world aware of the name but totally unaware of what it meant!

There is absolutely no point in using sponsorship to create name awareness and to develop an image based on association with an event if supporting, explicit information is not available to the audience of the sponsorship.

Another problem with the strength of messages available through sponsorship is the growing clutter in the marketplace. At present at least 70 per cent of televised sport is sponsored by a vast array of companies and products attempting to transmit a huge diversity of messages. The situation is not yet as bad as within conventional media advertising but the difficulty of using sponsorship for explicit messages, its increasing cost due to competition for top events, and the increased clutter, are all leading companies to make more creative use of the medium, as with the use of cause-related sponsorship, and to lever their sponsorship into other areas of communication. One has only to look at any major sporting event such as the Formula One Grand Prix series to see just how many companies and products compete for attention at each event via perimeter advertising, names and logos on cars and drivers' clothing, and any other mechanism that offers name exposure. While these companies and products may not, if they are very lucky, be in direct competition in the product marketplace, they are in competition for attention and can seriously damage each other's ability to portray a clear set of messages.

Another thing to consider about the strength of messages available to a company sponsoring an event is its suitability for the targeting of small, sub-set audiences and for the receiving of messages from these publics. In the rush to achieve name awareness with the consumer audience and to transmit messages about image via association with a particular event, many sponsors forget that among the advantages offered by sponsorship is the ability to target a range of audiences and to position oneself for two-way communication. Of course, the consumer audience usually has greatest importance but if you can use the same event to create staff incentives, to entertain key decision-makers, to provide competitions for your distributors, to influence your shareholders, to learn the views of these audiences by allowing the public to sample your product for instance, why not bring all these needs together within the sponsorship? Use the event as a theme and then devise as many uses as possible and you will find that the combined effect raises the total profile of the sponsorship and makes the most cost-effective use of your expenditure.

Matching the event to the objectives

Since the messages that most sponsorship activities transmit are implicit rather than explicit the most important aspect of selecting what to sponsor is matching the image of the event to the image you wish to project for your product or company. When sponsorship works well you will usually find that there is a natural marriage between the audience's perceptions of the event and the messages the sponsor is trying to put across to the main audience. As we shall see in the next chapter this marriage also extends to targeting the exact audience you wish to reach.

By linking your product or company with an event through sponsorship you hope that you will be able to 'borrow' the image of the event and use it to enhance your image with the audience for the event. It is this transfer of image that often causes us to consider product endorsement by sporting stars or celebrities as a form of sponsorship; the principle behind it is exactly the same.

The importance of matching the chosen sponsorship to the objectives for corporate or brand promotion is central to the requirement for those objectives to be identified *before* the sponsorship project is chosen. Image transfer from an event to the sponsor happens most readily when there is an obvious link between the event and the sponsor or the sponsor's products. Thus, as suggested earlier, it is easier to use sponsorship to reinforce a company or product image, especially among existing users, than it is to alter an existing image or to create one for a new product. A company selling sports clothing and footwear would, for example, have a good fit with international athletics, soccer or similar sports while an insurance company, cigarette brand or alcoholic beverage would have a harder time building the logical links that aid consumer acceptance and recognition.

Credibility is all-important if a sponsor is to achieve the desired goals. If the audience perceives a natural link, the sponsorship will be accepted and appreciated as a logical, sensible and 'comfortable' relationship between commerce and sport. If, on the other hand, the audience cannot see a natural link between sponsor and event the relationship may be subconsciously filtered out as having no relevance bar pure commercial exposure.

Credibility also extends to how the sponsor is seen to 'care' about the sponsorship. If a company regularly goes in for short-term sponsorships, switching between events and types of sponsorship on a seemingly casual basis, the effect on their perceived image may be that they are seen as an 'unfaithful' sponsor with little or no interest in achieving a two-way relationship with their chosen events. The same may also apply to sports or events which are not faithful to their sponsors or which do little to support and keep existing sponsors. The image of these sports and events in the eyes of potential sponsors could be seriously damaged in the long term.

In terms of image transfer the most powerful events are those that have a status of their own that is separate from their relationship with commercial sponsors. An event that is respected and achieves substantial publicity on its own account is the most valuable sponsorship vehicle since it will almost certainly have a powerful image or aura of its own among a wide public. Unfortunately, such events — examples of which would be the Olympics, the World Cup, Wimbledon, the Royal Henley Regatta, the Superbowl, the Kentucky Derby, etc. — are the hardest to buy as sponsorship vehicles, cost the most, and are extremely difficult, or impossible, with which to form name links.

At the opposite end of the scale are the events created by sponsors that have no track record as independent events with existing public images. Such events have to have their image created, and will require considerable effort in order to achieve media exposure and public awareness. While such projects can work, as demonstrated by the Virginia Slims Tennis tournaments, a sponsor should be aware of the long time-scale that will be required to build the event and of the considerable amount of time as well as money that go into creating a successful sponsorship.

In addition to marrying the sponsorship requirements to the existing images of events that are available, the sponsor must also be careful to analyse the natural audiences for these events and to match these to the audiences he wishes to reach. The question of audiences for sponsorship will be explored in the next chapter.

Media coverage

While still considering the messages you wish to put across to your audiences you should remember the importance of the media audience. Many sponsors think of the media only as a conduit to the wider public audience and forget that before the media can, or will, pass on messages to *their* audience they must be influenced to project the event and sponsor in a way consistent with the objectives. If the media do not support the event or the validity of the sponsorship you can be certain that they will project a different message from the one you wish to portray.

The media have historically had a difficult time accepting and adapting to the influences of sponsorship on sport especially, but also increasingly on the arts and other vehicles for sponsorship. Press, radio and television journalists who specialize in sports are usually suspicious of, or at best ambivalent to, commercial sponsors and many still require persuasion to include coverage of the sponsor in their reporting of events. This problem can only be tackled by an understanding of the media's attitudes and problems and by an honest approach to all dealings with them. Take time to identify the key media and provide them with the maximum amount of information, not only about your sponsorship of the event but also about your reasons for taking on the sponsorship. I can see few reasons for refusing to talk about this aspect of your sponsorship; the sort of information that you need to give the media to help them understand you and your aims rarely need to be kept secret, yet the paranoic attitudes still prevalent among many sponsors tend only to make them suspicious of questions from journalists who are only interested in understanding the relationship between you and the event.

Take time to understand the media who attend your events, get to know them and be honest with them, and you stand the best chance of ensuring that the messages you want to portray to your audience are the ones reflected in the media coverage of your events.

Sport, the arts and other properties

When selecting a sponsorship property you will need to consider the different imagery projected by the various types of properties. Sport, the most commonly used sponsorship vehicle of all, has, as you would expect, a competitive image and lives by creating winners and losers. Since business is also competitive the two can fit very well together but you have to be aware of the possibility of backing a loser. That may not matter if your sponsorship is carefully thought out and well structured, but if an association with winning is vital to your plans you will have to be careful to minimize the risks inherent with sports sponsorship.

It has been claimed that since sport is brash and, on occasion, abrasive, there are fewer problems associated with sponsorship exploiting sport. This may be true but I doubt it; the audience may accept brashness in their sporting stars but that doesn't necessarily mean that they will accept the same behaviour from sponsors who will go to any lengths to make their message heard amongst the clutter of sponsors all trying to use sport for exposure. Although sport, as a form of entertainment or relaxation, suggests very general images — of health and fitness, competition, aggressiveness, dedication, etc. — each different sport has its own images that can be used to match with the ones you are trying to present. Unfortunately the general image of many sports has become tarnished over the years as professionalism (and the availability of large financial rewards) has increased the pressures on competitors and on individual sports. Drug abuse and violence have crept in and there are increasing signs that audiences are becoming tired and disillusioned by these trends. All these factors mean that you should be careful, if you choose to sponsor sport or an individual sportsperson, in matching your image and awareness requirements to those of the sport. A mistake in selection could be very expensive to your image and may take a lot of time and money to rectify.

Compared with sports the arts have a clean, non-competitive and sophisticated image. Whether you are considering the fine arts or the popular arts you will not be thinking in terms of winners and losers but of images such as relaxation, the quality of life, creative talent, individual energy, style and good citizenship. Unlike sports, the arts in general do not deliver large audiences but the images you can utilize may be more important. Only by clearly defining your needs can you decide which vehicle is right for you.

Outside sport and the arts are other properties that may be right for the images and awareness you wish to create. Television, film, video, radio and book sponsorships can all deliver useful imagery and awareness to certain target audiences as can sponsorship links with charities or community projects. Once you have determined your requirements a careful exploration of all the opportunities available will provide you with a selection of projects, probably in different fields, that can be used to get your messages across. When you then match the visibility each can provide to your audience needs you are on your way to finding a sponsorship that will work for you. Do not automatically assume that you have to use a sports sponsorship because that is the most popular area. It is also the most crowded, and the clutter of other sponsors may make it impossible for you to get your messages across even if, on paper, the selected project looks ideal.

Expectations

It is important to keep in proportion your expectations of what sponsorship can achieve in terms of image and awareness. It is very easy to get carried away with assumptions for performance that would not be tolerated in the traditionally more formal world of advertising. Sponsorship is a subtle medium that takes considerable research, commitment and effort if it is to work effectively, and even then the results may differ considerably from those you expected due to difficulties with prediction, especially if you are experimenting in areas new to you.

It is essential that, if you are using sponsorship for objectives that include affecting awareness and image in large target audiences, you do not overstate your expectations by ascribing to sponsorship unrealistic powers to make major changes in these fundamental factors of audience perception. Especially important is to avoid stand-alone sponsorship campaigns that are supposed to contribute awareness or image benefits. It is a rare sponsorship indeed that can provide anything more than a temporary effect on these factors unless run over a long period and supported by all the communications tools at the marketer's disposal to supply the continuous reinforcement that these factors require.

6

Who's the audience?

While you are considering the type of messages that sponsorship
has to portray you must also decide on the type and size of
audience you want to reach. Do you want to use sponsorship to
reach the general public, or your existing or potential consumers?
Or do you need to be able to reach a smaller, more tightly defined
audience such as your staff, shareholders, the salesforce or key
decision-makers?

In practice it is likely that you will find that sponsorship works
best when you use it to reach a combination of audiences using different techniques built around the sponsorship vehicle. For
instance, you could decide to use a well-publicized sports sponsorship to raise product awareness in a wide, general public audience
that includes current consumers and potential consumers while
also using the sponsorship to provide staff incentives, trade promotions, and as a hospitality venue to entertain key decision-
makers, shareholders, etc. The possibilities are virtually unlimited
but before you can begin to use them you must analyse the type of
audiences you wish to reach.

The general public

If yours is a very large company, probably internationally based
and with a very broad general awareness within your key markets,
it is likely to be a household name. Examples are IBM, Philips,
Guinness, MacDonalds, Rank Xerox, etc. Such sponsors will
normally use corporate sponsorship as a means of indirect mar-

keting, to reinforce public awareness of the company name, and to present themselves as synonymous with their particular market. They will also want to project a particular type of corporate image that will depend on the particular market sector they are in, and which may change over time to reflect the current perceptions of that market. Thus, while the tobacco industry is perceived as being marginally immoral, individual companies will seek to project a public-spirited image linked with healthy, and probably youthful, activities. While the banking sector is seen as boring, faceless and dominated by automated systems, individual banks will try to present an image of friendliness, approachability and humanity.

The growth in corporate advertising over the last few years has been phenomenal. To a large part this has been due to the growth in corporate takeovers which has led companies to promote their name and image in order to progress or defend against takeover bids. There has also been an increased understanding of the importance of corporate image as the larger companies have grown in size and tended to dominate their marketplace. Companies in certain industries, such as tobacco, the oil and chemical business and the drug industry have also had to deal with poor public perceptions and have increasingly turned to image and awareness campaigns aimed at the general public on a national or international basis.

Advertising campaigns of this nature are very expensive and, with the increased need to communicate, more and more companies have turned to sponsorship as a cost-effective solution. While not being an alternative for advertising, sponsorship does help to reduce costs while at the same time providing a 'hook' on which advertising and PR campaigns can be built.

In these cases the sponsorship vehicle required will have as its desired audience the wide pool of the general public on a national or international basis. Little in the way of audience definition will be required since the type, or quality, of the audience is of less significance than high visibility for the sponsorship within the widest possible audience.

Another reason for targeting the general public is the case of direct product marketing where the product has such a wide consumer or potential consumer audience that it is a significant part of the total, general public audience. Once again, the audience for this type of sponsorship is the widest that can be achieved so the visibility of the sponsorship, coupled with the correct messages generated, are the essential factors to be considered. Tobacco and alcohol brands are most commonly associated with this wide audience targeting, although other large consumer brands in other product categories are increasingly experimenting with sponsorship to achieve visibility coupled with correct product imagery.

When the highest possible visibility within the general public audience is what is wanted the amount of research into the type or quality of the audience does not need to be detailed; what matters most is guaranteed visibility for the sponsorship and the ability effectively to link the corporate or product name with the sponsored event.

An example of this type of sponsorship, which actually includes corporate and product promotion, is the Mexico World Cup soccer tournament sponsorship undertaken by Philips. The company's objectives for the sponsorship are particularly interesting. Philips wanted to support and, if possible, improve awareness and image at both the corporate and product level. In addition, the company wished to improve its association with the event at the expense of its competitors. Philips' sponsorship came under the 'home products' category and the company's target audience was the general public reached by this global event. The company achieved its objectives through a combined communications exercise based on the sponsorship. We shall look at the Philips example in more detail in Chapter 7.

Product consumers

For most companies the target audience for consumers or potential consumers of their products is a smaller subset of the general public audience. Depending on the size of this consumer audience there may be no point in targeting the general public and the company will be more interested in sponsorship vehicles that can deliver an audience that is as close as possible to the target audience for the product while projecting images that are consistent with those desired for the product.

The first thing to consider, then, is the detailed information that should be available on consumers of the product. If, for example, the product has a particular consumer profile, say 25–40-year-old affluent males, the sponsorship chosen should demonstrably be capable of delivering this target audience. Unless considerable research is undertaken, both to determine the correct profile of the desired audience and that capable of being delivered by the sponsorship, there is a strong chance that you will end up spending considerable sums promoting your product to an audience that is not ideal for the promotion.

While any company should already know the profile of its typical consumers, since these requirements are no more than would be expected when planning an advertising campaign, it is likely to be more difficult obtaining audience profiles for many of the sponsorship projects that are available. The situation is improving, but many sellers of sponsorship have not done their homework and cannot provide this sort of detailed information. Do not enter into any sponsorship aimed at a consumer audience unless this research is in place and you can be reasonably certain that the chosen sponsorship can deliver the audience you require.

Other audiences
All the other audiences beyond the general public and specific product consumer audiences are a much smaller subset of the total achievable audience. Whether the group you wish to reach are your workforce, salesteam, wholesalers and retailers, shareholders, key industry decision-makers or the local community, you are dealing with relatively small groups who need careful and specific targeting. Obviously a large-scale promotion aimed at the general public or consumer audience may also reach the smaller, specialist audiences, but its effect on them could actually be the opposite of

what you would wish for. A sponsorship aimed at the general public or consumer audience will be designed to send specific messages that could, conceivably, produce mixed reactions in other audiences closer to the company. The workforce or shareholders, for example, may feel disillusioned if they are not specifically targeted or able to understand the rationale behind the company's sponsorship.

Once again it is very important to know as much as possible about each specific audience. How much do you know about your workforce, for instance? Do they fit into a certain age range? Do they have a typical range of interests or type of lifestyle? Do they live in one particular area, have common interests in sport or the arts? Does your workforce have particularly strong company sports teams, clubs or other recreational activities? The same questions can apply to any of your audiences and you will operate far more effectively in sponsorship if you undertake the research that allows you to know your audiences in as much detail as possible.

Lifestyle marketing

In an earlier chapter I mentioned that I much prefer the term 'lifestyle marketing' to that of sponsorship. From what we have discussed above and in the previous chapters you will have noticed that I believe that sponsorship should only be undertaken when you know exactly what messages you wish to project to which audiences. The most successful sponsorships are those which correctly target their audience, match the messages of the event to those they wish to project as a company or product, and which match the audience delivered by the sponsorship to the audience they wish to reach. In order to do that it seems best to regard sponsorship projects as a way to reach a specific audience *through their own interests*. By approaching your audience through what interests them you shift the communication from the commercial level, where many of the audience are resistant to being sold to, onto a level on which it is far easier to communicate since you are doing it in a seemingly more personal manner.

This philosophy of lifestyle marketing can take in any aspect of sponsorship and is not limited to sport, the arts, community projects, media sponsorship, bought-in or created events. Essentially you can use any vehicle you can find for reaching your audience as long as it is of interest to the audience on a personal level.

Central to the whole question of lifestyle marketing is knowing your audience. The research information you need in order to be able to do this is, in many cases, already in place, and sophisticated techniques exist to gather and analyse this type of information. The problem usually is not in finding and analysing the information, but in perceiving the need to do so and in using the research tools that are available, built on the needs of the advertising and sales promotions industries, to help build more effective sponsorship promotions.

The study of demographics — the social condition of communities and societies — is well understood and various measures are available to define audiences. These range from the social grading system that classifies people according to occupation, interests and social backgrounds on the assumption that those who fall within each classification will behave in a certain way, to systems that classify people according to the type of area in which they live using published Census statistics. The idea behind the latter type of measure is that people who live in areas that have similar demographic and social characteristics will share common lifestyle features. The extension of this is that these characteristics influence purchasing patterns and hence the marketer can target campaigns at the appropriate audience.

Using these research tools you can not only define the audience for your product or corporate image or awareness campaign but you can also identify audiences for particular sponsorship projects that match the audience you wish to reach. An extension of these techniques that is increasingly sophisticated but less common is the use of psychographics. This research technique studies how individuals see themselves, their view of the outside world, and how they see themselves and the outside world getting along together. Such research material allows you to learn about the individuals who make up your target audience, or the audience of the sport or other event you are considering sponsoring, and how they are likely to perceive both you, your product and the event.

The geographical reach

Another thing to consider is the geographical spread of your target audiences. If your company operates in the international market-place, like the example of Philips given earlier, you may well be in the business of using sponsorship on a global or multinational basis. On the other hand, you may want to target a single national audience or operate on a smaller scale within specific regions or local communities. If the latter is the case you would obviously be wasting your time and money going in for a sponsorship that achieves national exposure however good that may make you feel. Matching the reach of the sponsorship with your desires to reach your audiences is important for the final success of the project but is often harder to ensure with sponsorship projects than it is, say, with conventional media advertising where reach is easier to ascertain.

INTERNATIONAL EXPOSURE Needless to say, achieving international exposure from a single sponsorship tie-in is going to be expensive. With only a few exceptions this type of sponsorship is limited to the largest of companies and requires considerable resources to be made to work effectively. Within this category exist different types of events. At the pinnacle, especially in the sense of cost, are the large, abstract sponsorships such as the Olympic Games and the World Cup. Such events offer powerful imagery and awareness to a huge, global audience and provide the sponsor with properties that can be exploited in all the communication media. Only a few companies can fully exploit these opportunities however, not only because of the cost factor but also because few international organizations have the structure that allows the integrated use of such projects to be coordinated in all possible markets. In addition to the buy-in cost of such sponsorships are the additional budgets that must be put behind these events in order to utilize all the associated opportunities.

One of the problems with such events is the fact that the sponsor cannot achieve title to the events, can only take designation within specific categories, and has to deal with the competition from several other sponsors. There are usually very few opportunities for audience contact or for on-site promotions that can usually be incorporated into smaller events, and it is often very difficult to achieve product tie-ins.

Among the companies that sponsor this type of event one usually finds several that operate in industries with a very limited number of market leaders. In these cases the reason for sponsorship is often a defensive strategy. Kodak will attempt to protect its position from Fuji and Coke may buy a sponsorship to keep out Pepsi but these are very specific reasons for purchasing sponsorship opportunities that apply to very few companies.

An example of this type of sponsorship is that of VISA and 3M's sponsorship of the 1988 Olympics. Some months before the Olympics sources within VISA — a network of member banks and hence a difficult organization to pull together to achieve effective utilization — were already claiming that business had increased by 27 per cent even before the event, attributable as far as the company was concerned to their Olympic sponsorship. Indeed, they were already considering how to use the 1992 Games even more effectively.

3M is another interesting case. This multi-product, multi-market and multinational company had a turnover in 1987 of $9.4 billion, employs more than 82 000 people in 49 countries and produces about 50 000 product lines yet enjoys little corporate awareness among the customers for these products. Market research showed that consumer awareness of individual brand names such as Scotch and 3M video tapes, Thinsulate insulation and Scotch adhesive tapes were far higher than that of the company and that, because of this, its target audience were failing to link its name with that of its branded products. A major problem lay in the fact that only 20 per cent of their sales are consumer-based with the rest being in the business-to-business category. Much time was spent considering the various options available and sports sponsorship was found to be the best solution. According to the company, sports sponsorship 'provides an ideal medium for communicating domestic brand names. One of the major advantages of the Olympics is that it is a global activity, with substantial television coverage providing mass audiences and prolonged exposure for sponsors. Consumer markets to which other forms of access may be limited are made available through the printed word, and image and corporate identity is endorsed by association with this major event.'

3M had been approached with a view to having their Scotch brand products as the official audio and video tapes for the Games but they responded by approaching the IOC with a different proposal; to take 'official product' status for four of 3M's product categories. In addition other products were designated as 'products of a worldwide sponsor of the 1988 Olympic Games'.

In support of the sponsorship each autonomous 3M product group throughout the world devised individual promotion campaigns. The sponsorship has been used in all marketing media to take advantage of the international medium provided by the Games that, according to the company, 'transcends linguistic and political barriers. The Games offer the opportunity for 3M to reinforce its image as an innovative worldwide manufacturer of quality products and allows the company to maintain its corporate unity by providing *an overall theme to link specific product activities*. Providing visible sponsorship opportunities through television and the use of the Olympic logo on products the sponsorship allows 3M's diverse range of products and markets to be interlinked by the ideals behind the event; those of quality, innovation and success. It gives the company a unique opportunity to reinforce bonds between its family of employees, customers, dealers and distributors by uniting them with a common objective.' That is the company's official line on its sponsorship activities. It is too early to tell if the objectives have been met but it does appear that, for the particular objectives of 3M, the Olympic sponsorship holds the best opportunity for effective exploitation. Only a full-scale post-event analysis will confirm if the objectives have been satisfied.

Another type of sponsorship event that offers international exposure is the travelling series of events that, usually, cover several countries, and which obtain international television exposure. Among such events are the Formula One Grand Prix series, World Cup skiing and, increasingly, athletics. Such events gain their international recognition from television and can reach vast numbers of people, but also offer the sponsor a series of locally-based events that can, sometimes, be used for audience contact and on-site promotions in addition to hospitality, Large-scale, infrequent or one-off events such as the America's Cup, Live Aid or a Papal tour (yes, the Vatican does deal with sponsors and employs an agency for this purpose) also offer a degree of international exposure since competitors or participants come from a number of countries and the hype and prestige surrounding the event can attract a level of television exposure that justifies their inclusion in this category.

NATIONAL EXPOSURE   National exposure can be achieved from two main types of event; those in single or multiple locations. Single location events like the Grand National, Kentucky Derby, the FA Cup Final or the Superbowl achieve national exposure from their status and the consequent media coverage, especially television. (In many cases these events will also receive international exposure through television but this is usually only an added bonus for those sponsors able to take advantage of it.) Often it is possible to achieve title status at such events and they have the additional advantage of being good audience draws with consequent opportunities for a variety of on-site promotions. The big problem with this type of event is the general lack of availability. Since the number of good events is limited, and many sponsors are always on the lookout for new opportunities, it can be very difficult to purchase an event that suits your objectives. Also, it is very difficult to create new, single-location events that can win national exposure in their early days or without significant expenditure and effort on the part of the sponsor.

Multiple-location properties, able to deliver national exposure by staging a series of events across the country over a substantial time-frame, are often forgotten by sponsors seeking national exposure but they have many advantages. Events in this category include music tours, travelling festivals (even circuses can be sponsored!), mall-marketing, road-shows and multi-location sporting series or art exhibitions. Such events achieve their national exposure by visiting many towns, cities and counties achieving considerable local and regional publicity en route and offering the bonus of considerable local impact.

Such events offer a lot to the sponsor since organizers are often able to be more flexible than the organizers of single-location, one-off events and can tailor the travelling promotion to suit the sponsor. When a sponsor wants to target a range of audiences as discussed earlier, the travelling promotion offers one of the most effective ways of securing this objective, especially when dealer or sales support in regional markets is important.

The multiple-location event also offers the benefit of a longer-term promotion, the event is not over in just one or a few days, it lives for far longer and, indeed, can often be extended to be almost a full-time promotion in a large market such as the United States.

This type of sponsorship also offers more opportunities to enter the arena than the single-location national sponsorship since there are far more possibilities and the sponsor is not relying on the national media or television to promote the sponsorship nationally. The local media are always ready to cover quality events in their locality and, if the event has the right profile and presentation, you may still have the bonus of national media coverage at some stage of the tour.

LOCAL EXPOSURE   Local events aimed at local exposure can be the most targeted of all sponsorships and will certainly be the least expensive. Sponsoring a local fair, festival, the smaller sporting occasion or any other local event can offer market-by-market exposure to discrete audiences and can prove to be most effective. This not only applies to the smaller, local or regional company which cannot operate on a national basis, it also applies to the national or even international company which wishes to target specific audiences. Thousands of opportunities for this type of sponsorship exist in every market and sponsors can achieve highly cost-effective promotions that are relatively easy to implement.

These sorts of event are, in fact, harder for large, national companies to identify and run than for the smaller local or regional companies. The large companies will not usually be able to identify or run such local events out of head office. They won't have the time or the local knowledge required to handle these specialized requirements so the successful implementation will depend on a field staff who have the training in sponsorship management to do the job. If the larger company has the structure to allow such local sponsorships to be utilized then dealer tie-ins can work very effectively and you might even find a suitable event to use for a national programme in the future. Spreading the corporate knowledge and understanding of sponsorship into the field, through regional and local managers, sales staff and the dealer network will allow the larger, national company to identify and exploit short-term local promotional opportunities and to build programmes for the longer term.

Matching the event to the objectives

As we discussed in the previous chapter, it is essential to match the events to the corporate or brand objectives and this applies as much to the question of who the audience is as it does to the message requirements. Similarly, it is vital that you match the audience for your event to the audience you require for your corporate or brand messages. Every company is searching for the perfect match and, while this may not be easily identified, you should be aware that it is not impossible to adapt a merely good event into the perfect marriage provided you understand the requirements. Sponsorship is, and always will be, a buyer's market. There are far more events looking for sponsorship than there are ready and willing sponsors, so never be afraid to look for opportunities that you can adapt to suit your requirements.

Many sellers of sponsorship do not understand the true nature of the audience for the event, few can provide any serious research material and *all* oversell their product. Always insist on research into this important requirement, carry out your own checks and carefully evaluate the true visibility and quality of the audience the event can deliver. If you discover that the situation is not what you had hoped for, or have been led to believe, don't automatically dismiss the proposal. If an event has the type or quality of audience you require but falls short on numbers or reach the situation is not lost. Unlike the image of an event, the sponsor stands a better chance of altering the audience by his own efforts with promotional activity. If the event is basically sound the audience numbers can be built on, provided you are prepared to give it some effort and allow the promotion time to develop.

Since the audience you require to meet your objectives and the expected audience for the event are far easier to define than image or awareness factors, it is a simpler matter to match event and objectives but this should not dissuade you from putting plenty of research behind the evaluation process. This applies especially to claimed amounts of television exposure for an event. Many sponsorships are based on the reach generated by television or other media coverage and this is the main area where inaccurate claims are made or where unrealistic measures for the effectiveness of editorial coverage are employed. We shall look at how you evaluate media exposure in a later chapter, but always take the claims made by event organizers or promoters with a very large pinch of salt! Finally on this subject, please make sure that you are certain you can strongly link your corporate or brand name with the event, preferably through sole title sponsorship. Unless this can be achieved it is irrelevant if the event audience matches your target audience since unless you can project your sponsorship involvement to that audience, the whole point of your effort and money will have been missed!

The media

As before when we looked at image and awareness the media are a most important audience on their own account. With most sponsorships aimed at the larger target audiences the media are crucial to your succeeding in achieving your objectives. This applies not only to the general public or consumer audience, the media also matter when it comes to the trade press and your reach among your own industry and your dealer network. Television is, of course, usually the most important medium. Unlike the press or radio, television can deliver both words and images and it is the latter that will make the most impression on your audiences as long as you can achieve name branding in the pictures that are transmitted. If you or the event organizers handle the media badly you will severely limit the effectiveness of your sponsorship to those who attend the actual event; that could be disastrous. The best events from the point of view of media coverage are often the most difficult to achieve branding and this should be borne in mind from the outset. Do not assume that because you have just bought a property that traditionally achieves significant media exposure that you will easily be able to add your name to that exposure even if you have title rights. The opposite will probably be the case. The media are almost certainly going to be reluctant to add your name to their coverage of an event that they may have covered for years and which is known to the public under its own name. While you are likely to achieve plenty of coverage in the trade press this will not make up for the feelings you get when you open a national newspaper or watch a television item that fails to mention your company after you have spent considerable sums on the sponsorship. These are the occasions that sort the professionals from the amateurs and which help discover who has the staying power to make sponsorship work. Unless you are very lucky it is going to take time to link your name with the event and to win over the media. The job is by no means impossible but it requires understanding of the way the media work and the way they perceive their role in your sponsorship; and a lot of time and tact to achieve the recognition you may have thought came with the cheque you handed to the organizers! But don't give up, work hard at getting the media on your side, use some of the techniques you will find later in the book, and you can end up with the exposure you hoped for.

Sport, the arts and other properties

Different types of sponsorship yield different types of audience as well as different types of imagery, but the huge number of opportunities now available to all types of sponsor means that you should never be short of a sponsorship vehicle that can target the audience you wish to reach. At the risk of boring you with repetition the key to a successful choice of sponsorship vehicle is knowing the audience you wish to reach and marrying that objective with the type of audience the event can deliver. If you are looking for a mass market audience, especially if it is on an international scale, you will probably end up with a sporting property since few others can deliver this type of audience. Sport receives far more television exposure (about 12 per cent of TV airtime) than the arts or any other potential sponsorship vehicle, and major events attract very large on-site audiences. Many sporting events allow perimeter or other on-site advertising and some sports allow the sponsor to advertise on players' clothing all of which help, in theory at least, to increase the sponsor's exposure. But this does not apply to all sports or events.

Within the overall sports picture are thousands of individual sports, participants and events, each of which can deliver different audiences. Boxing, athletics, sailing or polo all have different sizes and types of audience, and even within one sport there may be differences from country to country. If you're looking for a broad international audience your scope will be further reduced since relatively few sports are truly international. Soccer, for instance, may be good for a European or South American audience but it won't do much for you in North America or Australasia.

In general, the arts — whether the fine arts or the popular arts — will not be able to deliver audiences that can compete in size or international scope with those of sport. Television and the rest of the media give comparatively little coverage to the arts and on-site audiences are usually small. Branding of an event is also harder to achieve than most sporting events and a company's handling of an arts sponsorship needs to be more restrained and understanding than with sport. However, many arts sponsorship can provide tightly targeted audiences that may be just what you are looking for. If your company is in the business of selling an up-market product in low volumes to affluent consumers, an arts sponsorship could be just the one you need. Similarly, if you are targeting a small group of key decision-makers, dealers, distributors, the salesforce or your workforce a form of arts sponsorship could be the right vehicle.

Beyond the most commonly thought of sponsorship vehicles of sport and the arts are many other opportunities that can deliver a diversity of audiences. Sponsored television, video, radio or cinema programming can, if you select the right programmes and where regulations allow, deliver huge audiences.

Books are another area that has great flexibility and access to large and closely targeted audiences. Then there are charities, conservation projects, local community projects and just about anything you can conceive of. All will have a natural audience and it is your job to determine if that audience fits with the one you wish to reach.

Expectations

In the preceding chapter I warned about too high a level of expectations concerning the creation of images and increased awareness. When we are talking about sponsorship's ability to target a wide range of audiences, however, one needs to be far less cautious. In terms of targeting specific audiences sponsorship is at least as effective a medium of communication as advertising. Where advertising would be inappropriate or wasteful for reaching small, specialist groups, sponsorship, if correctly researched, can deliver that audience cost-effectively. The key, as always, is to research your real needs and to continue that research into identifying the best sponsorship vehicle.

7

A communications package

In the previous chapters we have seen how a marketing policy for the use of sponsorship is essential to its successful exploitation and we have also seen how detailed objectives are a central part of this policy. Throughout this discussion on the use of sponsorship I hope it has become clear that I believe it to be imperative that sponsorship is used as part of a cohesive communications strategy that includes the use of advertising, point-of-sale activity, public relations, merchandising, hospitality and any other form of promotion that is available and relevant to the campaign. Before we move on to discussing the selection and use of sponsorship in practice let's take a look at how some companies have used a total communications approach to good effect.

Gillette and sport
Gillette's relationship with sport began with baseball in 1910 and has continued at an increasing rate ever since, with involvements in many sports and with sports broadcasting. Gillette now devotes a reported 65 per cent, or $308 million, of its advertising and promotional budget to support its safety razor division with more than half of its television advertising budget spent on sports programmes. A commitment of this level is done for only one reason: Gillette's promotional efforts using sports results in demonstrable benefits to its bottom line, especially in the short term, with some brands

achieving a third of their total annual sales volume during promotional periods around major events.

Gillette's sponsorship and related marketing activities are continuous and involve brand managers, marketing staff, advertising staff, and agencies and other specialist external agencies.

Gillette puts its main emphasis on consumer promotions built around its sports properties. Sweepstakes or contests linked to events are designed to shift products using a complete mix of marketing, advertising, trade and consumer promotions. According to the company's marketers they work hard at transferring fan loyalty and interest from the sport to the brand.

To do this the company chooses promotional activities that have the widest possible appeal with consumers. Whether it is a trip to the Superbowl escorted by a famous football player, a visit to the World Series with a baseball star, or an all-expenses paid prize to the Monte Carlo Grand Prix or the British Open, Gillette's product promotions are designed to appeal to fans and consumers.

Gillette also spends considerable effort on working with its retailers, including providing them with everything required to market its promotions at the point of sale. The company gives five reasons for this activity at retail level: to enhance the company's sports image with both the trade and consumers, to build high levels of consumer interest and through store traffic, to encourage the trade to support Gillette's sports activities over a long time-scale, to get the best in-store displays for the company's brands, and to provide the best incentives to the trade to feature the company's products.

In order to create exciting consumer promotions Gillette works closely with other companies involved in sports sponsorship and produces cross-promotions that work for all concerned. The company also advertises heavily around its sports promotions in order to add to the transfer of loyalty from sport to brand. All of this activity achieves its aim of attracting the consumer. So far the record participation in a given promotion was five million consumers — a figure any company would be proud to reach.

The Xerox Marathon campaign

This campaign was created to support the launch of a new line of photocopiers designed to re-establish Xerox's position in the copier market. The marketing strategy was for the new product line to be introduced internationally with a common theme and the decision was to use sponsorship to link in with the product advertising campaign. The company and its agencies undertook extensive research to determine the attributes purchasers of copiers wanted in the product. This research showed that the most important factor in consumers' perceptions was that the machine did not break down — it should have the ability to run indefinitely.

Because of the international introduction the company had to develop a common marketing strategy with a universal message. Once again research was used to determine that the name 'Marathon' produced the same perceptions in all markets, perceptions of endurance and strength. The advertising campaign used to launch the product used the marathon runner theme in print and television advertising in the US, Europe and Latin America.

The objectives for Xerox's use of sponsorship were to get increased exposure for the new product launch on an international basis, to attract media attention, to provide a means to inform the salesforce, and to attract existing and new customers. Alongside these objectives was the determination to integrate the Xerox advertising campaign with the sponsorship of events. Every element used in the advertising was incorporated into the sponsorship and associated promotions.

Fortunately for Xerox a major boom in running coincided with the launch of the new product line, so the company, since it was prepared to react quickly, became a major sponsor of international marathon events under the Marathon label. Also, the company discovered that the demographics of marathon participants were the same as the Xerox target audience so they were easily able to target the business audience they were looking for. Most of the marathon events Xerox sponsored achieved television coverage, and where this occurred the company placed television product advertising within the coverage. Among the events the company sponsored was the Rotterdam Marathon which brought together for the first time the two best marathon runners of the day and achieved significant television exposure. Xerox also sponsored the New York City Marathon along with many regional events that were tied in to local Xerox offices and their customers. The company sponsored the World Cross-Country Championship, held for the first time in the United States, as well as the US Men's Olympic Marathon Trials and the Los Angeles Olympic Games. All of these events achieved significant television exposure that included corporate branding.

At all these events the company and its agencies worked hard to get the Xerox name across to both on-site and television viewers. Xerox branding was placed on every conceivable object that would be viewed on-site and by the television cameras. Finish line tape, blankets to wrap competitors in as they finished, runners' bibs, signage and banners all had Xerox identification.

With event sponsorship in place the company created their own team. Team Xerox comprised a team of top-class marathon runners who competed in most of the events the company sponsored, kitted out, of course, in a Team Xerox uniform. Finally the company organized a promotion called the Xerox Corporate Marathon Relay aimed at bringing together the company's salesforce and their customers.

These events were unique in that entry was by invitation only and that invitation for a team entry had to come from a Xerox representative. Invited corporate teams comprised ten runners, at least two of whom had to be women, and each team member had to run just over two and a half miles. The top three teams won an award and the winning team received a trip to the Xerox National Championship held in a different location each year.

This newly-created sponsorship provided the Xerox salesforce with the golden opportunity to go directly to its customers and invite them to enter the company's event. All invitational packages were sent to the Xerox district offices and the salesforce then took on the job of inviting their top 100 customers.

At the event the salesteam were able to meet once again with the customers or potential customers and mix with them in a social and sporting environment. After the race the salesteam would return with results and photographs for all the teams. At just one of their events Xerox had the opportunity of bringing together over 1500 customers — the sort of opportunity that most companies would dearly love to have. In 1984 the winning team in each of the Corporate Relay events was given a trip to the Xerox Relay Championship held just three days before the Olympic Trials. The winning team was also given a trip to the Olympic Games at Xerox's expense. According to Xerox these promotions had very beneficial results. Not only did extensive publicity impinge directly on their target audience but the promotions aimed at the corporate clients reached that audience and impacted on the company's salesforce who were very enthusiastic about the campaign. In addition to the tremendous amount of goodwill the promotion generated among existing and potential clients, the company also sold 400 000 Marathon copiers in the first 21 months of the campaign — an effect that is directly measurable on the bottom line and amounts to a very successful new product launch.

Philips and the 1986 World Cup

I have already mentioned the Philips sponsorship of the 1986 soccer World Cup but will do so again because it is another example of a coordinated and well-researched approach to event sponsorship. Philips took on this major sponsorship, in the category of 'home products' — which included domestic and personal products, lighting, telephones and printers — at a very late date but with the intention of improving the association between Philips and soccer at the expense of competitors; and to support and improve the awareness and imagery of the company and its products. The target audience for this promotion was very broad — the general public in all the markets affected by this international sponsorship.

Philips exploited the event through perimeter advertising at the tournament matches, utilization of the designation of 'Official Sponsor of the World Cup' in its media advertising, together with the use of the official mascot and logo, and exploitation of the use of Philips' broadcast cameras for television coverage of the event.

Despite having just five months lead-time to exploit this major sponsorship Philips managed to organize themselves on an international basis to make maximum use of the opportunities on offer. The company initiated a steady flow of information to all its international offices to instruct them on how to utilize the sponsorship. This included advice on how to use the emblems, official designs, advertising and promotional concepts, premiums, point of sale promotions and all other ways of using the sponsorship. A regular newsletter was used to inform all offices and to provide the opportunity for countries to learn from each other's activities. The delivery of the broadcasting equipment was used in every country in Philips' advertising, and on the day of the opening ceremony in Mexico nearly 40 of Philips' national sales organizations around the world placed the same conceptual advertising in newspapers with the same campaign running in the international media. The theme of this campaign was 'Good morning, you'll be watching Philips for the next four weeks'. While this was a great example of a coordinated international activity one should point out that it was nearly wrecked by the problems encountered by the host broadcaster that resulted in appalling television coverage for the early games and the consequent uproar from around the world by media and viewers eager to see quality coverage of their favourite sport!

Before the event Philips coordinated a number of international advertisements related to its sponsorship of the event. The delivery to Televisa, the leading television station in Mexico, of broadcasting equipment was made the feature of a video tape story provided free to the world's two major television news agencies, Visnews and Worldwide Television News, for offer to their worldwide network of client stations. Various public relations campaigns were utilized in different countries with the common theme being the World

Cup sponsorship, while dealer trips were organized from different countries to the event with the object being to allow the invitees to exchange ideas and views in the atmosphere of a major international event.

Local Philips organizations were free to use a wide variety of advertising and sales promotion activities based on the World Cup, each of which was influenced by the different national cultures and their differing attitudes to the World Cup in particular and soccer in general. According to Philips it was this local exploitation that was the key to the success of the sponsorship.

These three examples of very different uses of the sponsorship medium do, I think, demonstrate that the medium is extremely versatile, can be used to target a variety of audiences with a range of messages, and has a demonstrable place in the mix of marketing tools.

These examples also show that sponsorship alone cannot deliver the goods. It must be used with all the tools at the marketer's disposal if it is to be truly effective, and should be considered only after extensive research has been carried out, both into the company's objectives and the particular attributes of the sponsorship project under consideration.

If sponsorship is used as a vehicle that allows the creative use of advertising, public relations, sales promotion and any other tool available it can prove to be the most effective use of the corporate or product marketing dollar. If these rules are not followed, however, you may well be disappointed with the results.

Having explored in some detail the place of sponsorship within the marketing armoury we shall now move on to consider the ground rules and techniques for making sponsorship work in practice. Bear with me; I hope you will find it worthwhile in the end!

Part Three

Getting it right

8

Selecting the sponsorship

So, you now have a sponsorship policy thought out and written down that covers, in broad outline, your expected requirements and uses of sponsorship and its relationship to the broader marketing policy. You know the communication requirements you hope to achieve — which audiences for what messages — and you have made explicit the importance of building sponsorship activities into your total communication package. You will have also created a system that allows for your sponsorship activities to be managed by an experienced executive, supported by a special department if you are planning an extensive use of sponsorship, and you have accepted the need to use formal research, where possible, to help you achieve your aims.

Right, let's go and buy a sponsorship. But where do we start? How do we choose between all those proposals that form a steady stream through the postbox? Should we go for a long-established event, take a risk with a new one, cut out the middleman and create our own, sponsor a team, an individual sportsman or artist; do we want to be involved with sport, or the arts, or perhaps we should look at media sponsorship? Or what about a community or charitable link? In other words, how do we analyse all the available options in terms of our own requirements?

Consistency
What we want to achieve is a consistency between the audience for the sponsorship and the target group — its type, size and

geography — for the corporate or product promotion. Similarly, we want a sponsorship that provides consistent messages in terms of visibility, quality and explicitness with those we wish to project for the company or product. And above all, we should be looking for a sponsorship that adds an extra dimension to our marketing plans and builds substance for the lifestyle characterization of our product or corporate image. These goals are quite complex and are certainly more detailed than the question one often hears, 'Will it give us publicity?' The goals for any sponsorship you take on should always be more than 'publicity' since this is very speculative, varies tremendously in its extent due to circumstances beyond the sponsor's control, and is, in any case, only one part of the overall criteria that must go into any sponsorship selection.

An evaluation system

Before you rush out into the marketplace it is important that you take the time to design an evaluation system that suits your own requirements. Such a system will be unique to you and meaningless to anyone else but it will allow you to quantify proposals and ideas against pre-established criteria. Using such a system will also prevent the occasional rush of blood to the head and the purchase of an unsuitable product through initial subjective enthusiasm by forcing you to be objective in your evaluation and decision-making. Once such a system is designed and in place it will also aid you in allocating financial and human resources to each project, will assist with budgeting and will make life easier when you are planning next year's activities.

By now I hope you are comfortable with the concept of analysing your corporate and brand requirements before considering sponsorship and you will, hopefully, have produced a formal list of key criteria for each possible brand user of sponsorship. This may have been done by brand management but it is better if your research department, or outside agency, is given the task. It can then interview brand managers using standard research techniques and eliminate the danger of brand management's personal, subjective views interfering with the assessment. With these requirements in place you can then readily identify the specific criteria of sponsorship projects that are important for meeting your requirements.

Evaluation criteria

You may wish to arrange your specific criteria under headings of Image, Audience, Sales, etc. or you may prefer another system, but the following criteria are examples of those you may choose from for your particular evaluation procedure.

IMAGE AND AWARENESS

- Does it provide a good fit with the brand or corporate positioning?
- Is it unique, or is there a danger of its being submerged under other similar activities?
- Does the event have a legitimacy and identity of its own, or will it rely on the sponsor creating an identity?
- Is the activity strongly associated with other sponsors? Is sponsor 'clutter' a problem?
- Can the event be incorporated into your mainstream advertising?
- Does the event/sport or activity have a clean image, or is it associated with violence or hooliganism (like British soccer), or drugtaking (like athletics)? Will that image affect the sponsor?
- Can the sponsor's name be associated with the event?
- How visible will the sponsorship be?
- What level of media coverage is expected?
- Will television cover the event?
- Will the media include the sponsor's name?
- Is signage available? What will be the amount, location, percentage of total and quality of the signage?
- Will competitors have access to signage? Remember that perimeter advertising or other signage can, like hospitality,

brochure advertising and many other links, often be bought at events without becoming a sponsor

- Will the audience be confused by co-sponsorship deals?

AUDIENCE

- What is the audience for the event?
- Do the event participants fit with a target audience in terms of demographics and psychographics?
- How many participants can be reached?
- How many fans will attend the event?
- Do non-participant fans fit with a target audience?
- How do fans of the proposed activity compare with average consumers of your brand? (If the sponsorship is for a brand of gin, say, you may discover that an average gin consumer drinks ten measures a week, an average soccer fan drinks two measures a week, while a yachting fan averages fifteen measures a week. Thus you can relate participants and fans of any activity to your average consumer for your product.)
- What level of fan involvement is there with the activity? Do they relate to it in an active manner?
- Do the audience for the event tend to be loyal brand purchasers?
- Do you want to reach loyal brand consumers or to make converts?
- Is the target audience geographically correct? If you are looking for a local or regional audience are you wasting money on an event that produces a national or international audience?
- Can the event be used to reach special interest groups or specialist markets?

SALES

- Has the sponsorship the potential to effect sales (on a regional basis perhaps)?
- Does it have sales promotion potential?

- Are there any distribution benefits, either wholesale or retail?
- Can your distributors get involved or be reached by the sponsorship? Are there any other trade tie-in possibilities?
- Are there any on-site sampling opportunities?
- Are there on-site sales outlets?
- Are competitors able to sell on-site?

MISCELLANEOUS

- How difficult or easy is entry into the sponsorship?
- Is it a sole or co-sponsorship opportunity?
- Are co-sponsors acceptable?
- What level of advertising and PR activity will the promoter/ organizer invest in the event?
- Does the event provide employee motivation or training opportunities?
- Are there chances for personality or charity tie-ins to enhance the sponsorship?
- What manpower will the sponsor need to put into the project?
- How much control will the sponsor have?
- Does the event have continuity or is it a one-off?
- Can the event be extended or transferred to another region/ country if successful?
- Are there possible long-term benefits or opportunities?
- Is it a simple or complex event?
- Are there spin-off or mini-events surrounding the main event that can provide added benefits?
- Is the event manageable and do the organizers have the necessary experience?
- Are there any legal restraints (tobacco or drinks companies need to be especially careful on this point), or are there dangers of controversy with the sponsorship?
- Can the event be test marketed — produced on a small or local scale before extending to the main market?

- Can results of success or failure be measured?
- Does the timing of the event fit with the timing needs of the promotion being undertaken?
- Are there merchandising opportunities?
- Are there hospitality opportunities that will appeal to your key guests? Do the right facilities exist?
- Does the event add an extra dimension to your communication activities that aids the projection of a product lifestyle image?
- Are there revenue possibilities associated with the event?
- Will your involvement aid the event?

Some of these criteria may cause a few raised eyebrows — especially those that ask whether revenue can be gained and whether the sponsorship link aids the event — and I shall consider some of these in more detail later.

No company should expect to include all, or even the majority, of the possible criteria listed above in their own evaluation process since it would result in a clumsy system that would defeat the object of clarifying the process. Rather, each company and brand should devise its own unique list based on what is important to them. Such a list is unlikely to number more than fifteen separate and clearly defined criteria and should provide an effective summary of all the key brand or corporate requirements from sponsorship.

Most corporate users of this type of system apply a numerical weighting to each criterion to reflect its relative importance and then allocate a score, out of 100, say, to the event's ability to satisfy each criterion. The total figure gained by adding up the score for each criterion multiplied by its weighting is the final score for the proposal being assessed. The figure, whatever it is, is purely arbitrary and will have no meaning to anyone else. It simply allows you to compare each proposal you receive against each other using a fixed scale of criteria that relate to your previously identified corporate or brand objectives. If you then divide the cost of the project by the total score you get another, relative cost figure that can be used to compare projects.

This technique can be improved over time by comparing the predictions given by the system to actual experience with events. You will probably find that you need to adjust the relative importance of the criteria by adjusting their weighting in order to refine the system but after a year or two of practical experience you should find that it provides a reasonably accurate and objective system that is infinitely better than the personal, subjective basis on which too many sponsorship decisions are made.

In addition to helping you evaluate sponsorship proposals or ideas developed in-house, this system will also help to plan your actions and assign effort and manpower to each criterion according to its relative importance to the overall success or failure of the project. In effect, the criteria you have developed for selecting your sponsorships are also the criteria for a successful (for you) event and can be used, with their mix and weighting, to form the objectives for the running and promotion of your sponsorship of that event.

The brilliant match

All this talk of measurement and objectivity, while vital to the successful application of sponsorship to the communications mix, should not detract from the need for intuitive flair or the benefit to be gained from the brilliant fit. Just occasionally an event and a sponsor come together in a perfect marriage where each complements the other and the combination forms a very powerful communications tool. It is this perfect marriage that is the goal of each sponsorship executive and although the use of an evaluation system will greatly aid selection, only an intuitive feel for the brilliant idea, an ability to react quickly, and a certain flexibility of management attitude will allow a company to take advantage of such opportunities when they arise.

Cornhill's sponsorship of the cricket Test series described earlier proved to be a perfect marriage of an established company in a traditional industry acting to save an established competition in a traditional sport. Both sides benefited; the Test series was saved from a very real threat and Cornhill received significant media exposure and acknowledgement as a 'worthy' sponsor. Xerox's sponsorship of marathon events was another inspired fit that delivered significant benefit to the company and was easily understood by its audience. Similarly, the Mars sponsorship of the London Marathon, Virginia Slims sponsorship of women's tennis and Subaru's sponsorship of US skiing all show an added ingredient that provides the additional benefit that we are all looking for from our sponsorships. In each case an objective evaluation system would have pointed to the benefit of these sponsorships, although such a system was not used in some of the examples, but it often takes an individual's insight to spot the great deal as opposed to the good one, especially when the real benefits of a sponsorship are achievable only in the long term.

The amazing thing is that some companies' personnel don't seem to be able to spot a brilliant match even when they've already found it. The recent dropping of the London Marathon sponsorship by Mars is a case in point. The Mars London Marathon was, in my opinion, a perfect marriage. A product that is sold on its energy-giving properties linked with an energy-sapping event like the Marathon with all the branding and spin-off promotional benefits a sponsor could dream about. Inexplicably the UK company dropped the sponsorship following a change in personnel and, even more astounding, have also been heard to complain about the time it will take to break the link between the company and the event that has so effectively been formed in the public's mind! And, while the UK company was busy ridding itself of what many believe was a perfect sponsorship link, the European arm of the company was actively looking for vehicles to help develop the link with marathon running across Europe. Sometimes this business does make one wonder about the effectiveness of communications within, especially, multinational companies!

If you ask any of the big players in the sponsorship game what they are looking for from their next new sponsorship deal they will almost certainly tell you that they dream of the brilliant match that adds an extra, almost indefinable dimension to their promotion.

These are the ones who see almost every major proposal doing the rounds; virtually nothing is new to them or their departments, if they haven't had it presented they have thought about it themselves, yet almost without exception they recognize that somewhere out there is an idea that can be developed into the perfect marriage. That is the goal of the sponsorship executive, and while a proper evaluation system will help you make the most of sponsorship, will help ensure that you do not buy many dud projects and will bring a degree of objectivity to an area of marketing that too often lacks this discipline, only an understanding of the ultimate goal and a large helping of luck will give you the chance to find that single perfect match that will make your competitors drool with envy. In this sense sponsorship has a lot in common with advertising. You should be looking for the pioneering idea, the one that offers a breakthrough in your search for the route to your target audience, the concept that grabs you in the guts and which you then work on to develop the logic that will convince management! One of the problems of introducing the idea of an objective evaluation system is that such a rational process never throws up this brilliant idea. Such ideas are born out of that sudden rush of realization that may come as a single-page proposal through the postbox, may hit you while daydreaming in the bath, or as you beat yourself to death on a squash court. It won't come at the end of a lengthy evaluation procedure unfortunately. I'm sorry to have to tell you this but, like all other creative areas, sponsorship — and it should be a very creative business — is one in which logic will not produce the brilliant idea. You have to feel it first and then have the guts to run with it, mould it, change it if necessary without losing that essential spark that made it brilliant in the first place.

Budget matters

Budgets! Quite a change from brilliant ideas but, like it or not, budgets have to be under control and the time to get them into this state is at the pre-planning stage. Many of us hate dealing with budgets. 'How can we come up with a budget when we are not sure

what we are going to do with the event?' is a normal cry. Nobody
hates the discipline required for working on budgets more than I
do but I have to admit that it can be done and is an essential part of
making a project run well.

Let's assume that you have started on the search for a suitable
sponsorship project with a total spend budget for the year, or the
quarter, or whatever time-period you chose to work with, already
in place. With this as part of your evaluation criteria you will be
able to reject those projects that are obviously too expensive.
However, don't allow the formality of a supposedly fixed budget
ceiling limit your selection too much. You might, for instance, be
lucky enough to run across one of those brilliant ideas we have just
been talking about that, on the surface, appears to be ruled out
because it is too expensive to fit in with your budget planning. Now
is the time to review your budget, not to throw out the idea! If the
idea shows promise of being more cost-effective than your
previous activities it's worth seeing if you can increase the
budget — but you had better be right! Or you could look for ways
of using co-op budgets. Maybe the idea has cross-use potential for
the advertising or PR departments. What about the sales promotion budget? How about doing a deal with your distributors, or
retailers? Or what about bringing in some non-competitive co-
sponsors to fill out the budget? Don't give up on an idea you
believe in just because, on the surface, it looks as if it's too
expensive.

But back to the more normal situation. You have found a project
that looks as if it will work. Your evaluation procedure has
indicated that the proposal can meet your targets and the outline
budget you have been given fits in with your spending plans. Now
is the time to go back to the proposer and ask for a full budget
breakdown. Just where and how is that $1 million going to be
spent? If the promoter doesn't want to tell you, say goodbye! He
will either be back in your office the next day with the required
breakdown or you will have avoided what is likely to have been an
expensive mistake. Never, repeat never, accept a total figure from a
proposer without seeing a complete breakdown. This is not to say

that most proposers are deliberately dishonest, but sponsorship has, unfortunately, grown up as a medium which far too many promoters have seen as a way of getting rich quickly.

The budget breakdown should let you identify the true costs of the event, and with the aid of your evaluation procedure that identifies those areas of the project which are more or less important, will allow you to question any particular cost areas that seem too high, or which have not had enough funding allocated to them. You will also be able to see how much the respective parties, agent, promoter, organizers, etc., are making on the deal and you may wish to question these or other areas you are unhappy with. Never accept an original budget without going into a full analysis of the different cost areas. You may well find that, with your help, the costs of various elements to the project can be reduced. Often a sponsor can achieve better prices on printing, advertising or other event costs than can the organizer and it is then worth removing these items from the event budget and taking them on yourself.

From the budget breakdown and your own evaluation criteria you can work out how much additional expenditure you will need to put behind the project in order to achieve your objectives. Extra cost areas not built into the sponsorship fee may include your own media promotion, event-related advertising, merchandising, hospitality, film or video coverage and a number of other promotional opportunities that you will want to build into your programme.

A typical range of promotional costs versus the sponsorship fee is from 1:1 to 3:1 and you should beware of any proposal that requires you to exceed these guidelines. A promotional spend less than an equal amount to the sponsorship fee (or the organizational costs if you are creating your own event) suggests that you are not spending enough to secure the proper level of benefits for *you* — as opposed to the event. It is very rare that the promotional activities built into the event package, and designed to promote the event, is of sufficient quantity or targeted in the right way to ensure that you, the sponsor, receives the benefits you are looking for, hence the need to create and pay for your own promotional package. This is especially the case in the larger event in which several co-sponsors are all looking for promotional returns from their sponsorship.

If the ratio exceeds 3:1 you should also question whether the event is right for you since such a disparity between fee or organizational costs and the promotional costs implies that the event is too small to achieve your objectives and you should begin the search once again.

The sources you can tap to fill the required budget vary from company to company. Sometimes you will find a centralized or brand sponsorship budget, but more commonly budgets will be made up of contributions from brand marketing budgets, advertising, sales promotion and public relation budgets. Each controller of the different budgets will want to reduce financial involvement as much as possible while getting as much use out of the sponsorship as possible. It will be up to the project manager to produce a complete budget for the project, including fee, direct costs and promotional spend and then to find the money needed from the various budgets that might be available.

Budget sources may be available from outside the company through co-op deals with dealers or distributors if you can demonstrate the benefits of the sponsorship to their local business. If you are the major or title sponsor you may wish to consider bringing in non-competitive and complementary co-sponsors. Where possible, if you are taking a title sponsorship, you should insist on the right at least to veto unsuitable co-sponsors, and preferably to choose them yourself. You may well be in a better position than the agent, promoter or organizer to sell the deal to other companies you would wish to work with and it is often worth taking on this job since a close relationship between co-sponsors can make all the difference to a multi-sponsor event.

When drawing up a contract between yourself and an event organizer you should always try to ensure that payments are phased throughout the period of the event with the last payment not being made until the end of the project. Payments should also be related, where possible, to the performance of the event organizer or competitor. The recipient should not object to this if the promises made can be delivered, although given the unpredictable nature of many sponsorship projects you should be prepared for changes to your plans and be willing to use a degree of flexibility in interpreting your agreement.

Another point on budget matters not often considered concerns the funding of events that are new and which could not take place without the sponsor. Too often promoters of this type of event come to a sponsor with requests for what is in effect start-up finance. Usually this means the sponsor takes all the risk, which is often substantial, while the promoter pockets a hefty fee. The promoter, or the organizers, then often have the ability to attract further funds from other marketing of the event that is now guaranteed because of the title sponsorship. The scenario then sometimes continues to the point where the event becomes firmly established in the sporting or artistic calendar, rights fees escalate, and the original sponsor becomes priced out of the event.

I am not suggesting that promoters and agents should not make a profit from introducing projects to sponsors but there is a strong case, which some companies are now beginning to recognize, for these early payments that ensure the running of an otherwise unfundable event to be treated as high-risk investment funds that are rewarded by a share in the event and its future earning potential. The original sponsor would then be in a position to take a share in any profit centres that the event can generate.

Linked to this concept is the approach that some sponsorships can be used as direct revenue earners for the company. More and more sport sponsors now look for sponsorships that can at least be self-liquidating by providing income in the form of merchandising, television rights fees, co-sponsorship deals, cross-sales promotions, co-op deals with distributors and retailers, and directly related product sales. I anticipate that more companies will adopt this approach, especially since the supply of major events available for sponsorship is well below demand. This will force more and more sponsors to take on undeveloped events or to create their own. This trend will, however, mean that companies will have to take a far broader view of event marketing than they have done previously since they will have to become much more intimately involved in the business aspects of events. This will also mean that such companies will need personnel experienced in the broader skills of event marketing as well as corporate sponsorship.

Give it time

The first point about time is to give yourself that vital commodity. Give plenty of lead-time to the planning of all projects. Unfortunately, this is often confused with decision-making time. Any system you use should be able to provide a decision on whether or not you are interested in any particular proposal within a day or two. There is no excuse for receiving proposals and then taking weeks or even months before saying yes or no. Not only is this unfair on proposers, it is very poor public relations and will also severely restrict your ability to snap up the best proposals and get them into the planning stage as soon as possible. Most of the major sponsors can make a rapid decision on any project since they know their own requirements, have a good idea of what they are looking for in a project, and have an action system that moves fast to ensure they can stay ahead of their competitors. You should do the same. It does no harm either if, when you reject a proposal — as you will far more often than you will accept one — to take the trouble to suggest alternative companies if you know of any. I'm not suggesting you give projects to your competitors, but once you have been in this business a while you will start to come across a lot of other sponsors and will begin to swap intelligence. You may have a good idea that so-and-so down the street could be interested in the project. You might even be in the position of referring the proposer to another brand manager or department head in the same company or group. Give the proposer this sort of help and he will remember you for ever and is likely to return with another proposal at a later date that could just be that brilliant match you are always looking for!

Back to the subject of time; this time your annual strategy. You need to have all your plans for the next year — it could be the financial year but it is usual to work on calendar years — in place well before the end of the preceding one. You will still, however, want to try to retain sufficient flexibility to allow yourself to respond to that once-in-a-lifetime opportunity that demands not only an instant decision but rapid action. Budgets will need to be agreed for a quarter, half-year or year ahead depending on your particular system, and you will also have to plan for the manpower requirements, advertising and promotional activities well in advance of the event. Advertising is one of the major determinants of lead-time, in fact, due to the time required to prepare and place advertising in the media.

You will also have to allow for the time-consuming matters of contract negotiation and for planning the nuts and bolts of the project. Whatever the project there is always an enormous amount of detail that has to be taken care of if the sponsorship is to be successful and the lead-time never appears to be enough, especially as the deadline approaches.

It is for this reason that only the most experienced companies with the most responsive agencies at their call can really undertake last-minute sponsorships. Many of these occur because a company simply cannot refuse the offer in case their key competitor is able to respond and steal a march. In such cases the organization is really tested. Only organizations with considerable experience can pull these last-minute deals off, and then only by following the rules and guidelines they have laid down through countless events, both successes and failures. If you are new to the game, and if you don't have the money to spend on an agency that you trust implicitly, don't even consider a last-minute deal. Let it go and get your experience with events that allow you plenty of time to plan ahead.

The other major point about time is to ensure that you allow sponsorship to work for you by giving it the time to do so. Sponsorship is not a good medium for creating long-term effects from one-off actions. You need to be involved with an event, individual, sport, music or art sponsorship for some time to obtain the true dividends the medium can offer.

When taking on the sponsorship of an event or a particular sport plan to be in that event or sport in three or five years' time. The first year will be spent learning about the event or activity, making contacts (and probably quite a few mistakes) and finding your way in this new area. The second will start to show the potential you are hoping for, while the third should, if you have done your work correctly, see the benefits accrue, the audience accept your presence and motives, and the media to be comfortable with linking you with the activity.

Don't expect instant results, they can be painfully slow in coming. And avoid one-off event sponsorships like the plague if you cannot see a way of turning them into long-term involvements with the sport or activity. If you take them on you may notice a very short-term awareness reaction amongst your audience but there are unlikely to be any positive image benefits. Once the event is over any awareness you gained will melt away like ice in the Sahara.

Take the time to develop an evaluation system, make quick decisions on proposals but then take the time to plan your actions thoroughly and stay with the plan for sufficient time to reap all the benefits that are available from long-term associations.

Dealing with requests

Most companies of any size regularly receive requests for sponsorship and once it is known that you are an active sponsor, or are looking for opportunites, the flow of requests will increase considerably both from agencies and individuals.

Many executives complain about the numbers of proposals they receive but in my view any company that wishes to use sponsorship seriously should welcome proposals. After all, you want to know what is available, to receive and analyse the opportunities before your competitors, and to enable yourself to develop a pro-active rather than reactive ability to selecting and creating the right projects for you.

What is important is that you have a standard response system in place to deal with all these requests as quickly as possible. A large company with perhaps many different brands all with their own requirements from sponsorship should create a central clearing system for all requests that come into the company through any route. Proposals will arrive in many different departments, especially if, from the viewpoint of the proposer, the structure of the company and of its brands is not clear.

Proposals will either be sent out on a scatter-gun approach where all possible targets are circulated, or the proposer will try to target brands or companies that he feels are right for the proposal. Since it is impossible for an outsider to know what your objectives really are, and since there may be no obvious focal point for a proposer's entry into the company, you will often find proposals landing on your desk which are not relevant to your needs but which may be just right for another brand. Unfortunately, you may be as much in the dark about another brand's requirements as the outside proposer. In order to deal with this problem brand management, corporate advertising or public relations departments may choose not to attempt to evaluate the proposals that land on their desks but refer them instead to the sponsorship department for a central evaluation.

If you have been through the process described earlier in which your central unit evaluates all the corporate and brand needs the sponsorship department will be in a position to evaluate any proposal against all brand and corporate requirements. By developing and summarizing these brand and corporate requirements, and doing the same to the benefits and disadvantages of each proposal you receive, you will be in a position to cross-check and match the attributes of each project with the requirements of any brand or department.

If you don't have a structured system in place to handle all the offers that will arrive by various routes into the company you will find executives having to spend considerable time dealing with requests and may well lose potentially useful projects within the system as letters get passed back and forth before being rejected or ignored. You could also find that several brand managers are all busy evaluating the same proposal that a scatter-gun mailshot has delivered to several different departments, all without the knowledge of the others' involvement!

The sort of system you use will depend on your company's structure, the number of people who need to be involved, the amount of sponsorship you undertake, and the number of proposals you typically receive. You may choose to forward all requests to the sponsorship department for evaluation and reply, or the recipient may handle the initial evaluation and reply based solely on individual requirements before passing on the details for central evaluation. The most sophisticated systems will utilize a central computer data-base which can be accessed by all interested individuals. Details of each proposal received and the responses will then be available to all users of sponsorship and periodically all proposals can be cross-checked with each brand's requirements.

The first response to a proposal should always be sent as soon as possible and could be one of two types of reply. A polite 'no thank you' together with the information that the details of the proposal have been circulated to all other users of sponsorship who will reply directly if they have any interest will be the most common response. Alternatively, if the proposal appears interesting, a sensible second stage is for the proposer to be asked to complete a standard questionnaire that can be easily evaluated against corporate and brand requirements. You can base this questionnaire on the one you will have used to determine your own requirements as we discussed earlier.

If this second stage continues to demonstrate the proposal has merit you would normally progress to a meeting at which you will begin a full evaluation, based, preferably, on conventional research techniques.

9

Nuts and bolts

With all your strategy for the use of sponsorship in place, with specialist skills for the use of the medium available to you, and with an evaluation procedure ready to go, you can now get on with the more interesting business of choosing and running your sponsorship projects!

Types of project

One thing you won't be short of is projects to choose from. There are literally thousands of projects available for sponsorship in every country and many available that will give you international, or even global, reach. The only problem is selecting one that is right for you and, since despite the extent of available projects few will match your requirements, you may have to get involved in designing your own event or at least adapting one that is offered.

One question that is often asked by the prospective sponsor is, 'Should I be in sport or the arts?' Nowadays this question is a bit restricting since the field is no longer limited to a straight choice between sport and the arts. Indeed, you can sponsor virtually anything that requires funds or services. You could choose to link yourself with any conceivable sport or physical leisure activity (I was recently sold hard on the supposedly latest craze to hit the States — walking!), events, teams or individuals. Then there are the modern or fine arts, charity or community projects, competitions, expeditions, fêtes and fairs, circuses, scientific lectures, the provision of social services, even a Papal tour — the choice is wide open and limited only by your imagination.

Many sponsors first choose the broad type of activity they wish to sponsor before selecting an event. In many instances this is a practical approach, but ruling out certain activities before evaluating them does bring the risk of missing opportunities you are not aware of.

The most common practice is for a sponsor to assume that sport, say, is the one and only medium able to communicate the required message to the target audience. This may be true but it is a dangerous assumption to make unless you have actively researched the other options open to you. As we shall see, sport is an increasingly difficult area for new sponsors to use effectively, while some of the other opportunities offer what may be significant advantages for the newcomer to the medium.

SPORT   Sport is by far the single largest market for sponsorship and is also the one with the longest history. The advantages of sport from the sponsor's point of view include the huge interest and awareness level of sports fans, the fact that many fans 'consume' several sports, and the fact that it attracts a very large percentage of television airtime since it is cheap to make, varied and popular, thus providing a cost-effective alternative to mainstream advertising for many companies. Sports fans are spread widely across the full range of demographic and psychographic types, so sponsors can use sport accurately to target specific audiences by their choice of sport, or can go for a wider, scatter-gun approach to reach large-scale audiences. Sport also has the ability to cross national frontiers and cultural barriers that may prove to be obstacles for conventional advertising, and it can do so comparatively cheaply.

The huge range of sports available to the sponsor means that virtually any audience can be reached and a variety of messages implicit to each sport are available to choose from. Sports events can last just a few minutes in the case of a horse race or a boxing match, or they can last days, weeks or even months. You can choose from events that cost as little as a few hundred dollars up to a few million, that attract local or regional audiences, or are watched by huge live and television audiences on a national or international scale. The sport you choose can be amateur or professional — just because the sport itself is amateur does not prevent events from being sponsored — can be played by teams or individuals, a spectator sport or one built on strong participation, can be long established or relatively new and little known.

Despite all these very significant advantages of sport there are a few equally significant disadvantages. Sport is bulging at the seams with sponsors, or at least most of the valuable properties have a problem of clutter. Having read that statement there will now be many organizers and supporters of the 'minority' sports reaching for pen and paper to complain that their sport offers much but so far has few sponsors. Believe me, I sympathize. But the fact remains that in most cases, sports that can deliver an audience of sufficient size and of a suitable type, and have organized themselves to do so, are already crowded with sponsors all trying to put their message across.

There are now too few top-class events to go round. These major events are often in the comfortable position of not even needing to sell title sponsorship since their earnings from television rights fees, gate receipts, advertising signage and the other profit-earning centres reduce their need of corporate sponsorship, which even if it is available, will be extremely expensive.

This excess of demand over supply has led sponsors into trying to develop less-known events, often with notable success, into the creation of new sports, activities and events, and into ever more intensive marketing of sponsorship projects through the television medium. Some current sponsored events classified as 'sport' probably would not exist without their title sponsor's money and promotional efforts, and this fact always tends to devalue the sponsorship message since fans tend to recognize this type of sponsorship as being close to overt advertising and offering little to the longer-term benefit of sport.

The attitude of fans to sponsors has changed considerably over the last twenty years. Commercial involvement with sport is generally well accepted today but there is also growing evidence that some fans are becoming disillusioned by activities that they perceive as too overtly commercial and designed only for advertising purposes. The pressures on professional sports stars to perform at all costs in this increasingly commercial world, including very significant financial inducements to ensure they do so, is seen by many to be responsible, at least in part, for the increase in unsporting behaviour in many sports, of drug-taking and of cheating. These trends clearly worry some fans and many administrators and must also be addressed by sponsors who hope to communicate through sport.

Since sport relies on its ability to provide sponsors with the right sort of implicit message generated by the activity with which the sponsor associates, and since sport is one of the worst vehicles for the transmission of explicit sponsorship messages, it is vital that you are convinced that the chosen event will provide you with not only the audience you wish to reach, but with the image with which you want to be associated.

Look at it this way; you've chosen your event, it has a large international audience through television, and the sport has seemingly the sort of image you wish to link with. At the event the only way you can communicate with the major part of the audience — the TV viewers — is through perimeter signage, perhaps, or by having your logo on competitors shirts, caps, etc. Fine so far, but what happens if the event is struck by violence on the field, or allegations of cheating or drug-taking? Or the competitors who wear your logo are guilty of bad behaviour, of using foul language to the umpire, of fighting on the field or some other form of unacceptable behaviour that is becoming increasingly common at sporting events? What happens then to the images you were hoping to exploit? Do you really want your logo exposed in this way? The argument that bad behaviour attracts the TV cameras and helps expose the logo — and anyway all publicity is good publicity, isn't it? — totally misses the point. You went into the activity for, presumably, clean image association. If you get the opposite, the promotion may have done far more harm than if you had not sponsored anything at all.

The above examples of possible down-sides to sports sponsorship are not intended to send you out into the marketplace determined to sponsor anything but sport; the range of sports is so great that you have many opportunities to choose from, most of which probably do not suffer from many of the disadvantages given. You simply need to be aware of potential dangers when making your choice. From athletics to yachting, archery to volleyball, there are hundreds of sports to choose from. The first task is to gather information on selected possibilities that you can match against your evaluation criteria. Most importantly you will want to know the demographics of the participants and fans for these sports, the size of the audiences each can reach, and the images fans and competitors have of the sport and themselves. Such information should be available from any sport that seriously wants, and is ready for, sponsorship involvement.

Sports that already have a history of commercialism will have done the most work on this research and will probably have their own departments to work with and advise sponsors. New growth opportunities are likely to come, however, from less established sports and activities that have not yet been heavily exploited by sponsors. Such sports may be run by amateur enthusiasts and are unlikely to have the in-house marketing skills to provide detailed information and services to sponsors. In these cases you should expect to use your own research staff or an outside agency to conduct audience research on the activity.

While you will want to learn as much as possible about the sports under consideration you may run into a problem that is symptomatic of the less commercially developed sports. If you talk to an enthusiast participant or organizer involved in any one of these sports you will be dealing with someone who is totally committed to that sport. To say that their perspective is distorted is severely to understate the usual case! Listen to these people and it is hard to understand why their sport doesn't achieve prime-time television every night of the week and have millions of participants in every 'civilized' country! Quite simply, they are too close to the activity, they love it and cannot understand why no one else seems to recognize its potential.

Your search for information about any particular sport should always start with the international or national authority if there is one, since these are the organizations who should be able to provide the background you need. Bearing in mind the problem of dealing with enthusiasts, however, always check the sources of all claims made for audience size and type, unless the sponsorship deal is so small that you are prepared to risk losing your investment.

Even if the sporting authority you are dealing with doesn't suffer from this problem they are still unlikely to understand the needs of corporate sponsors unless they have already worked with some before. This is where your understanding and delicate handling of the situation are required. Even in today's commercial sporting world there are still many individual sports that have little or no experience of dealing with sponsorship. Many of these are naturally protective of their sport and, despite needing funds for development or just plain survival, require gentle handling by any prospective corporate partner.

Even if you have been attracted to a sport by an agent or representative of a particular event I would recommend that before making any decisions about specific events you take the time to learn about the activity in some detail and the experiences of any sponsors who have been there before you. In Britain the Sports Council, the Central Council for Physical Recreation, and the various national sporting authorities are able to provide information on sports sponsorship while similar organizations exist in other countries.

THE ARTS   If you think that sports are varied in the opportunities they offer then take a look at the world of the arts. From popular arts such as rock music, modern theatre and festivals through to the fine arts of music, opera, theatre, ballet, etc., there is a huge range of opportunities available to you. Sponsorship of the arts may be a long way behind sport in terms of quantity or experience but it does have a long history of patronage. Nowadays the arts, both popular and traditional, are relying on either the state or individual patronage, are facing up to the world in which they have to survive, and are embracing the concept and practice of commercial sponsorship.

Compared with sports the arts have a far lower profile, smaller audiences, considerably less media coverage and do not always travel as well across national frontiers. The major area of arts sponsorship that is not covered by these very general observations is popular music which has seen a great growth in sponsorship involvement in recent years. Sponsorship of rock music has given marketers a valuable means of targeting a young audience that has proven to be relatively hard to reach via sport. Pepsi's sponsorship of Michael Jackson is probably the most newsworthy example of this type of sponsorship but there are many other recent successes that demonstrate that this vehicle is going to be far more heavily used in the future.

Sponsorship of today's rock stars has the advantage, not shared by many other artistic vehicles, of providing the potential to reach an audience size as big as offered by most sports, also of attracting television coverage, and of providing a versatile promotion that can feature well in mainstream advertising and product sales promotions.

Like sport, the arts offer the ability to reach accurately targetable audiences, and while these may be smaller than most audiences for sport sponsorships, they often offer the advantage of more up-scale demographics and of providing images that are also associated with up-market activities. Projects can be had at prices that can range from the provision of some simple services like printing and basic promotions with no fee involved, through to major international sponsorships costing hundreds of thousands of dollars.

The lifestyle association of the arts offers sponsors a valuable means of reaching a variety of audiences but the means used to do this tend to be far less overtly commercial than most sports sponsorship. The sponsorship of an artistic event or individual does not buy the sponsor the opportunity to employ the heavy-sell techniques they may be able to get away with in sponsorship of

sport. Heavy branding of artistic events and the explicit endorsement by performers and artists of the sponsor or the products are
not benefits that the sponsor should expect; rather more subtle
approaches must be devised and the sponsor must be satisfied with
the 'quality' or 'artistic' image links that sponsorship of the fine or
popular arts can bring.

Sponsorship of the arts can be used to target a very wide range of
audiences but one of the most common uses for this type of vehicle
is to reach <u>small groups of key decision-makers</u>, the workforce,
shareholders or other target groups who can be entertained in an
unusual environment using the sponsorship. Sometimes product
consumers can be directly targeted if the product has a consumer
profile that spells sophisticated, quality and expensive tastes.
While an automobile manufacturer such as Volvo can effectively
use tennis sponsorship since the demographics of the tennis
audience match the demographics of the Volvo consumer, a
manufacturer like Jaguar can use arts sponsorship, through the
entertainment of very small groups of potential clients, to sell
its automobiles.

As with the selection of a sporting event for sponsorship it makes
sense to talk to a number of people in the arts world before committing yourself to any one event, in order to get an overview of the
market. Once again, you should try to obtain research material for
the audience provided by the different types of arts sponsorships
but this is likely to be more difficult than with sport since the arts
world has generally less experience of the needs of the commercial
sponsor. In Britain a potential arts sponsor can obtain supporting
information from the Arts Council and the Association for
Business Sponsorship of the Arts while similar organizations exist
in many other countries.

EVENTS OR INDIVIDUALS Another fundamental question
you will want to answer is whether you wish to concentrate on the
sponsorship of events or to become involved with individual competitors or teams, or whether your objectives can best be met by an
approach that combines these different types.

Sponsoring an individual involves the same principles as sponsoring an event. You will have chosen the sport or artistic activity that best suits your audience and image requirements, but you will then have to identify the individual whose personal audience and public image can best be utilized for your purposes. You will nearly always want to pick a high-profile competitor with a winning record although you may decide to go with a less well-known competitor who won't cost as much, but who will, you hope, develop into a star during the period in which you are involved as a sponsor.

Sponsorship of an individual tends to carry a higher risk than an involvement with an event since you are almost totally reliant on the individual's performance and, more importantly, on his or her behaviour while in the public spotlight. Unfortunately, today's pressures on sporting stars especially often boils over into behaviour with which many sponsors would not wish to be associated. If an individual you are using to promote your image behaves badly in public, cheats or abuses drugs, the spin-off damage to you could be significant.

Commercial involvement with individual sporting stars comes in many forms; you may simply buy advertising rights to put your logo on their clothing, equipment or transport, they may be contracted to endorse your products — by using them, playing with them or appearing in endorsement advertisements — or you may have a package sponsorship deal that buys you some or all of these plus the right to have the star attend promotional days you organize to entertain key clients, distributors or other decision-makers. These different forms of involvement imply varying degrees of 'approval' by the individual for the sponsor or his product. It is important that you decide clearly in advance just what you wish to achieve from a relationship with an individual.

Extraordinary high sums are now often paid to top athletes in return for their wearing corporate or product logos on their sports clothing. These logos are often very small, are hard to identify even when the television camera moves into a medium close-up, and rely on the image of the athlete to transmit any messages about the sponsor to the audience. Personally I would question the spending of hundreds of thousands of dollars for the right to this sort of advertising unless some other significant benefits are included in the deal.

Sponsoring a sports team or artistic group reduces the problems associated with linking your name and image to a single individual. A team is less likely to develop a poor public image than a single star, and the possibilities for effective promotional use of the group should be increased. But do make sure that individual members of the team are not already sponsored, especially by your competitors. If all team members wear your logo this will help increase its visibility, and the public's impression of a team sponsor may have more of the 'supportive' image characteristics than sponsorship of a top individual which is often perceived as the sponsor riding on the coat-tails of a successful star.

In general, I would suggest that a sponsorship involvement with an individual or a team should come after you have chosen the sport or artistic field that is best suited to your requirements, and after you have built up strong links with the activity by sponsorship of events. Event sponsorship helps you build a close association between you and the activity in the public's mind. Once that has been achieved team or individual sponsorship can be utilized to develop further opportunities for exposure within the existing sponsorship umbrella.

THE TOP END OR GRASS-ROOTS LEVEL?   When considering sponsoring an event, individuals or teams within a selected sport or other activity you should first decide whether you wish to enter this involvement at the top end or at the grass-roots level. All sports or activities can be thought of as a pyramid; at the top are the winners, the top performers, those of excellent ability. In the professional sports or arts these top performers are often very highly paid and have celebrity status. Below this level are the merely good performers, sometimes able to earn an income out of the activity, but often holding down a regular job to pay the bills. Below this level are those of average ability. While at the base of the pyramid are the grass-roots participants — the casual players, novices, beginners and young potential talent.

Sponsoring a top sportsman or artist can link you with excellence, a winning ability, or a rare talent, but it also carries substantial risks and may be difficult to utilize effectively. An involvement with the grass-roots, especially youth talent, may provide less exposure through the media but will almost certainly be far cheaper and can often be used very effectively in promotional activities. You may even strike gold and find that a youth talent you support now becomes a major talent of the future.

INTELLECTUAL PROPERTIES   This group includes properties that are protected by the law of copyright such as film, video, television or radio programmes; theatrical and musical works; books, magazines, newspapers and other publications. Any of these could be sponsored but the most valuable is television programme sponsorship.

Sponsorship of a television programme has the advantage of linking the corporate or product name with the editorial content of television rather than its advertising. While viewers can, and do, filter out television advertising messages in a number of ways, the messages given by a sponsor's link with a programme are set in the context of non-advertising. Viewers tend to relax their guard against advertising outside commercial breaks and to accept more readily the messages given to them. The value of this to advertisers is obvious from the efforts taken by major brand names to ensure the placement of their product in major movies.

Sponsorship of broadcast television programmes (and many of these comments also apply to radio) involves the payment of a fee for the rights to associate one's corporate or product name with a programme. The programme could fall into the categories of drama, comedy, music or light entertainment, but by far the most popular at present, and almost certainly in the future, are sports programmes.

The amount of branding the sponsor will be able to achieve will

depend on any rules governing programme suppliers in a particular country. These rules differ tremendously around the world
and often vary within any one country depending on whether the
broadcaster is a national or public service channel, an advertising
channel, or a supplier that delivers its programmes by cable or
satellite. Some suppliers will not or cannot accept any association
between a sponsor and a programme, while others treat sponsorship as an important source of income (or as a means of reducing
the cost of purchased programming) and are able to offer a
sponsor name association, and excellent audience targeting
and reach.

The current level of programme sponsorship outside the US is
small but the indications are that it will grow tremendously in the
near future. Indeed, I would not be surprised if, in say ten years'
time, that television and radio programmes form one of the most
popular areas for sponsorship. After all, if you can sponsor the
television coverage of golf, say, and achieve high association and
recognition with the golfing audience, you don't necessarily need
to sponsor an event or player and have the attendant trouble of
ensuring that television covers your event. Obviously, an event
sponsorship can offer other advantages outside television
exposure but airtime is often the most significant attribute. By
sponsoring the programme you can go directly to your audience
through the most powerful medium of all.

Resistance to programme sponsorship is usually based on two
factors. First, many programme-makers argue that it distorts or
undermines the editorial integrity of programmes, especially in the
minds of viewers, even if the sponsor has absolutely no editorial
influence on the programme. Secondly, station executives will be
concerned with the financial or legal implications of sponsorship.
Some broadcasters are prevented by charter or other regulations
from carrying advertising in order to be supposedly independent
of any commercial influences, and the use of sponsorship will then
normally also be restricted or prevented. Even the executives of
commercial stations may well have reservations about sponsorship
since they may argue that advertising revenue may fall if sponsors

have direct access to programmes and an alternative to the rapidly increasing costs of television advertising.

Rapid changes in the international television industry do, however, mean that programme sponsorship is almost certain to become far more common. Television throughout the world is becoming increasingly open to competition, stimulated by the advent of cable, and even more importantly, of direct broadcast by satellite (DBS). The rapid increase in television airtime in many countries brought about by an increase in channels and a trend towards twenty-four hour programming means that the demand for programming has risen strongly. Programme repeats cannot continue to fuel this increased airtime but a failure of programme budgets to rise in line with the increase in hours to be filled means that suppliers are increasingly anxious to obtain inexpensive quality programming.

The cost of making programmes is probably reducing in real terms as new technology and the demise of the restricted practices historically endemic in the television industry combine to allow more effective utilization of resources. It is, however, never a cheap business to make the quality programmes that suppliers require if they are to compete with an increasing number of rivals. Since advertisers seem increasingly reluctant to put up with ever-escalating airtime costs (coupled with a possible decline in the effectiveness of TV advertising due to fragmentation of audiences and growing competition for a finite audience from other activities and media) the only practical route for programme suppliers is to use sponsorship to help reduce or eliminate programme purchase or production costs.

Programme sponsorship has the advantage of directly using the television editorial medium to reach a sizeable audience who can be targeted and attracted through their lifestyle interests without the necessary complications of event or individual sponsorship. Also the medium has the advantage that it can be used inter-nationally or on a global basis. An international sponsor can use the medium to reach his audience in several countries and, since sponsorship based on lifestyle activities typically crosses cultural,

linguistic and national boundaries far more easily than does advertising, the sponsor will not have the same problems as are
associated with designing an international product advertising
campaign.

We have already taken a look at the use the Gillette Company
makes of sports sponsorship so it should come as no surprise to
discover that Gillette was one of the first to use international programme sponsorship with their Gillette World of Sport programme. A general sports show such as this suits Gillette very well
but I am sure that, in the future we shall see many more dedicated
sports shows — motor racing, athletics, cricket, tennis, golf, sailing
etc. — funded by sponsors who wish to reach the audiences
provided by each particular type of fan. This sort of programming
could lead the way in the development of true narrow-casting, as
opposed to broadcasting, in which smaller but more identifiable
audiences are targeted by programming. This trend will benefit the
sponsor but is also likely to be welcomed by viewers who complain
at the lack of coverage given to their favourite subject or activity. If
there are enough fans or participants to be attractive to a sponsor
someone somewhere could benefit from targeting that particular
audience.

Specially attractive areas to sponsors of programming in the
future will be sports shows and programmes aimed at the youth
audience — an audience that is proving increasingly important yet
difficult to reach through conventional television advertising.

Although we can expect, at least in Europe, that it will be cable
suppliers and the operators of DBS services who will be most
receptive to using sponsored programming, I am sure that the
terrestrial broadcasters, and even those in the national broadcasting area, will soon be forced to consider sponsored programming. Moves such as those in Britain whereby broadcasters
are required to take a sizeable percentage of their programming
from independent producers will increase the need for alternative
funding sources, since broadcasters will be unwilling to pay the
whole cost of production. This will push producers towards sponsorship funds as well as co-production finance.

One crucial point for sponsors who might be tempted to rush into this area is that rigorous research must be conducted into audience figures and the degree of branding that will be allowed in each market before committing to such projects. And of even more importance is the need to ensure that the programming is of the best quality and standard possible. It may appear attractive to produce low-budget programming, especially if there is no competition at present in the market for your programme, but this is a very shortsighted view. First of all, the audience generally is used to seeing quality programming and any drop from this accepted standard will undoubtedly prove unacceptable to viewers. Secondly, a sponsored programme carrying substantial branding is a powerful awareness and image tool. If the programme quality is poor, you cannot expect the audience perception of your product to be any better. Do the job badly and you can be sure that a competitor will step in and do it better, such is the competition for quality programming within the television industry.

Television programmes can be a very useful sponsorship vehicle not just because of their direct reach to a targetable audience but because they also allow the sponsor to build an integrated campaign around the programme that will add value to the sponsorship. Video copies of the programme can be offered through the specialist press, event sponsorship can be incorporated to build the links between the sponsor and the activity and to provide hospitality opportunities, books and other publications can be developed for the audience, merchandising can be sold, and advertising can utilize the sponsorship theme, often in and around the programme.

One final point on the sponsorship of television programmes. As a journalist and programme-maker I am convinced that sponsorship can be used by programme-makers without having to relinquish their much valued editorial independence. Indeed, I believe that sponsors should not ask for such control and that producers should never relinquish it. Apart from the ethics of the situation there is a good practical reason for this. The success of the sponsorship will depend on the programme appealing to the target audience and this is best achieved by letting television professionals do what they are good at doing — making programmes for audiences. If the programme is made with too much commercial bias or presentation, or the level of branding is offensive, the result will be to alienate the audience. They are watching the show because they are interested in the content. If a sponsor's involvement is giving them something they like, and which they have not had available before, they will have positive feelings towards the sponsor. If, on the other hand, you overplay the branding at the expense of the programming, you will only succeed in alienating your audience.

The level of branding you will be able to achieve will depend on the rules under which the supplier operates. Indeed, if you are producing a programme for international distribution you may well have to alter the level of branding for each programme outlet. Ideally, you will want the programme to have a title that includes your brand name during the top and end titles, going in and out of commercial breaks, and whenever a caption is seen on the screen. For some markets all these are possible, as are having sets designed in the corporate style, your logo used on screen and with presenters dressed in the corporate colour scheme. In other markets you may have to restrict the branding severely, especially in the title of the programme, but always remember that there are many ways of achieving audience recognition of your sponsorship apart from the direct approach.

Official films of major events can usually be sponsored, sometimes separately from other involvements in the event. Unlike ordinary television programmes official films are often designated for cinema showing as well as for television release and home video distribution. The 'shelf-life' of an official film is often longer than topical programmes designed solely for television but the production time is also often longer. If the film is destined for cinema release it will be shot on film rather than the now normal video tape used for most television sports coverage. The use of the film medium can often give creative film-makers more scope for producing interesting and evocative portrayals of events. Branding such films can be quite difficult but for a sponsor interested in using all methods to make an activity his own, the official film of an event can be a useful sponsorship vehicle.

Book sponsorship is another medium in which sponsors are showing increasing interest. A book can be aimed very effectively at a target audience with many of the lifestyle-related advantages discussed above. Branding can be explicit, it can be targeted at a national or an international market, can reach very particular audiences and is highly flexible. Whether your market calls for a glossy, coffee table publication or a paperback you can find a subject and format to fulfil many requirements. In book sponsorship the sponsor puts up the money or shares the risk with the publisher and should also expect to share in royalties. Book sponsorships allow a sponsor to extend his campaign to reach an audience through a new route that is complementary to many other promotional and marketing activities, and to do it in a way that can often become a revenue-earner. So a major sports sponsor could produce an annual publication dealing with his chosen sport to reinforce the overall campaign and to approach the audience through a different and effective route. Like television sponsorship, and indeed the sponsorship of virtually anything, the activity itself should have a purpose other than to promote the sponsor. If a book does not stand up on its own merits and is seen merely as a form of advertising, the value of the sponsorship will be lost.

Many products lend themselves to book sponsorship. A manufacturer of burglar alarms could, for instance, sponsor a book on the subject of preventing burglary in the home or office; a manufacturer of tools for the do-it-yourself market could produce a guide to home improvements, while a company producing food products for babies could sponsor a manual of child care. Products can often be used in illustrations, but once again these should be used because they support the text rather than merely to sell the product.

Books such as the *Michelin Guides*, and the *Guinness Book of Records* and the *Wisden Cricketers' Almanac* are all examples of successful publications that have become standard works and continue to carry the sponsor's name to a wide audience. In order to achieve this sort of success the sponsor should work with an experienced publisher and a professional writer or author. The sponsor should not attempt to interfere with the editorial process except by providing any specialist knowledge you have in the subject, and ensuring the accuracy of any material pertaining to your business.

OTHER SPONSORSHIP OPPORTUNITIES   Outside the broad coverage of sport, the arts, teams and individuals, and intellectual properties lay many sponsorship opportunities in areas as diverse as competitions, expeditions, charity or community projects. fêtes and fairs, aerobatic demonstrations and firework displays. Or how about the American idea of mall marketing where a sponsored show or theme activity visits shopping malls on a regional or national tour? Such opportunities, whether existing or born of your imagination, stretch the boundaries of sponsorship to new limits. Few specific rules can be laid down for the exploitation of this type of opportunity except to say that whatever the activity you should still expect to research the likely audience for the sponsorship and the messages that the activity itself is likely to generate.

Many of these opportunities offer relatively unusual ways of reaching an audience and of gaining publicity and it is the uniqueness of many of this type of project that can make them stand out from the crowd and get you noticed. The important thing, when evaluating projects that don't fit comfortably into any particular type, is to keep an open mind and to undertake enough research to give you the answers you need to make an informed decision.

Buying the project

Now that you have selected your sponsorship vehicle you have to begin the task of ensuring that all the details are in place before the project gets underway. At this stage you may be feeling excited by the project, eager to get on with it, and excited — or maybe overawed — by the countless details that you will have to organize

Figure 9.1   A sponsorship link with a charity can prove effective, especially if a well-known personality such as British Chancellor of the Exchequer Nigel Lawson helps launch the promotion. (SOURCE: HELP THE AGED)

before the event begins. STOP. Now is the time to take one last look at the research information you have and to run through the reasons for entering into this sponsorship. Are they still valid? How conclusive is the research? How impressive are the organizers? Has the situation changed since you analysed your

requirements? If the answers to these questions are all favourable
you must still ensure that the process of buying rights in the
property is carried out in a way to minimize your costs, exposure
to risks and any possible tax liabilities.

WHO DO YOU DEAL WITH?   The question of whom you deal
with is most important. You may have been dealing with an agent
during the preliminary negotiations, or you may have been dealing
directly with the rights holder. At this stage you will certainly want
to finalize agreements and arrangements with the rights holder as
well as the people who will be organizing your event should they
be different from the rights owners. You will probably also have to
bring in your own specialist advisors for matters such as contractual arrangements, financial, tax and insurance implications, and
you may also have to deal with the media to ensure coverage
of the event.

The most important thing at this stage is to identify exactly what
rights you are buying and what you are paying for each one. Do not
accept an 'all-in' price without seeing a complete, itemized breakdown. If you have been dealing with an agent in the early stages of
negotiation do insist on knowing what commission arrangements
have been agreed between the agent and the rights holder. If you
find that you have been approached by several agents all claiming
to be representing the rights holder don't deal with any of them if
you can help it. Go straight to the rights owner and let him or her
sort out his or her own arrangements with the various agents. This
situation happens too often and is usually caused by a rights holder
who is reluctant to give exclusive selling rights to one agent and
tries to play the field, often at the expense of finding a sponsor
since the number of agents in the game tend to confuse the
market.

Do insist on knowing what commission is being paid and do not
accept the argument that since it comes out of the recipient's
income from sponsorship it should be of no concern to the
sponsor. Of course it is, since you will eventually be footing the bill
for the agent and an excessive commission will be reflected in the

amount you have to pay. Tales of agents taking up to 70 per cent of the fee may be unusual but it does happen. Typically an agent will expect between 10 and 30 per cent of the sponsorship fee but you may wish to discuss this with the rights holder and the agent if you feel that the level of effort the agent has had to put into the sale fails to justify the commission. The only time to sort this out is before signing anything and only in consultation with the organizing authority and the rights holder.

Make a list of everything you expect to receive from the sponsorship, that is, those things that are to be provided by the organizers, and ask for a breakdown of the fee allocated against each of the headings. For instance, you may expect to have your name included in the title of the event, advertising on players' shirts, signage around the stadium, your name and logo on all printed matter, a number of pages of advertising in the official programme, hospitality facilities from a certain number of people, and a set number of tickets to the event. These, and many other expectations, will be what you require from the event. List them all and ask the organizers to break down the costs for each one. Remember that at many events you can buy some or all these rights without becoming a sponsor and you will want to ensure that you are being charged no more for any particular privilege than other advertisers who are not taking sponsorship rights. Indeed, you should expect a healthy discount on many of these items compared with what a simple advertiser is expected to pay since your sponsorship package will be of far more value to the organizers.

Now is also the time to explain to the organizers exactly what you hope to do by way of promotion, over and above that which will be done by them or included in your package. Discuss your sponsorship objectives with them, as well as the details of what you wish to do, so that there can be no question later of misunderstandings and so that they can adjust their activities, if possible, in order to help you achieve your aims. By the time you have listed *all* the details of the sponsorship and the extra activities you will undertake to make your sponsorship work you will have a list that will probably be daunting in its size. In fact, this list should become the most useful aid to running your sponsorship.

I prefer to use a loose-leaf folder with separate pages for each activity or detail that must be organized. At the start of the project you will simply have a list of headings but you should also include your overall aims for the sponsorship on the title page, and the particular aims for each activity right below the heading of each section. This folder will become your event bible, will help ensure that you do not forget any of the vital details, and will be invaluable when it comes to organizing this and subsequent events. It will also be an extremely useful aid in finalizing your personnel requirements and the total spend budget and will help ensure that you do not omit some crucial element that foils all your careful financial planning.

The question of the experience and reliability of the event organizers or the governing body of the activity you are sponsoring must be addressed before you commit yourself to the sponsorship. Have they run this event, or one like it, before? Will you be able to rely on them? Do they have the personnel needed or is it a small organization that will be overwhelmed on the day? Will they have the funds required to complete the event or will they need to secure other sponsors before you can be sure that the event will take place? Are the funds you are providing really more of investment finance than a straightforward sponsorship fee and if so can you obtain a share in the future of the event? Do the organizers have the authority to deliver all they are claiming? Has the media really promised to cover the event as the organizers claim? And do they have the experience to build the publicity level for the event? These and other questions must be answered before you finalize the deal. Do not be afraid to ask for supporting evidence of all claims, especially ones made about expected media coverage. If a television station is really planning to cover your event they should be prepared to confirm that in writing. If you are sponsoring an event with co-sponsors do take the time to meet them and discuss what you each expect to achieve from the project. Make sure that the organizers or rights holders are making the same claims to each of you and look for differences in the deals under offer that could cause problems later in the relationship. If you are the title sponsor try to retain control over the type of co-sponsors who will be invited to join the project. If necessary, work with the organizers in finding and selecting secondary sponsors so as to ensure that they are compatible with your aims.

CONTRACTS   You should always write a contract to cover even the smallest sponsorship project you undertake. Sponsorship is a business deal between two or more parties but the special nature of the sponsorship medium usually means that the deal is quite complicated. The only way to make sure that you and the recipient get what you had expected to receive is to write it all down at the beginning of the project. A sponsorship contract will be covered by normal contract laws but it may also involve laws covering copyright, the use of trademarks, charities and some other legal niceties that you may not often meet in your normal course of business. You will need to involve your in-house or external legal specialists but it is usually best if you sketch out the clauses to the agreement before having it vetted by professional opinion.

The main problems you should be seeking to protect yourself from are concerned with non-delivery of promised benefits, outright deception, the cancellation of the event, a change in image of the sponsored activity or person, and possible accidents. The recipient will want to be covered against a withdrawal of funds or a change of heart (or management) on the part of the sponsor, a change in the objectives for the sponsorship, and any misunderstanding on the question of which party is responsible for the various supporting activities that must be undertaken.

The danger of non-delivery of promised benefits will be much reduced if you have gone through the discussion and itemization processes described above so that everyone involved knows and understands the objectives and their roles in meeting them. Any difficulties that might arise from circumstances out of your control should be thought through and an appropriate response worked out in advance. If, for example, an important benefit of the sponsorship hinges on the attendance of a VIP do work out in advance what the effect would be if the celebrity was detained for some reason, and what you would do about that eventuality.

Outright deception is highly unlikely although it has occurred, but the processes you will have gone through already should have eliminated that possibility. The cancellation of the event for any reason would be a serious problem, especially if you have already handed over most or all of the funds you were committed to. If cancellation could be a possibility then a deadline for such an eventuality should be set and the reasons that would cause such a decision to be made must be clearly defined. In such cases I would advise that you do not commit too high a percentage of the fee until you are sure that the event will go ahead as planned, and that you investigate the possibility of insurance cover.

A change in image of the activity or individual must be guarded against. If you have chosen the sponsorship on the grounds of its image benefits, a change in the circumstances, such as a scandal concerning drug abuse or violent behaviour, could make the activity wholly inappropriate. If the image of the activity is vital to your requirements you would be justified in making sure that you had an option to cancel or end the sponsorship if such a serious alteration in the situation took place.

The recipient will obviously wish to ensure that you do not withhold funds for any reason not covered in the contract since to do so could put the entire event in jeopardy. While on this point you must make sure that contracted payments take place on time. Don't treat your sponsorship organizers as a business supplier you can get away with paying 90 days after invoice. The organizer will often need your money when it is budgeted for and any delay could threaten the solvency of the event. You will recall, I hope, that I advised you earlier to try to arrange for stage payments based on set performance levels. These terms should be spelt out in the contract but you should also exercise a degree of understanding when applying them, unless of course, the recipient had been grossly deficient in his performance, in which case you may well wish to use your option to withdraw. For your part make sure that you pay on time and do not add to the organizer's problems by your own behaviour.

The project plan you drew up earlier will be of great help in writing a contract since it should have defined exactly what you wish to achieve from the overall project, the aims of each part of the event, who is to be responsible for what, and the expected costs. These headings will be almost directly translatable into contract headings. As a minimum the contract should include the identity of all the parties involved, the capacity in which they are parties to the agreement and the rights or benefits that are involved in the contract. You should clearly define all rights that are exclusive and who is responsible for their delivery. Also to be included are details of payment, including dates when stage payments fall due, and any grounds for payment to be withheld. Any titles, names, logos, mascots or emblems involved with the event should be covered and protected by the agreement, and you should also ensure that the contract protects your company's name, logo or emblem from misuse by the organizers. All grounds for termination must be included, as should the eventuality of the event being cancelled. Make sure that you do not lump together all the benefits and rights offered by the sponsorship. Itemize all the benefits you expect — title, signage, shirt advertising, hospitality, media coverage, etc. — with separate sections for each covering the rights, costs and actions to be taken if any benefits cannot be delivered.

Obviously one could go on at great length, if one were an expert on contract law — which I am not — but the above will help you to draw up a workable contract for the legal department to tidy up as necessary. One clause that I would advise you to include, however, and which most lawyers may fail to mention is what a past colleague of mine called the Japanese clause. He maintained that the reason why there are so few lawyers in Japan is that every contract there includes a clause stating that, in the event of a dispute, all parties to the contract must meet and attempt to resolve their differences before resorting to legal action. This seems to me to be eminently sensible. A sponsorship arrangement is often a business deal between parties who operate in totally different environments, do not understand each other's businesses, and who have different aims from the deal. Sponsorship is a complicated procedure to get right but, in the vast majority of cases, it is an arrangement which works very well provided all parties take the time and effort to understand one another's needs.

SPECIALIST ADVICE   You are likely to require specialist advice or services at some stage during the sponsorship project, whether for legal, taxation, insurance or promotional purposes and some of these relationships may require separate contracts. These should not, however, be as complicated as the main sponsorship agreement since they will be covered by the normal provision of services arrangement common to business.

Do consider the tax liabilities of the sponsorship, however, before you commit yourself. For the most part sponsorship activities, as long as they are of a revenue rather than capital nature, are tax deductible as a promotional expense although you may find certain restrictions placed on your activity. For instance, if your sponsorship includes a large element of hospitality the tax authorities may, depending on the country, refuse to allow all the costs as a tax-deductible expense. I have already talked about the possibility that you may be able to treat the sponsorship fee as a start-up investment in a new event with the aim of creating a revenue earner in the longer term. In such cases you may have to treat the payments as capital investments for tax purposes.

Depending on the tax regulations in particular countries you may find that sponsorship of a charity will be dealt with differently from sponsorship of non-charitable organizations and special procedures may have to be used to minimize tax liabilities.

Another important consideration is insurance against circumstances that may affect the sponsorship project. While the organizers can be expected to insure against accidents or unusual circumstances affecting the event you will almost certainly wish to insure against accidents or problems that affect your investment in the project. Virtually any circumstance can be insured against, whether it is the weather or other eventuality that interferes with the performance of the project. You would be well advised to take specialist advice and to insure against anything that could seriously harm your investment.

10

Exploit the sponsorship

Now that you have signed the papers and are committed to your chosen sponsorship the hard work begins! It is vital to realize that the success of your project in terms of meeting the objectives you set for it depends on the way you run and support the activity. Sponsorship is a communications medium that requires continuous effort if it is to work well; there can be no question of handing over the cheque and sitting back and waiting for the benefits to deliver themselves, you have to make it happen. Do not forget, though, what I said in an earlier chapter: sponsorship should also be fun for all concerned and should help develop new skills among your marketing team. The activity has many real, tangible benefits but no one can deliver them for you. This chapter is entitled 'Exploit the Sponsorship' and the use of the word exploit will, I expect, cause some eyebrows to be raised amongst readers who are involved in the business of sponsorship as a recipient. Exploitation seems to be a common fear on the part of organizers, occasionally, perhaps, for good reason. My use of the word is, I hasten to add, intended to refer to the way in which the sponsorship project must be used to its maximum. The opportunities for creating substantial benefits should be there if you have done your research and planning properly, it is now up to you to make use of them. Sometimes the desire to do this can cause problems for the recipient or the activity and it is up to you to listen to their fears and to avoid exploiting the benefits of sponsorship to the extent that the event itself suffers.

When you are planning the way you will run your sponsorship and the support activities that will deliver the benefits you hope for you will find that there are numerous points you have to consider and act on covering a wide variety of marketing and promotional skills. Unless you have all the necessary skills amongst your sponsorship team you will have to bring in specialists from other departments or outside agencies. The most important specialist skills required in the support of sponsorship activities are those provided by publicity and public relations practitioners with further input often being required from advertising and sales promotion staff.

Figure 10.1 Sometimes sponsorship activities allow you to take a light-hearted dig at the opposition. Here Heineken's T-shirts make a play on the fact that Heineken's powerboat finished a race while Carlsberg's sank!

In order to bring all these skills together to get the best out of your sponsorship you should spend some time planning your activities. In order to ensure that you don't forget any important element it helps, especially in your first few projects, to produce a manual of operations that can be referred to by all those involved in the activity. The level of activity you have to undertake and the degree of complexity will depend on the scale of the sponsorship. What may be inappropriate in a project costing only a few thousand dollars may be imperative in a million-dollar sponsorship but whatever the project you should run through a checklist of possible activities to ensure that nothing is forgotten. In this chapter we will take a look at some of the key areas that you must consider when running any sponsorship project.

International, national and local

The areas that will be covered in this and the next chapter are concerned with how to maximize the effectiveness of your sponsorship. The actual techniques that are used for any particular sponsorship and the degree to which they are used will depend on the size of the project, its inherent potential for exploitation and the geographic spread of the project. As is to be expected, international, national and local projects differ in their scale and in their complexity.

Large international companies sometimes use global sponsorship vehicles to reach massive audiences — such as the Olympics, World Cup, America's Cup, etc. — but it should be remembered that while these can be hugely successful they also entail considerable difficulties and require vast support budgets if they are to be made to work effectively.

It might appear that such international sponsorships offer the best opportunity to use the various devices for exploitation but one often finds a major stumbling-block in the difficulty most companies have in directing and controlling the support activities of their satellite companies in the different national markets. The complications that arise out of a promotion aimed at more than one country demand experienced personnel and as much lead-time as you can give them. They also need a clear understanding between the operating companies in the different countries of their roles in the promotion. When the use of discretionary budgets are added to the complications the situation can become nightmarish as executives in each country have to be 'sold' on the idea of backing the project.

By contrast most national or local projects are much more straightforward although the budgets available are obviously much smaller. In some ways a national sponsorship undertaken by a large company is easier to run and make use of than local projects run by the same company. National projects are usually run out of head office where specialist expertise is available and where senior marketing management can take a personal interest. Local promotions are often bought, run and promoted at the local branch, regional office or dealership level. The people running such projects may be considerably less experienced in the utilization of sponsorship and may not appreciate opportunities that are available. It may also be quite difficult for head office to make use of the promotion in other markets unless this is considered from the beginning and the structure exists to make it practical.

The same problem exists for international companies whose national operations buy and operate sponsorships aimed mainly at their particular national market. In some cases one subsidiary or division may select a sponsorship that has the potential to be used by the company in other countries. Unless the central structure is designed to allow such cross-use of projects and unless there is a free flow of information and ideas between sister companies, many opportunities may be missed.

The tools available for exploitation of sponsorship projects and the techniques that go with them are essentially the same whatever the scope or size of the project, it is just that the suitability of individual techniques and the emphasis placed on them will vary from project to project. The observations made here about what should be considered for the successful exploitation of a sponsorship will need to be tempered with the reader's personal objectives and the size, complexity and budget of each project; there are no hard-and-fast guidelines to help but mostly it is quite obvious and a matter for simple commonsense.

Figure 10.2 White Horse used their 1986/87 sponsorship of the America's Cup in a number of markets. Their activities included producing a limited edition special blend whisky that reflected their sponsorship.

Working with organizers

The key to working with event organizers or individuals you may be sponsoring is to ensure that all parties understand each other's aims and hopes for the sponsorship and to try to conduct all your dealings on a friendly, personal level. Beware of bringing to sponsor-ship dealings the intensity that may be present in other commercial relationships; organizers are often not used to the commercial world you operate in, may be intimidated by it, and could feel threatened if you are insensitive to their position. Handle the relationship correctly and the recipient will be anxious to give you value for money and to ensure you receive the benefits you expect.

On the other hand, some organizers and many agents are very experienced in the commercial world and will understand your business needs. In such cases you need be less concerned about sensitivities than when you are dealing with amateur organizers and indeed you may need to be careful that you are not out-manoeuvred by some of the sharp business practices that some-times occur in sponsorship! By the time you have gone through the contractual negotiations with the organizers and their agents you will know which type of organization you are dealing with and can plan your strategy and approach accordingly.

The person in charge of your sponsorship must arrange a direct link with the organizers in order to create easy communications and to avoid the confusion that can arise if too many people are involved in making necessary arrangements. Hold regular meetings between the organizers and your team to keep in touch with the latest developments and to make sure that your plans and theirs are proceeding on schedule. Any decisions taken at these meetings should be minuted and circulated to all the people involved in turning plans into reality and you should also ensure that your own staff are kept aware of all developments. If you have created a project team to handle this sponsorship you should soon find that everyone fits into their roles and gets to know their opposite numbers within the event organization. Encourage this to happen by holding informal gatherings as well as regular business meetings so that an ideas forum can be created in which people will be happy to suggest new ways of utilizing and improving the sponsorship.

Do expect these ideas to develop as you go along. It is a rare sponsorship indeed that follows the path exactly as you had envisaged. New opportunities arise, some aspects you expected to be significant may prove to be less so, and new ideas will appear as your project team get used to the activity and the organizers become more familiar with your business and objectives.

If the event or individual you are sponsoring is part of a larger activity, such as a series or championship event, you will probably have to work with other organizers and sponsors. Try to coordinate important activities such as press liaison and hospitality functions so that they achieve maximum impact for all parties. Work hard to avoid any conflicts since these will almost certainly damage your own sponsorship and are likely to be picked up on by the media. The same applies to activities in which you are involved as a co-sponsor. I have already mentioned that, if you are taking title

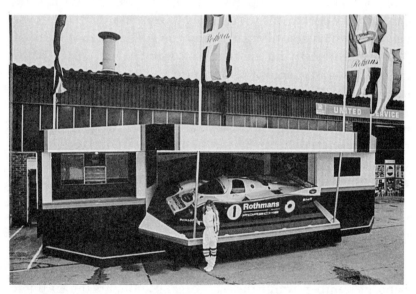

Figure 10.3 A travelling exhibition can help bring the audience to you at events where you may be competing with several other sponsors.

sponsorship to an event that needs subsidiary sponsors, you should try to ensure that you choose your co-sponsors. If you have been able to do so you should have a working relationship with them before the event begins and, depending on their relative investment and interest, you should involve them in much of the pre-planning. Co-sponsorships can cause additional problems but when the sponsors are well matched, and are in non-competing businesses, some additional opportunities can present themselves especially in the area of sales promotions and other consumer promotions.

It is not unusual for sponsored events that attract many top stars — who are often highly paid — to be run by enthusiastic amateurs who receive no financial rewards for their efforts but do it out of their love for the sport or activity. This situation can be fraught with difficulties, especially if one of these expensive stars is insensitive enough to be rude to the helpers. It may result in these essential organizers asking for financial rewards or being reluctant to put themselves out. Believe me, you will need people to perform beyond the call of duty and it is essential that you inspire everyone concerned and demonstrate that you appreciate their efforts. One way of doing this is to talk to these staff regularly, ask their opinions and let them know what is happening. Hold a party just for them before the event and afterwards; hold a raffle for them, give them some of the event merchandising, or find some other way to say thank you. After all, they may well be customers of yours and even if they aren't other people who are, or the media, will soon sense any bad feelings that pervade the event or your sponsorship involvement. All of this is basic public relations yet it is amazing how often it is ignored by sponsor's who assume that, just because they have handed over a fat cheque, they are entitled to treat unpaid event helpers in a way that their own staff would never tolerate.

Design

The question of design is one that is often not given enough atten-tion by many sponsors yet it is not only important, it is fundamental to many of the other aspects of making sponsorship work. Design

Figure 10.4a, b Sometimes it can be difficult to brand certain events visually. Johnnie Walker whisky make use of their famous logo (top) and a human version (bottom) to help link them with their speedsailing and Ryder Cup sponsorships.

is concerned with the visual presentation of your sponsorship and includes the style of your set for press conferences, the use of corporate colours and logos on all written material, the uniforms worn by organizers and competitors, give-aways to the media and countless other aspects of the sponsorship that many people fail to recognize as part of the overall image. It is pointless for you to spend hours analysing the image benefits of particular activities if you then fail to ensure that all aspects of the design related to your sponsorship activities are consistent and present the image you wish to portray.

If you are new to the game take a look at how established sponsors handle the design elements of their sponsorship. Look especially at the tobacco companies who are amongst the most professional in the field. If yours is an extensive sponsorship you will probably have to create your own design handbook in order to ensure consistency across the range of activities in which design will play its part in getting your message across. Because so much of sponsorship's effectiveness depends on visual messages being received and understood, often amidst considerable clutter from those of other advertisers and sponsors, you should never underestimate the importance of effective design.

You will, of course, have to live within the design constraints of the event itself and other, more senior sponsors but whenever possible you should attempt to brand the event, not only with your name, but also with your house colours, logo and any other recognizable design characteristics. If the event has its own logo or mascot you will want to incorporate it into designs for advertising, sales promotion material, merchandising, written material and other visual aids you use. But if there isn't one then you have the opportunity to create one that is specific to you, perhaps making use of your existing house logo.

Try to get your colour scheme, logo and/or name on as many aspects of the event as possible. Organizers can wear the sponsor's uniform, transport can be painted in house colours, finishing tapes can carry your name, soft drinks can be given to athletes in cups carrying your logo — the list is endless but demands that you use

10.5a

your imagination to get the best possible results. The Xerox
Marathon sponsorship we discussed earlier is a good example of
what can be done. Xerox's agency concentrated on achieving clear
brand identification not only for the on-site audience but also for
the cameras. Xerox had their name on strategically placed
banners, the runners' numbers, the finish line tape, the blankets
used to wrap competitors when they finished and their own team's
T-shirts. These and other name displays ensured that Xerox made
the impact they wanted on a large audience.

10.5b

Figure 10.5a, b   Sponsor's branding and endorsements are taken to the limit in Formula One motor racing. Hardly any space is wasted on the cars or the drivers' clothing, and even the smallest logo can cost tens of thousands of pounds.

Do make sure that all designs you use are legible, not only to the on-site audience, but also for television and photographers. Some designs and colours just don't work well on television — they distort or flare, sometimes to the point of illegibility. A good designer used to working in the television medium will be able to advise you. It is usually best to keep designs as simple as possible so that they are easily assimilated and do not confuse.

Figure 10.6   If you plan to present a cheque to the winners, make sure it is a
large one and that your name is clearly visible.

Your design handbook should contain specimen artwork so that
all those who may use the material can produce consistent designs.
It should specify the style and size of lettering and the colours to be
used in reproduction of logos and other designs.

Hospitality

The opportunity to entertain various groups of important people is
another significant reason for many companies utilizing sponsorship. While hospitality can be undertaken without the need for
sponsorship, and indeed is becoming a major industry around
top-class events such as Wimbledon, sponsorship does provide a
'hook' for entertainment and adds value to the activity. Guests are
likely to be more impressed and feel more important if they are
invited to an occasion of which you are a sponsor.

The extraordinary growth of the hospitality business in the
eighties is the only evidence you need to see how companies are

nowadays entertaining far more than ever before. Best-selling venues are, as you would expect, the major sporting occasions. Most such events now enjoy large revenues from selling space for this sort of entertainment. Unfortunately, this growth should give cause for some concern. The large numbers of companies fighting for space at these events risk devaluing the sporting content of the events. The fight for tickets needed by the hospitality operators reduces those available to true sports fans and pushes up the black-market price. The sight of row upon row of identical hospitality marquees disfigures many major sports venues while those who are the recipients of this lavish corporate entertainment rarely watch the sporting action, even if they are lucky enough to be entertained in a spot within sight of the competition. The level of corporate entertainment allowed at some events has reached such proportions that sporting authorities may soon have to consider whether the revenues earned are worth the possible long-term damage to the event. Wimbledon is an example of a quality event that is not only bursting at the seams with official hospitality operations but is also home to many unofficial operators whose venues are outside the ground, often some distance away, with marquees pitched on any available space, including the lawns of private houses. Such operations have nothing to do with sponsorship or with sport. They are merely the somewhat unsavoury end of an essentially parasitic industry. In my view it is far better, if you are considering hospitality, either to utilize it around your own sponsorship, when the added value of being seen to be part of the event will make your hospitality something different, or choose a stand-alone hospitality package that is different, that takes your guests to an unusual venue, and which is not going to be lost among a sea of identical corporate hospitality tents.

Used properly, and preferably based around a sponsorship activity, hospitality offers you the opportunity to target groups that are important to your business and to communicate with them in an atmosphere that is based on leisure activities and outside the normal business environment. Don't expect to do much hard selling at such an occasion; the object should be to open new lines of communication and to provide different reasons for the individuals concerned to have warm feelings about your company.

The sort of groups you may consider inviting to such occasions include your own workforce, salesteams, dealers and retailers, suppliers, key customers, institutional and government decision-makers and the media. You also have the choice of whether to mix different groups of people at one event or to run separate hospitality functions for particular audiences. The former is often a good idea provided you have the room since it adds interest to the occasion and allows new links to be formed.

THE VENUE   The facilities available for hospitality should have been determined before you signed your sponsorship agreement since they can make a considerable difference to the perceived value of the occasion. The best situation is a venue from which your guests can see the action without leaving your party; the worst is a tent or marquee in a row of other hospitality sites at the back of the site, half a mile away from the action. Unless the event venue has existing entertainment facilities, which is unusual, you will have to bring in mobile facilities — usually a marquee. Such venues are not ideal especially where the weather cannot be guaranteed, but you may not have much choice in the matter. Do ensure that the facilities are adequate for the number of people you wish to entertain and don't be tempted to cram more people into the space than can be comfortably accommodated. If necessary, and if the event goes on long enough, you could choose to hold several receptions for different groups rather than cram everyone into the venue at one time.

For small groups you may have the option of using a mobile hospitality unit that can be hired for the occasion or, if you are undertaking considerable sponsorship activity, you may choose to buy your own unit and have it painted in the corporate livery and equipped to your own requirements. Do remember to make all arrangements for any equipment that must be hired well in advance of the occasion and arrange to have quotes from a number of different suppliers — the quality and cost of these services varies widely.

DESIGN   You should give serious attention to the design aspects of your hospitality venue since this will reflect the quality of your activities and will affect the guests' perceptions of your company. Do not overstate the commercialism of the occasion but try to brand the event in a subtle way. Don't settle for what is supplied by the organizers or outside suppliers; take the trouble to arrange a coordinated decor based on your house colours with your logo incorporated wherever possible. For a small extra cost you may be able to have the room or marquee decorated in your own style with nice touches such as the place settings personalized to your company. Allow plenty of time for the arrangement of such details and consider using a professional designer experienced in such occasions to help add a touch of style to the proceedings, if you think that such points are a waste of time or money, remember that there is no point in staging hospitality events that fail to impress or which merge into an indistinguishable muddle of competing occasions.

INVITATIONS   Your invitation list should be completed well in advance and circulated within the company or project team to ensure that no embarrassing omissions are made. Send out the invitations at least three weeks before the event to give people time to plan their schedule and reply. Personalize your invitations as much as possible and aim to make your guests feel that they are of special importance to your occasion. Invitations should give all the necessary information needed, including date, time, details of venue and the occasion, a guide to dress, and whether partners and/or children are included in the invitation. Since such occasions are usually meant to be informal opportunities for people to meet and enjoy themselves it is normally best to invite partners. If you don't you may find that fewer people accept and you risk antagonizing the very people you wish to impress. The question of whether to invite children depends on the event, but if the occasion is suitable it is often a good idea. Give executives' families a good time and they will find it hard to resist the positive feelings you wish to encourage. If you do include children in the invitation make sure that you cater for their needs, not only in terms of food and drink but also by the provision of facilities that will keep them occupied while their parents relax and enjoy your hospitality.

Monitor the replies and acceptances to your invitations so that you can ensure that numbers are kept appropriate to the venue and to allow you to invite extra people if necessary. When calculating the numbers of guests don't forget to allow for your own staff you will need for the occasion. You should have enough of your own people in attendance to be able to mix with the guests and look after their needs without outnumbering them. A ratio of five to one is usually appropriate depending on the size of the occasion.

When advising people on what to wear consider the type of event, the normal dress of spectators, and the likely impact of changeable weather. If bad weather could cause a problem you may decide to provide umbrellas or foul weather gear for guests, branded of course with your corporate livery.

Just before the event send guests details of travel, any tickets or passes they will need, copies of the programme and perhaps a guide to the event. On the day have a commissionaire on the door to check invitations and turn away gatecrashers but also have one of your staff nearby who can deal with the possible problem of genuine guests who have lost their tickets. Leave a visitors book at the entrance and ask all guests to sign it so that you have a record of attendees.

TRAVEL   Arrangements for getting your guests to the venue need some thought, especially if it is a major event that will attract large numbers of the public with the consequent likelihood of traffic jams and queues at the gate. Whenever possible you should aim to insulate your guests from such frustrating problems since you want them to arrive relaxed and happy. You may choose to let guests arrive by car — preferably with their own parking area that avoids queues for the public car parks — you may bring them in by coach or fly them in by helicopter. The latter adds an exciting element to the occasion for many people but do remember that some people may be terrified of flying so offer an alternative arrangement whenever possible. The same points apply to returning guests after the event. If you have brought them in by your own transport make sure that return services are available from well before the time you expect the event to end since some people may wish to leave early.

CATERING Depending on the event you may have to accept the caterers contracted by the organizers or the site owners or you may have the freedom to bring in your own suppliers. The latter situation is usually preferable since you have a choice and the opportunity to negotiate over quality and cost. When discussing menus and other arrangements with caterers tell them exactly what you are aiming to do, the type of guests you expect, and any time constraints on the serving of meals. Make sure you check the references of the caterers since this aspect can make or mar an event, and detail all the agreed arrangements and costs in writing so you have some recourse should reality not live up to your expectations.

Try to match the catering with the type, style and quality of the event, choose the best standard you can afford, and do try to arrange a choice of meals to cater for the increasing number of vegetarians — also for religious groups — i.e. no ham for Muslims and Jews. The supply of alcoholic refreshments needs some thought. While you will wish to entertain in style and would not want to be seen as stinting on liquid refreshment, equally you do not want your event to turn into a drunken party. Waiters circulating with drinks usually means that people drink more than if they have to visit a bar for a refill. Offering soft drinks or non-alcoholic alternatives should help limit consumption to a moderate level. If you suspect that some of your guests may take more than is good for them make sure that at least one of your staff is detailed to keep an eye open for any behaviour that may disrupt others' enjoyment of the event. This job requires considerable tact so do not allocate it to a junior member of staff who may be overawed by the importance of some of the guests. It should go without saying that your

staff should not drink too much and should stay in control of the
proceedings but those who have not been involved with hospitality
functions before may need some instruction in the specific
requirements of corporate entertainment.

THE SOFT SELL While the whole purpose of hospitality
functions is to achieve corporate objectives that are ultimately
aimed at improving the bottom line, the quickest way to spoil it is
to treat the occasion as an opportunity for a hard sell. Do this just
once and you will scar your reputation for a long time, so temper
your urge to push the company's products and find more subtle
ways to get the message across.

We have already talked about branding the venue in a way that
remains in good taste but don't forget other opportunities for reinforcing the corporate image. Have a photographer on hand to
record the proceedings, and if you can have a celebrity or competitor present, set up a production line for photographing guests
with your star, if possible with the celebrity dressed in a branded
sweater or other clothing. After the event you can send each guest
their own picture as a memento which is bound to be well
received. Small keepsakes for the guests always go down well, as do
small touches like presenting the ladies with a rose as they
arrive or leave.

Although it is often inappropriate to have products on display it
is sometimes possible to get away with this especially if you are
entertaining customers or dealers, or if you have a particularly
unusual product or one that has particular relevance to the event
you are sponsoring.

Speeches can be an area of particular difficulty. If you must
include one — and there is rarely a strong reason why they must be
given at such occasions — keep them short and try to make them
appropriate to the occasion, preferably with a touch of humour or
self-deprecation. Unless you are particularly skilled at preparing
speeches have them professionally written for the occasion. Rather
than make your own speech consider having a celebrity say a few
words on your behalf but make sure that the person you choose is

articulate and comfortable in this role. If you are planning speeches don't forget to let the caterers know so that they can arrange their work to avoid disturbing the proceedings.

If you are sponsoring an individual or a team try to make sure they are available for at least part of the time but don't expect competitors to disturb their schedule just to play host to your guests.

Advertising

There are several ways of using advertising in a sponsorship project to the benefit of both the project and a company's advertising objectives. The important point is to integrate advertising with the sponsorship from the beginning of the project and to involve your in-house advertising staff and your agency in the campaign from the start.

ADVERTISING THE EVENT   The purpose of event advertising is, of course, to attract the public. A well-established event will require little advertising beyond reminding the public of the dates and venue, while a new event that needs to attract a large public audience may require extensive promotion using press, radio and television advertising. The amount of advertising planned for the event should have been decided upon before you signed contracts since you may wish to take on this task in return for a reduction of the sponsorship fee. If you are a large-scale user of mainstream advertising you may be able to secure lower rates than the organizers, and your agency may also be able to produce better ads. Beware, however, of new or unproven events that require significant levels of event advertising — it may be a sign that the event as planned is not really viable. Whether you handle the event advertising directly or leave it to the event organizers, try to ensure that your name is mentioned in all copy and, if event advertising has been promised as part of the deal, do monitor it to ensure you get what you expected.

ADVERTISING THE SPONSORSHIP   Since you want the world
to know of your sponsorship link with the event, you may well wish
to use advertising to help convey the message. If you are organizing
the event advertising then you can tie in your sponsorship advertising
at the same time using posters, print, radio and television advertising.
When Philips sponsored the 1986 Mexico World Cup they used
newspaper advertising in nearly forty countries on the morning of
the opening match to tell the world that Philips was a sponsor of
the event and the supplier of television broadcasting equipment.
The advertising used the same conceptual theme in all the markets
Philips wished to target. If yours is an international campaign do
try to coordinate the activity in this way. The benefits of doing so
can be large.

    During the period of the sponsorship you should have a number
of opportunties to advertise your activities. You would normally
expect to have space provided free in any brochures or event programmes and you should try to reach an agreement that prevents
competitors securing advertising in these publications. When
designing advertising for use at and around the event don't
automatically run your standard ads. Tailor the advertising to the
event and the audience or you will lose a good opportunity
properly to utilize your sponsorship activities. While you should
obviously look for every means of linking your name with the event
and of presenting a sales message you should avoid an overkill. It is
possible to go overboard with advertising and name mentions to
the extent that the audience begin to feel under attack. If this
happens you will probably do more harm than good to your
image.

SIGNAGE   The quantity, size and position of signage available to
you through your sponsorship fee should have been detailed in the
agreement, as should who is responsible for providing the banners
and signs. It is sensible to have one of your own people at the event
responsible for ensuring that your banners are in position and that
they do not get moved, stolen or obscured during the event. Try to
have a couple of movable ones so that you can react to a situation

The America's Cup

THE SPIRIT TO WIN

The White Crusader in action

The America's Cup is gruellingly tough. It is highly prestigious. To compete it takes a superb aerodynamically crafted, twelve metre yacht. It needs a truly dedicated topflight crew. Then there's a great backup team ashore.

THE WHITE HORSE CHALLENGE
THE TEAM SPIRIT

And, of course, the right spirit. White Horse Scotch Whisky.

White Horse was not only the official Scotch Whisky to the America's Cup. It was also the major sponsor of the British challenge led by the *White Crusader.*

As a world class yacht it was amongst the world's best yachts and yachtsmen battling it out off the coast of Western Australia. You had to admire their team spirit.

Because for the *White Crusader,* and all the other international challengers involved, the bid to win the America's Cup was anything but easy.

It required teamwork, skill, a great deal of determination, a lot of experience and, of course, the spirit to win.

But then, much the same qualities are needed to blend as fine a Scotch Whisky as White Horse. It owes its specialness to the quality of its malt and the skills of its blender. Just as the America's Cup owes its specialness to the quality of the yachts and the skills of the yachtsmen.

White Horse
Scotch Whisky

The official Scotch Whisky to the America's Cup.

Figure 10.7a, b   White Horse Whisky used their America's Cup sponsorship in mainstream advertising in international markets.

where the television cameras decide to focus on one particular spot, perhaps for interviews after a race. It may not be possible to get signs in place — the television director may object — but unless you have signs that can be moved you will not be in a position to try.

Although signage is classed as advertising, and can usually be bought without having to become a sponsor of an event, it is very rare that it can be used for any other purpose than to present your name; most advertising, of course, allows you to present a message as well. While signage can demonstrably increase name awareness during an event, the level of recall will drop rapidly after the event. And if your name is not already known, displays that do not incorporate any message, such as who or what you are, can have little benefit unless you can find other means to present the message.

The other problem with signage is the growing clutter at major events. Many top sports events have advertising boards around the ground, some of which may be bought by advertisers who are not sponsoring the event. In some cases signage at major stadia is bought on a long-term basis so it is quite possible for you to find that one of your major competitors is already contracted for signage at the event you are sponsoring. There is often little that can be done about this but you should check before you contract for the sponsorship, and wherever possible you should try to prevent competitors having access to signage.

The position of signage at televised events is usually crucial in terms of the number of times you get your name in picture and for how long. Study recordings made at the same venue or, if that is not possible, at a similar event, and work out the best positions for your signs before committing to any agreement. Also see if you can find out where cameras — both television and stills — will be sighted. Armed with this information you can work out their most likely field of view, and hence the best sites for displays. Getting signs incorporated in pictures is often a competition between you and the still or television cameramen. They will usually do their best to crop out as much advertising as possible, and are very good at doing so.

10.8a

10.8b

Figure 10.8a, b, c, d Perimeter advertising should be positioned where
possible so that it is clearly visible and is in the best location relative to television and still cameras covering the action.

10.8c

10.8d

There is much argument within the advertising industry as to the value of signage exposure in pictures, usually revolving around the question of whether the signs are in what is called the 'heart of the action' or whether they are peripheral to the shot, and for the length of time that they remain in picture. These arguments are, to my mind, somewhat academic — research suggests perimeter boards at events do increase viewers' recall of the advertisers' name in the short term. The question that bothers me is the value of advertising that can only present a name and not a sales message. For very established brand or corporate names the problem is far less acute than for the advertiser who is not well known, but even they will need to ensure that other means are used to present explicit messages to the event audience.

Don't always assume that signs have to be large to get attention. While large perimeter boards or banners can be read at a distance they are no help when television or still cameras zoom in to get close to the action. When this happens the viewer will only see a

Figure 10.9 Advertising at events does not have to consist of simple, and boring, banners or perimeter boards. If you can come up with a different idea you are sure to be noticed.

letter or two in the whole word. The way round this problem is to think small! Use small signs in strategic positions or print your name in smaller letters around the edge of a perimeter board as well as in large letters across it. And while graphic artists and designers may get carried away with creating subtle logos, don't rely on a logo alone for recognition and awareness purposes — how many companies can you identify from their logo?

MAINSTREAM ADVERTISING   Sponsorship activities can be very usefully used in a company's mainstream advertising especially if the sponsorship involves a well-known sport or other activity that has a large public audience in its own right. Thus Canon can use the Formula One motor racing sponsorship of the Williams team as a means of capturing attention and presenting messages in their product advertising while at the same time increasing the awareness of the sponsorship link. This advertising can work for a general audience but is even more effective when placed in media associated with the activity. You would expect a motor racing audience to be more receptive than non-fans to Canon's use of their Formula One sponsorship in ads placed in car magazines or the motoring sections of newspapers, etc., but even for non-fans such advertising will serve to present specific messages about the company and its products.

The use of sponsorship activities in mainstream advertising should be planned before the event so that photographs and film or video footage can be shot during the event rather than recreated afterwards. By planning and creating the sponsorship-linked ad campaign in advance the ads themselves can be placed for maximum effect during or immediately after the event. Such activities should obviously be planned in conjunction with one's advertising agency and it is important if an advertising link is to be exploited effectively that the agency is involved in the sponsorship planning so that they understand its aims and objectives and can provide advice and suggestions from an early stage.

Consumer promotions

The one great advantage of sponsorship as a communications medium is the number of opportunities it offers for building a huge range of promotions around the sponsorship activity. Nowhere is this more apparent than in the area of consumer promotions yet far too many sponsors who are supposedly using sponsorship for product promotions reason fail to use all the opportunities offered by sponsorship activities to reach their consumer audience.

POINT-OF-SALE PROMOTIONS The right sponsorship can provide a useful vehicle for promotions aimed at the customer at the point of sale. Depending on the product and where it is sold it may well have to compete with many other similar products in a clutter that must be overcome if yours is to attract the customers' attention. If a link with the sponsorship can be formed using on-pack or display promotions you may have the opportunity to utilize the attraction of the activity to stimulate your consumers. Although you may find a way to create an immediate promotion by adding a sponsorship-linked gift to the product at the point of sale (especially if this is the event venue) it is far more likely that you will use the sponsorship to create delayed promotions where the customer buys your product and then responds to the incentive offered on the packaging.

As long as there is a high enough level of interest in the activity you sponsor within the general public, or your product audience if that is a specialist one, you could consider using delayed promotions such as competitions based on the activity with prizes associated with the sponsorship — tickets to the event, dinner with a celebrity, etc. Other such delayed promotions involve free draws, charity promotions, coupons redeemable against entry to the event, or mail-in premiums such as free gifts that consumers can send for when they have accumulated enough vouchers. You may also be able to involve co-sponsors in cross-couponing promotions using the sponsored activity as a central theme. As with the exploitation of the event in mainstream advertising you should involve your sales promotions team in the sponsorship from an early stage if you plan to make the sponsorship work for you in this way.

COMPETITIONS   In addition to running on-pack competitions for point-of-sales promotions as mentioned above, there are several other ways of using the sponsorship in competitions aimed at the consumer. One excellent way is to form a link with media outlets to carry your sponsorship-linked competition. This can be done in all media including radio and television and can give the particular media outlet involved a strong reason to publicize your sponsorship through editorial coverage. An international sponsorship gives you the opportunity to run competitions in the media of each country you wish to target but you shouldn't forget that even a national or regional sponsorship often offers the possibility of running the same competition in more than one outlet. Instead of running one competition in a national newspaper, for instance, you may be able to achieve better audience penetration by running the same competition in several non-overlapping regional or local papers. Competitions can offer many different types of prizes linked to the sponsorship; free tickets to the event, event merchandising, sponsors' products, a chance to meet a celebrity are all possibilities, but you will find many more if you analyse your own activity carefully.

In addition to running competitions through the media, direct mail or by on-pack promotions don't forget the possibility of running a competition at the event. Depending on the size and type of audience and your particular product you could run a competition, draw or sweepstake for a prize — preferably linked to your product or event — to be presented at the end of the event.

DIRECT MAIL   Targeting an audience through direct mail is an increasingly popular form of consumer promotion, and sponsorship sometimes offers possibilities that you could consider. First and most importantly is the possible opportunity you may have for obtaining mailing lists from the sponsorship. Assuming that you did your research to prove that the audience for the activity and the event is a valid one for your product, then any names and addresses you can generate out of this audience should be members of your potential consumer audience. You may be able to obtain mailing lists from the national or international authority of the activity you are sponsoring but check this in advance. You may be able to acquire these lists as part of your sponsorship fee but if you leave it until later you may have to pay extra. At some events tickets are applied for in advance by mail or phone and this may allow you to build up your mailing lists.

When making mailshots to lists generated by the activity or event you are sponsoring you should consider using explicit sponsorship-related messages to target this audience. In addition to selling your product in this way you could also use these lists to sell your branded sponsorship merchandising.

PRODUCT SAMPLING   Sponsorship of an event that attracts the right numbers and type of spectators can provide a good opportunity for product sampling. Once again, if your sponsorship is in support of product sales and if you have done your research the audience at the event should be potential product consumers. So why not use every means of reaching this audience and converting them to your product? If you look at the activities of the tobacco companies who utilize sponsorship as a major communications tool you will find them using every means at their disposal to convert consumers to their particular brand. Yet while it is common for tobacco companies to use product sampling at events it is far less common among other companies who also use sponsorship for product promotions. Since this can be one of the easiest ways of using the sponsorship on-site and also adds to your visibility at the event (and can be tied in with an on-site competition) you should give serious consideration to whether you can utilize this sort of promotion.

MERCHANDISING   The selling of merchandising not only aids
the longer-term awareness of the sponsor's name but sometimes
has the potential to provide a revenue source. Merchandising sold
at events is very popular with audiences and is often used by
organizers as a means of earning revenue. If it is organized by the
event promoters on this basis the sponsor may get no financial
benefits and, unless the sponsor's name is included in the event
title, may receive no publicity benefit from branded merchandising.
You need to sort out with the event organizers in advance what
opportunities will be available for branded merchandising, both at
the event and for later sale to enthusiasts. Unless you feel that
handling the production and sale of merchandising will impose an
extra and unwelcome burden on your staffing requirements, you
should consider producing the merchandising to be sold at the
event. This allows you to retain control over the type and quality of
the merchandising — of which a tremendous variety is available —
and to incorporate your own branding on the goods. Such an
arrangement should also allow you to take the lion's share of the
revenue from the sale of merchandising — a revenue source that
can prove quite substantial at some events.

Whether you are able to come to this sort of arrangement with
the organizers will depend on the type of activity you are sponsoring
and the degree to which the organizers are already marketing it. At
the very least you should try to ensure that your name and logo is
incorporated into merchandising and that you have some control
over the quality of the goods. The latter is especially important
since poor quality merchandising carrying your name will reflect
badly on your image with the very audience you are trying to
impress. The point made earlier about the use of a logo alone on
signage applies here as well. Don't let the designer get away with
the use of a logo without your name; you want consumers to
associate strongly with your company and they won't do so unless
you provide a strong enough reminder of your identity.

You may feel that you don't want the trouble of organizing the
production of merchandising. But take heart, you don't have to.
There are plenty of firms who will handle all aspects of merchan-

dising for you from design through to selling. You should expect to
pay them a large fee or commission though, and so you will gain
far less benefit from this possible revenue source.

When producing merchandising for sale don't forget that you
can market it through other means than the event itself — direct
mail to lists of enthusiasts for instance. And in addition to selling
merchandising there are literally thousands of ways to create off-
site visibility through give-away products used as on-pack promotions, displays at the point of sale, at the event, or through
advertising or direct mail. Everything from stickers, pins, badges,

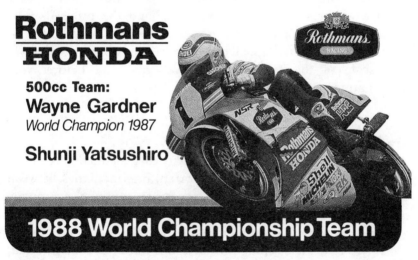

Figure 10.10   Give-aways such as stickers are a good way to extend the reach
and shelf-life of a sponsorship.

cards of every description, posters, calendars, the whole range of
clothing and anything else that the public collects. Think of a new
one and you could start a trend that always remains linked with
you — such are the dream goals of sponsorship.

PUBLIC RELATIONS   Much of the public relations activity surrounding sponsorship projects usually involves efforts directed at
achieving press coverage but there are often opportunities to direct

such activity at the consumer audience or other target groups. Some of the activities that can be classed as public relations efforts, such as hospitality, have been mentioned earlier, but there are often plenty of other promotions that can be designed to suit particular circumstances. Another example of the way Philips used their sponsorship of the 1986 Mexico World Cup shows how PR activity can be designed to take advantage of any particular event. In their German market Philips arranged for giant footballs with their corporate logo to be rolled through the streets of several cities with the public being invited to sign their names on the balls for a small donation. The footballs and the money raised were sent to Mexico at the time of the World Cup and the proceeds went towards the running of social projects. There are no rules for the creation of such activities; all depends on your objectives, the type and scale of the event and, as we have said before, your imagination.

Trade promotions

By trade promotions I mean any activity that is aimed at retailers, wholesalers and dealers — the important intermediaries between you and your customer. There are several reasons why a company may wish to target its trade audience — to encourage retailers to give your products prominence on the sales floor, to provide incentives to dealers selling product, to reward outside sales staff, to attract co-op sponsorship funds, and to provide a hospitality forum at which sales or marketing policy can be discussed in a relatively informal and unusual setting.

CO-OP FUNDING   In some cases you may wish to run sponsored projects on a multi-regional basis but with a common theme. In such cases the cost of the support activities may be prohibitive for you to fund from central budget sources but a possible solution could come from getting dealers to contribute in return for an involvement in regional sponsorship activities and an expected benefit in trade through the dealerships. In order to achieve this level of cooperation you will have to convince your dealers that the activity can have a positive effect on sales since there is little else that is likely to motivate them. They aren't, for instance, going to be too interested in providing funds for an event designed to improve your corporate image!

Creating interest in such projects with dealers is a notoriously difficult business and you may have to do a lot of convincing. A lot will depend on the relationship you have with your dealers and how much you know about them as individuals. You may find, for instance, that a majority of your dealers are enthusiastic motor racing fans. If a motor racing sponsorship is a viable means of meeting your other objectives this information could lead you to utilize the sport to encourage dealer involvement.

The main thing to remember when trying to involve your trade outlets in sponsorship promotions is that the more incentives you can provide the more likely they are to work hard to make the promotion a success. The first incentive you should try to ensure is an increased flow of potential customers through the outlets. We have already talked about running competitions or sweepstakes and these can provide a good means of increasing customer traffic provided you organize the competition in such a way that people have to go into a dealer to enter. Depending on the type of product and retail outlet you may find that you can provide sponsorship-related merchandising for sale in retail outlets or you may be able to offer to have a celebrity from the event visit the dealer for a point-of-sale promotion of the product.

If you expect dealers to become involved with your sponsorship you not only have to provide them with incentives, you also have to inform them on the promotional opportunities that are available. Produce a manual that explains all the ways each dealer can get involved and what the incentives are for doing so and you stand a much better chance of bringing together a group of dealers who are eager to promote and exploit the sponsorship. The more effort they put into it the better their bottom line and, of course, yours.

INCENTIVES   There are a number of ways that sponsorship-related incentives can be used to promote interest and activity at the trade level. Since we have just been talking about raising co-op funds for utilizing sponsorship on a regional basis (or, indeed, on a multinational basis in the case of an international sponsorship) let's move on to incentives by looking at further ways dealers can be encouraged to spend their own money promoting your product via a sponsorship project.

Suppose you wish to get dealers to share in the costs of local advertising of your products around the sponsorship event. You could argue that it is in their interests to do so as the sponsorship provides them with a 'hook' to attract customers into their premises but this argument may not be strong enough to encourage them to part with up-front money. Alternatively you could implement a scheme whereby the more a dealer spends on joint promotions the more 'credits' he earns. These credits can then be used to reduce the cost of incentive packages you create around the sponsorship that will be offered to dealers. You may, for instance, do a deal with a resort or co-sponsor to provide a holiday or a product at a cost-only price. If the opportunity is attractive to the dealers they will want to buy it and you can offer it to them at a reducing price dependent on the credits they have earned. The best thing of all is that such an incentive can be done at absolutely no cost to yourself, merely a creative use of all the possible links that can be created around many sponsorship projects.

Incentives can be used in a number of other ways to increase the visibility and the effectiveness of the sponsorship. Products that are sold through a large number of retail outlets are unlikely to be suitable for the sort of promotion described above, nor will retailers be interested in any special involvement with your activities. This sort of retailer can, however, be motivated to provide a prominent position for a point-of-sale display or to use other means to sell more products. By informing retailers of the coming event and by providing them with special displays linked to the activity they are likely to be ready to give you prominence over competing products. If you then offer sales incentives by giving prizes for the best sales results during a given period you are sure to stimulate extra activity.

As we have seen above, prizes for this sort of incentive can often be obtained from the industry associated with the sponsored activity or from other sponsors at very low cost. If skiing is the activity being sponsored, for instance, you will find that skiing equipment suppliers will usually be happy to provide goods for competitions in return for an advertising or promotional link with a non-industry sponsor. And if an automobile manufacturer is a co-sponsor you should be able to obtain a car as a prize in your competitions for little cost. You don't necessarily have to give incentives away free. As was described above in encouraging co-op funds, the offer of a prized opportunity at a very low cost depending on performance is often as good an incentive as the free prize and can usually be arranged to be cost-free to you.

Similar incentives can be organized for other members of the trade link with the consumer. Dealers can, for instance, be offered promotional packages aimed at their own sales staff. You can do the same for your own sales people, and wholesalers can be encouraged by competition to sell more product to the retail trade. The beauty of it is that you can achieve this without discounting the product price and at little or no extra cost to the sponsorship budget. It is these sorts of creative opportunities that makes sponsorship such a flexible form of promotion.

HOSPITALITY   All of these points made earlier about the use of hospitality at events apply to the entertainment of your trade outlets but there are a few additional points that you may need to consider. It may be more appropriate to hold a separate function for the trade rather than include them in a general occasion if your aims are to use the occasion for a sales promotion talk or for a more or less formal product discussion. There is nothing wrong with bringing your trade guests together with other groups, of course, but unless the objective is purely to provide a day out to create warm feelings about the company you are likely to be better off holding separate functions for different groups. All the points mentioned earlier concerning presentation and arrangements still apply but you can afford to have far more product-related display material at a trade function than you would at one for the media or other target groups.

Staff involvement

Another advantage of sponsorship as a promotional activity is the opportunities it offers to provide incentives for staff, to involve them in sponsorship activities as a training forum, and to target them directly for public relations purposes.

Incentives suggested by the sponsorship activity can be used as rewards for the performance of the sales staff or for increased productivity by the workforce in general. Since such incentives are linked with an existing company activity they can be extremely cost-effective and also carry a form of involvement that common, bought-in incentives lack, especially since sponsorship-related incentives are based on lifestyle interests — sport, the arts, etc. — that you may find appeal strongly to your own staff as well as your other target groups.

Involving your marketing staff in developing all the aspects of sponsorship promotions can be a very useful way of adding to their experience by means of a form of in-house training. Since the use of sponsorship is a very creative activity, in the sense of demanding new and fresh approaches to each project if it is to be exploited to its maximum, staff can enjoy wide-ranging experiences that they probably would not meet in most other forms of marketing. These experiences and the discovery of new approaches to promotion can be extremely valuable when later applied to other areas of marketing.

If you run your sponsorship support activities in-house it is possible to create project teams for each sponsorship. These can be run by full-time experienced sponsorship staff supported by others drawn from the different disciplines within the company. After the event they can return to their own department armed with new ideas and approaches and, hopefully, stimulated by the experience of working on a project team trying to produce commercial benefit out of an activity that often involves working with non-commercially-oriented organizations.

Sponsorship can also be used to target the workforce for staff relations reasons. This can be done by using the spin-off benefits of a sponsorship project that has as its main target another group — consumers or trade for instance — or it can be done by sponsoring some activity aimed only at the workforce. This could be the provision of sporting facilities, or a crèche for working mothers — perhaps for both employees and those in the local community — or the provision of activities that can be enjoyed during the working day — a sponsored concert in the company dining room at lunch time for instance, or a special performance of a play in the evening.

Problem areas

Mismatching and misunderstanding are probably the most common problem areas found in sponsorship projects and usually cause the sponsor to blame the recipient for failure to perform. In fact these problems are usually the fault of the sponsor not having done his homework and research properly before signing the deal. The recipient can never know your objectives when he offers the sale, despite the many proposals you receive that tell you this project is just right for your requirements, so the responsibility for ensuring a good match between event and objectives is yours. So is the task of ensuring that misunderstandings do not occur. These usually arise when the parties to the agreement have different views as to who will do what to exploit the sponsorship. The way to avoid this is to go through every possible element of the project beforehand and to agree the areas of responsibility. These details should be included in your contract so that in the event of any disagreements the original arrangement can be referred to. These problems only arise when a sponsor has an incomplete understanding of the medium and assumes that benefits will flow naturally without extra promotional effort. As we have seen, this is not the case; the project has to be worked on by all parties but it is the sponsor who must take the lead. Too often recipients concentrate on selling the proposal and give insufficient thought to servicing it. This is by no means always the case but you should look at every project as potentially requiring you to ensure or arrange all the support activities. That way if the recipient turns out to be well prepared and professional, and delivers additional benefits designed around your requirements, you will be pleasantly surprised. If you have problems in this area you may have to grit your teeth and put up with them this time but learn from the experience and improve your planning of the next event.

The most dangerous period of a sponsorship is the time when the honeymoon period comes to an end. Your initial press conference to announce the sponsorship may have generated good publicity and everyone should have left with warm feelings towards you. The period that follows, when everything often goes quiet, when publicity is hard to get, and when the details of the rest of the sponsorship are often still in the planning stage is usually the time when problems first emerge and when newly formed relationships suffer stress. This is often a time for the detailed planning of the main event and you should ensure that you keep in regular contact with the organizers during this period and that you work together to identify opportunities. If the organizers are naive about sponsorship and unclear about your objectives it is well worth while investing some time in educating them. If they are on your side, understand your needs and feel that they have a good relationship with you, minor problems that occur can be quickly dealt with without escalating into a major confrontation.

Be prepared for criticisms of your sponsorship. Some people, including quite a few journalists and editors, actively dislike sponsorship and are very ready to criticize new activities. Criticisms may also come from closer to home. Your own workforce or shareholders may view your activities with concern, especially if you are going through a patch when redundancies are occurring or profits are low. Tackle this problem early by informing key groups about your activities and your reasons for utilizing the sponsorship. Since sponsorship is a very public activity, or should be, you run the risk of upsetting various groups by your actions unless these are well considered. Before going into battle with organizers over the site of competitors' banners, the non-attendance of a celebrity, or your wish to change the event in some way to suit television's requirements, bear in mind any PR implications there might be if the argument becomes public.

The relationships between individuals involved in your activity can sometimes cause the most problems. Sponsorship is a medium that requires that people from many different disciplines work together for mutual benefit but in an area many may not have worked in before. Not only will you have your own project team incorporating talent from marketing, public relations, advertising, sales promotions, finance and management, but you will be dealing closely with event organizers, agents, promoters, the media, specialist suppliers and outside agencies in the various marketing disciplines. Each will have their own opinions on sponsorship, many built on very little experience, and each will have his or her own ideas as to the best way to exploit and run the activity. These differences can cause tensions that may undermine your ability to get the best from the event. The best way to avoid these problems is regular communication in a forum that allows all involved to air their views and discuss problems. An event run by a project team who stay with it from start to finish of the sponsorship goes a long way to encouraging a sense of involvement in the project and will usually ensure that you avoid serious problems.

The biggest problems often come when you are using outside agencies for some of the support services you need. Advertising agencies have been among the most reluctant to accept sponsorship although the situation is changing fast, and you may find that your account team are less than keen on becoming involved in the marriage of sponsorship and advertising. Don't allow your agency to get away with this. If they are not enthusiastic, but cannot demonstrate that your reasons for entering into the sponsorship are flawed, then let them know that you will go elsewhere to find a team that is able to utilize sponsorship effectively.

The worst problems, in my experience, come from public relations agencies. Usually, a sponsor will already have one or more agencies working on corporate, financial and product PR accounts and the temptation is simply to hand over the exploitation of a sponsored event to the relevant agency and sit back and await the results. Since many of the areas of sponsorship exploitation fit within a broad definition of public relations there is some excuse for this approach. The problem with it is that it abrogates responsibility for an activity that can only really be effectively handled if full-time control is kept in the hands of an experienced company marketing executive. Secondly, the agency you use may do a good job for you on other accounts, but how experienced are they at exploiting sponsorship opportunities? Some specialist agencies exist and some of the larger agencies have specialist departments, but to date I have to admit to being singularly unimpressed with the ability of such agencies really to think themselves into the requirements of their client and to apply a flexible enough approach to identify the opportunities that exist.

Far too often they concentrate simply on achieving media publicity, and most of the ways they have of doing this are boringly conventional and uninteresting. Many of the problems I have encountered have stemmed from an agency, usually public relations, mishandling the relationship with the recipient. Too often they start from the attitude of working for a client — the sponsor — whose interest they have to protect through a technique of confrontation with the recipient. They fail to appreciate that even if it is the sponsor who is paying the bills the recipient is also their client. They are working for the event, even if their specific brief is to obtain benefit for the sponsor. This can only be achieved by viewing the activity as a whole. You cannot benefit the sponsor by harming the event or upsetting the organizers!

If you do use outside agencies, as you are almost bound to in a large project, make sure they work as part of your project team and insist they take the time to learn something about the event and the activity involved. When the event is in full swing these people are going to have to deal with enthusiasts and experts in that activity, as well as to communicate with a specialist press and a knowledgeable audience. If they don't know anything about the activity and are obviously disinterested in it yet try to exploit it they will quickly antagonize all these groups who will recognize the lack of knowledge immediately and are likely to be highly critical of their activities.

Other problems that can arise are clashes between sponsors. As with most problems you can do a lot to avoid them at the planning stage by ascertaining the exact situation regarding co-sponsors, sponsors of individual events on the tour you may be sponsoring, or sponsors of a championship in which an individual you are backing is competing. The main cause for concern will be if direct competitors are involved in the activity in some way, even if it is only as advertisers on perimeter boards at events. Unless you find out what the complete situation is before you start you could be in for a nasty surprise after the sponsorship has got underway.

Another problem — and I'm sorry to be going on so about potential difficulties but it is essential that you recognize them in advance — concerns the amount of support activity you put behind each sponsorship. If you are a regular user of sponsorship you will probably schedule major activities spaced throughout the year to reinforce your major sales periods. Let's say that you run one major event each quarter with minor events in between to maintain awareness. You will budget to include all the various support activities we have mentioned above in the plans for each major sponsorship and will attempt to extend its reach into the consumer and trade markets via advertising, sales promotions and public relations activity. When it comes to the minor projects, however, you may well not be able to afford all this support activity and will have to make do with the benefits of publicity coupled with some PR activity unless you can find a sponsorship that will attract co-op funds from your dealers. The problem then is to identify minor projects that will provide publicity benefits and PR opportunities without requiring significant expenditure in support of the sponsorship. For this purpose you should be on the look-out for smaller title or co-sponsorship opportunities around well-established events which although they may cost more in terms of a fee than newer events will not require so much supporting spend to achieve useful returns. Do not be seduced by a low-cost event that exaggerates its benefits. Although you may be able to buy in cheaply the chances are that you will have to spend considerable time and money to achieve any returns. Such events are not cost-effective in the role of minor, supporting events; they can only be made to work by a long-term strategy coupled with considerable promotional spend. Always define the type of event you want, how it has to fit in with your overall plans, and then look for the most cost-effective solution.

A few more points. To avoid the danger of getting so involved with an activity that you start to take it over. Many hard-up events are so ready for a sponsor's investment that they will agree to change some parts of the activity to suit the sponsor or television's needs. This is the thin end of the wedge and is loaded with danger. Go too far and you will quickly upset the fans or participants, while any arguments that develop will be seized on by the media. Try to remember at all times the reasons why you are involved in the activity. Whatever the particular ones they should all have a sound commercial basis. Your remit does not include the business of marketing the activity — you are there to market your product. Make sure that all your activities are valid from this perspective.

The same applies to the danger of overkill. While your main objective may be to achieve increased name recognition with a particular audience you should be sensitive to the danger of bringing too much branding to the event. Insist on placing banners everywhere and ramming your message down the viewers' throats and you could do more harm than good. Also, don't emulate the chairman of one company sponsoring Cowes Week, the premier British yachting regatta. He was so determined to ensure benefits from his sponsorship that he publicly warned competitors that unless they bought his company's office equipment he would not be back as sponsor for a second year! Here was a businessman talking to a crucial audience — many of the sailors in Cowes Week run their own business or make purchasing decisions, and others are influential in the wider business and investment community — and giving them nothing but threats. You can imagine the response! I can sympathize with this particular chairman. The sport he had chosen to sponsor could deliver exactly the audience he wanted but the established traditions of the sport plus the amateur and slightly supercilious way it dealt with its sponsors, meant that he had an uphill battle to make the deal work. One can imagine his frustration at the restrictions that were imposed on his ability to achieve results but that is no excuse for reacting in a way that can only damage your own credibility. Sponsorship demands that sponsors be credible if they are to get the results they hope for. You have to get to know your event and its audience and attempt to influence change in a less obvious way than forcing the audience to hear your message.

All sponsorships have a natural lifespan; the trick is in identifying the best time to end a project. Perhaps the time to do it is when people have become too familiar with you as the sponsor. At this point the organizers may have become complacent about helping you to achieve your objectives and the audience may have identified you with the event for so long that they now ignore your presence. The only way to be certain when the sponsorship results are beginning to suffer is to carry out continuous measurement of the effects of the sponsorship on your objectives. Once results start to fall you will look for new means of attracting attention. If these fail or prove to have a short lifespan you will have to consider ending the liaison. In any case you will have contracted for a given period, hopefully long enough for you to stand a chance of achieving results, and you should not consider pulling out before the end of the contract period unless there are serious problems with the event that force you to withdraw. When you decide to end the relationship always give the recipient ample time to find a replacement and offer any help you can. This is only fair to the organizers and competitors but it is also important from a PR point of view. The last thing you want is to end a relationship in a way that invites criticism.

It is not only on the sponsor's head that criticism falls when a sponsorship relationship ends. Too many organizers or their agents force founding sponsors out of events by escalating the rights fees once the event has proven successful. At the end of the first contract period you may have the unpleasant experience of being offered a new contract but at many times the fee you paid at the beginning of the event. Some increase may well be fair and justified but often the value of an event has been built by the early sponsors, not only by their money but by the promotional efforts they have put in to make the event a success. This problem is one reason why I suggested earlier that you consider making payments to unproven and untried events a form of investment finance rather than a straight sponsorship fee. If you retain some rights in the event it will be much harder for you to be outbid by richer sponsors once the event becomes valuable.

In this chapter we have looked at many of the ways you can support the sponsorship and exploit its strengths to the benefit of your commercial goals. The one thing not mentioned so far is the use of sponsorship to achieve publicity. This is often a major aim of a sponsorship project, especially when insufficient support funds can be invested to utilize other forms of promotion. The achievement of publicity largely depends on the event itself and the particular activity you are sponsoring, but whatever these may be you will have to exploit every option you can find in order to beat the sponsorship clutter. In this area of exploitation your target audience is the media and we shall examine the options available to you in the next chapter.

11

The media

Media coverage is often the most crucial single element within the reasons for a company entering into sponsorship and it is certainly the one into which most effort must be put if you are to ensure successful and consistent results. To handle press relations effectively you need at least one experienced publicist on your team, preferably an individual who understands, and is interested in, the activity you are sponsoring. Make no mistake, this area is crucial to the exposure of your sponsorship through the media and you should do everything possible to ensure its effectiveness.

Dealing with the media

Unfortunately, in my experience as a journalist covering many sponsored events for both the written media and television, the standard of publicists is woefully low. It seems that the art of bullshitting is alive and well and living in publicity land!

There is nothing worse for a specialist journalist than to be confronted by a publicist who obviously knows nothing about the activity yet pretends to be the font of all wisdom. Any journalist can tell stories of agencies or in-house PR staff who haven't done their homework, know little about the event or activity yet use a heavy-sell technique to achieve branding for their client. Nothing damages the media's attitude to a sponsorship more quickly than this sort of unprofessional behaviour and it is your responsibility as the sponsor to ensure that it doesn't happen.

If the activity you are sponsoring is new to you it is a good idea to take the time to meet a few of the specialist journalists who regularly cover the activity in informal, off-the-record meetings before you commit to firm plans for media activity. From these discussions you should be able to find out the general attitude to sponsorship within the organization of the particular activity, its participants and the specialist media. You may also be able to identify those agencies with good and bad track-records with the specialist journalists. Take the time to build a personal relationship with these key journalists since they will be the ones who give you the most regular coverage for the target audience and who will often determine the attitude and level of coverage of the general media.

The key to good relations with the media is not to treat them as a means to promote your sponsorship nor to give the impression that you think sponsorship is a means of getting free publicity. The media are in the business of satisfying their audiences not sponsors and they aim to do this by providing stories that are interesting and informative. If you wish to achieve exposure through the media it is essential that you start from the position of aiming to satisfy the media's needs. This means providing stories that will appeal to viewers, listeners and readers and only then working to achieve the level of branding that is appropriate to the story. The best tip I can give you about finding stories that the media will want to run is to look constantly for the human interest angle. Whatever the subject of your sponsorship the audience will be most attracted by stories about people, about personalities or competitors whom they can relate to on the personal level. The media know this and they will be delighted if you can provide these types of stories. Concentrate on doing so and then find the means to include your branding in the coverage and you will be well on your way to ensuring good relations with the media and satisfactory coverage of your sponsorship.

Before you rush to employ an agency to handle your press relations consider the possibility of recruiting a publicist experienced in the particular activity to your project team. The two most valuable assets a publicist can have from your point of view is a good working knowledge of and an interest in the activity, coupled with a personal relationship with the specialist media. If you can find such a person all the other requirements of dealing with the media can easily be handled in-house since they are a matter only of detail — design and presentation in particular — that you will need in any case for many other aspects of the sponsorship. The question of whether you or the organizers handle the majority of *event* publicity depends on the skills and experience available to the organizers but you will often be on safer ground if you either control the publicity operation or at least have a day-to-day involvement in it. If you are sponsoring a well-established event with its own publicity operation even a peripheral involvement may be difficult and you will be reduced to trying to interest the press in matters relating simply to your sponsorship. This can be a problem and it is certainly difficult to sustain continuing publicity on this basis. Wherever possible get intimately involved with the publicity operation and tie it directly to your sponsorship activities.

PRESS LISTS   Comprehensive and up-to-date press lists covering the specialist, technical, trade (yours), local, national and international media plus the international news agencies are an essential starting-point for communicating with the media. A good specialist publicist or outside agency should come armed with these lists since they are the most essential stock-in-trade, but you should make absolutely sure that they are accurate and comprehensive enough for your purposes. Some agencies or individuals may be reluctant to let you see or have access to their lists since they are valuable properties, but you must insist on knowing that they are sufficient for your needs.

The point about being up-to-date is very important since journalists tend to change jobs or move quite frequently and there is nothing worse than receiving invitations to events or press conferences that are out of date because they have been sent to the wrong address. I still regularly receive material sent to an address more than eight years old. You can imagine the impression that makes! Since it is only a question of an agency regularly up-dating their lists from published information, failure to do so demonstrates a lack of professionalism that reflects on whatever the agency is trying to publicize.

A comprehensive press list will carry not only the names and contact numbers and addresses of individual journalists but also the details of the editors of the various newspapers, magazines, radio and television programmes along with brief details of the type of stories most likely to appeal. While most of your mail-shots will target the journalists, it is often a good idea, when launching an important new sponsorship, to contact the editors of the most important story outlets and invite them to accompany their journalist to the press conference or event. Don't expect many to accept, but the very act of inviting them will help make them more aware of your activities and may assist the journalist when selling the story to the editor.

The most useful way of storing this considerable amount of information is, of course, on a computer data-base but do up-date it regularly, keep hard-copy printouts on file, and do avoid sending what is obviously a computer-generated circular letter or invitation to the media. Personalize your media correspondence as much as possible so that journalists are not made to feel like an impersonal part of a chain in your marketing programme — even if that's how you really view them!

PRESS RELEASES   The press release is the major means of communicating with the media but because everyone else is also sending out press releases — often on subjects that do not merit any form of communication whatever — it takes a lot of thought and presentation, or a really newsworthy announcement, to produce a press release that will attract the attention of journalists. When you were considering the design factors discussed earlier you should have given some thought to the visual presentation of your press releases in order to help them stand out from the many that drop through every journalist's mailbox. Your aim should be to produce a standard press release format and presentation that attracts attention by its design and is instantly recognizable as dealing with your event. The use of a colour heading and interesting design incorporating the event name and/or logo — without going overboard on the graphics — can greatly aid this recognition and it also helps if you can distinguish press releases from other information you send out, perhaps with the heading: PRESS INFORMATION or NEWS.

Publicists are taught that press releases should be typed with double spacing on one side of A4 paper with wide margins at the sides and bottom of the copy (to make it easy to edit the copy) and it is usually worth following these 'rules'. As with all rules, however, there are occasions when it pays to break them and if you are publicizing an event that requires you to send a considerable amount of information to the media, as with a long-term sponsorship of a major sporting series at which many top stars compete and for which the media require comprehensive information, you can get away with single spacing and printing on both sides of the paper.

What really matters is the content. In the above example the media will be interested in having as much hard information as possible so concentrate on presenting it lucidly and with a layout that allows them to retrieve whatever they need quickly and easily without having to hunt through several pages for some important detail buried away in the copy. If the information is more general, such as an announcement of your sponsorship or the provision of follow-up information you should concentrate on telling your story as straightforwardly as possible and in a manner that makes it easy for that particular recipient to use the story as directly as possible. You may well have to write different releases for the various media you are circulating. A sports journalist will need a different angle to the trade or general journalist, while the television or radio journalist may also require an alternative presentation or story.

Every press release you send out should contain certain important facts that must be readily discernible by the reader. Who you are, what is happening, when, where and why are the basic questions that must be answered by every communication and you should attempt to summarize these as close as possible to the beginning of the release before elaborating on them later in the copy. Please don't make the mistake of assuming that other people already know the answers just because you do and don't let invitations or releases go out without thoroughly checking the contents. It is a good idea to ask someone in the office, unconnected with the preparation of the release, to read it and check it for sense. That way you avoid mistakes such as the invitation to a press reception I received recently that told me where the meeting was to be but not when! Don't forget, too, to identify clearly who is the person to contact for further information. There is nothing more annoying than to wade through a press release, decide you want further information, and then not be able to find whom you should call.

The question of imposing embargoes on information you send out in press releases is a difficult one. Quite often the information leaks in one way or another and there is no more certain way of upsetting journalists than to have them respect an embargo only to find the story appear the day before in a rival paper. Some journalists regularly ignore embargoes, especially if they feel the information is not of earth-shattering importance. It is important that you keep things in perspective. While the sponsorship may be most important to you it will only be one of many similar stories to a journalist and you should not expect them to feel as you do about this particular story. If you must prevent the story from appearing before a particular date and are worried that some journalists may not respect an embargo don't send out a press release by mail but have it delivered to the important outlets by courier on the day — and don't give out any hints on the phone beforehand otherwise someone will almost certainly dig out the story before you want it released.

The best publicists understand the requirements of journalists and are able to write stories that in many cases, with just a little sub-editing, can go straight into the paper or magazine. If you don't have a publicist who thinks like a journalist (and perhaps was one), and is able to write stories acceptable to the media, then find one. Whatever the cost it will be repaid many times over by the increase in media coverage you will receive.

PRESS CONFERENCES   When thinking about holding a press conference consider whether it is really necessary or appropriate. Contrary to popular opinion journalists have other ways to spend their time than at press conferences and they are not likely to be pleased to be called to a conference when a simple press release would have sufficed. The most likely time for you to hold a press conference is at the start of the project when you announce details of your sponsorship. This is an important occasion since your presentation and attitude to the media will set the tone for future relations.

Determine whom you will invite then set a venue and time that will suit the majority of journalists who may have to travel to the occasion. The sort of hospitality you provide may depend on the standards set by similar events in the activity in which you are involved, as well as by the perceived importance of the occasion. A multi-million dollar sponsorship announcement may justify a lavish lunch or dinner after the announcement (but don't expect busy journalists to stay unless they can continue to learn more about the project) or you may simply provide coffee beforehand with drinks afterwards for a less important announcement.

Spend time making sure that the decor for the press conference is satisfactory and fits in with your overall design for the sponsorship. Don't overload the venue with your banners. The press have seen it all before and will not be impressed if you go over the top. Consider having the recipient make the announcement of the sponsorship and the benefits to the activity before you present your reasons and aims to the media. In most cases it helps if you are explicit in what you are trying to do. I never understand why so many sponsors are coy about their commercial reasons for indulging in sponsorship. We all know that you are involved for commercial reasons and most are happy that it should be so. Why not present your case and explain your objectives? You may find the media more ready to help you than you suppose. The thorny question of the amount of money involved usually crops up, and again many sponsors are unnecessarily shy on this issue. If you are one of those you may have included a confidentiality clause in the contract with the recipient and will probably refuse to answer this question, but before you do so ask yourself the question 'why?'. If it is a large sponsorship you will probably find that revealing the amount makes the story more newsworthy and certainly a degree of openness will set a good tone for future relationships with the media. If you do quote figures make sure that the media understands whether you are talking about the sponsorship fee or your total spend budget. It is usually the former that journalists are interested in since it is this sum that goes to the recipient, although your trade press will probably be interested in the total spend figure.

Do be careful not to allow yourself to get upset by such questions. At one major press conference I attended, at which a very large sponsorship deal was being announced, I asked the recipient if payments from the sponsor were dependent on performance. The person in question refused to answer the question and told me that such questions were damaging to the sport! The sponsor later took me to one side and apologized for the recipient's attitude and confirmed that indeed the payments were payable in stages depending on performance. The attitude of that particular event promoter remained hostile throughout the sponsorship, however, and demonstrated how a lack of understanding of the role of the media can damage the sponsor's return from the coverage.

It is sensible to prepare a list of possible questions you may anticipate at the press conference, including the hostile ones, and prepare suggested answers to deal with these. Hold a meeting with all involved before the conference to discuss such questions and answers and to decide how they should be handled and who will reply. Such planning can do much to help present a united face to the media and to avoid the surprise of unanticipated questions. If you expect a particularly hard time from some journalists over certain aspects of your sponsorship you may wish to consider ways of taking the sting out of the problem, either by raising the issue from the platform and answering the questions before they are asked, or having a friendly journalist pose the questions before the less friendly media can go on the attack.

The detailed planning of a press conference is important if it is to go ahead smoothly. And it is important that it does so if you are to reflect the kind of image you wish to portray. Arrange for people to arrive 15 to 30 minutes before you plan to start the conference. Offer coffee or drinks and make sure that there will be enough seating for the numbers you expect to attend. Incidentally, a phone-around the day before should enable you to assess accurately how many will actually attend.

If you plan to issue name tags — and they are useful to assist you and the event representatives in identifying guests — have them ready at the door with enough staff available so that arrivals don't have to queue. Asking all guests to sign a visitors book is a good way of identifying who actually attends and should be done as they arrive or you will be sure to miss a few. Make sure enough staff and representatives of the event are on hand to mix with the journalists before and after the event, both to answer questions and to provide a friendly, open face to your sponsorship.

Spend some time preparing a detailed press pack that covers all the points the press are likely to be interested in but try to avoid issuing so much paper that it never gets read. If you expect to send out a lot of press material in the future now is a good time to provide a simple filing system, such as a loose-leaf ring-binder in which future press releases can be kept together. If you plan to hand out give-aways the choice is almost limitless but try to give something that is either appropriate to the event or useful to the journalists. It should go without saying that whatever the give-aways they should be branded with the sponsorship message and should be useful or interesting enough so that they are not immediately discarded in the nearest rubbish bin.

If you have prepared special artwork for event logos or other design material you should include reference material in the press pack. By making it as easy as possible for the press to use this material it is much more likely that it will be used from the start of the sponsorship. In many ways the first press conference for the event will set the tone for the rest of the event, however long it lasts. Get it wrong at the first press conference and you will regret it for the whole project since first impressions are vital, especially when dealing with the media.

Don't forget to test the public address system before guests arrive and make arrangements for television crews to place their microphones near the speakers. If you do expect radio or television reporters at the conference and there is a possibility that they will wish to conduct interviews, set aside a quiet room for this purpose and make sure that all those who may be interviewed are available after the main press conference.

Once the press conference is over identify those who didn't make it and send them a full information pack as quickly as possible with a brief note saying that you hope to see them on the next occasion.

CONTINUING MEDIA RELATIONS   After the first excitement of the initial press conference you are likely to experience a lull in media coverage but this is no time to ignore the need for continuing media relations. After the press conference take a while to examine the amount and type of coverage you received. See if you can analyse which journalists gave you the most coverage, which were obviously sympathetic or antagonistic to your sponsorship, and which didn't mention the sponsor's name. This information, and that gained as the sponsorship progresses, will help you decide which journalists need to be targeted with more information or a different approach.

Keep up a regular communication with journalists on your press lists, keep them informed as the story develops, and learn what story angles they are interested in. Don't concentrate only on the established names within the activity you are sponsoring or those journalists who work as staff reporters for the major papers or television stations. The young freelance journalist of today could be the key reporter of the future and it costs you little to afford him or her the same privileges as more senior journalists — your efforts will certainly never be forgotten. While talking to journalists and selling your story don't forget to listen to their ideas or points of view. They are probably more experienced than you in many aspects of sponsorship publicity or the particular activity you are sponsoring and you are likely to pick up some good ideas.

If, as is likely, you find some media outlets refusing to mention the sponsor's name in reports, don't lose your temper and start an argument with the journalist. Such an approach is guaranteed to ensure that your name is never mentioned again in that particular paper or programme. Instead, try to find out why your name was not mentioned — it may be standard policy or the personal policy of the editor — and ask how you can help ensure a mention next time. You may find that the name of the event plus the sponsor's name is too long for inclusion in many written reports. This is a point often overlooked by those who make up event names. In general a three-word name, including the sponsor's reference, is about the limit if you are to get regular mentions. Don't forget that the media are not compelled to use your name. Indeed, many newspapers, and some commercial television stations, are becoming increasingly aware that sponsorship could potentially harm their advertising revenue and that freely to credit sponsors of events — especially sporting ones — in their editorial coverage simply increases the pressure on the advertising department. However, sport especially is a very important element in most newspapers and in many hours of television programming and since sport needs sponsors the media have to be careful to balance their approach to providing sponsors with appropriate credits.

As the sponsorship progresses continue to look for story hooks that you can use to generate publicity. Many people forget the local or regional media when handling a national event yet these can provide you with plenty of useful publicity provided you tailor your press releases to their needs. Every competitor in a major national or international event comes from somewhere and their local paper, radio or television station is probably eager to use something on them provided they are given the necessary information. It is up to you to identify these story leads and to present them to journalists on a regular basis.

As you approach major events within the sponsorship so you should increase the frequency of your press releases. Give journalists plenty of pre-warning of events, send them a complete information pack including tickets, copies of the programme, lists of competitors and background information, details of the press office location, phone numbers and the names of press officers, what facilities will be available to them, and details of local accommodation.

PRESS OFFICES   If the organization of a press office falls within your area of responsibility you must give careful thought to what facilities you will have to provide. Even if this will be the responsibility of the organizer, you must ensure that it is run effectively and that everything that should be provided is available to the assembled press corps. If it isn't you can be sure that you will share in their displeasure whether it is your fault or not.

Setting up a press office is actually quite simple yet it is amazing how many sponsors or organizers fail to provide even the most basic facilities and information while expecting the media to report effectively on the event. The first consideration is space; there must be enough for all the journalists you expect to work in (you can forecast this figure by asking journalists to register for accreditation in advance). You will need to provide telephones (if these are of the phonecard type then make sure you have a supply of these for sale in the press office), desks and chairs, typewriters (both electric and manual — some journalists still prefer manual typewriters), telexes, telephone points for personal computer modems, pin boards for information, an office area for the press officers, a separate relaxation area with a bar for coffee, soft drinks and alcohol, pigeon holes for messages, and separate working areas for television and radio reporters. You will probably also need an area for press conferences complete with a public address system, and you may want to install televisions in the various areas if the press can monitor activities via television.

Most important, however, are the press officers you use to run the press office. They must be friendly and knowledgeable, not only about the needs of journalists but also about the detail of the event. The rapid and accurate flow of information from the organizers to the press is the secret of a successful press office but is the one element that is too often missing. There is no excuse for this and you should do everything to ensure that your staff understand the absolute importance of providing the information the press need at the time when they need it.

Make sure that at all times there is one spokesperson available who can answer any question and deal with any problem. This is especially important when things go wrong, or when there is a major catastrophe with the event. At such times the press will descend *en masse* and will be demanding information. Statements must be issued quickly with regular updates if you are to keep control of the situation; at such times experienced press officers are worth their weight in gold and you must ensure that one is available even if you are not directly involved in the organization of the press office. This area of publicity is so important that it is worth writing into your sponsorship contract details of how it will be provided and who will be responsible.

PHOTOGRAPHS Photographs are an important element that can be used to extend your visibility throughout the sponsorship. Used in conjunction with press releases, photographs can extend your media coverage and provide a means to brand the coverage with your name or logo. Consider employing your own photographer to cover your event so that you can provide a continuous flow of photographs to the media. While black and white photographs are the most frequently used you should also have a selection of colour photographs and should find out which type the various newspapers and magazines covering your event would prefer. Never issue any photograph that does not include your visual branding, whether it be your name or logo, and always provide a clear caption on the back of the print or attached to a transparency.

Look for ways to illustrate every press release you issue and do try to make the pictures interesting. A bit of thought and effort applied at this stage can reward you with considerably more use for the press release than if it is sent out without illustration. Of particular importance is ensuring that the first pictures you issue, perhaps at the time of your press conference announcing the sponsorship, are of the best quality, and are clearly branded. These are the pictures that will probably end up on file and may well be used time and again. If you fail to ensure that these first photographs reflect your sponsorship you may find that they return to haunt you time and again throughout the sponsorship with little you can do to remedy the situation.

The same applies to photo sessions when press photographers assemble to capture your activities on film. Unless the level of branding and its 'subtlety' is well thought out these expert media photographers will find ways to take their pictures without including your branding. It almost becomes a contest between you and them, with you trying to find ways to ensure that your name or logo gets into each shot. Don't rely on background banners. These are often easy to shoot around or to edit out afterwards. Put all celebrities in your event clothing, which is of course branded, incorporate livery on any transport, and look for any other opportunity to ensure that photographs portray your sponsorship message.

Have every stage of your activities photographed and keep a library of pictures to which you can refer to fulfil any press requests. At any hospitality functions you host at which local or national dignitaries or celebrities attend make sure photographs are taken of guests alongside the person who may attract news coverage. Issue these to the media, both national, regional and local, and you may be surprised at the level of coverage you receive. These pictures can also be useful if you have guests from your trade suppliers or dealer network, or indeed any other group that you may wish to impress. A photograph of each guest alongside the celebrity or sporting star makes a useful present to remind each person of the day spent with your company.

Although you will be concentrating on supplying pictures to the media do not forget other techniques such as competitions for photographic clubs based on your event. These can add useful publicity, especially if you tie the competition in with a magazine or a film supplier.

If you are running the press office at your event do not forget the needs of the professional photographers. Make sure that vantage points are available exclusively for press photographers, try to keep them separate from television crews, and arrange to have a fast film developing service available, along with facilities to transmit pictures to the photographers' newspapers. Be very careful about trying to restrict photographic access to events, especially if they take place in the public domain. More than one sponsor or organizer has found that attempts to do so have back-fired with angry protests from the media. The most notable example of this was the 1987 America's Cup when IMG, the agency for the event, attempted to restrict severely photographers' access, and tried to insist that copyright on pictures taken was the property of the event! Naturally the world's media vigorously objected to this plan and the agency was forced to back down.

RADIO   Radio is often the most ignored medium yet it can be extremely useful in extending your reach for very little effort or cost. You will, of course, include all national and local radio jour-nalists, plus those from any specialist programmes that deal with the activity you're sponsoring, in your press lists, invite them to press conferences and provide suitable facilities for radio inter-views. In addition, however, you should offer to have celebrities or spokespersons available for studio interviews and you should also consider offering syndicated tapes covering your event.

The policy of radio stations towards syndicated material varies from those who will never accept it to those who are extremely grateful for any usable material they can get. If you do decide to produce syndicated tapes have an experienced radio journalist do it for you and make sure that you do not try to include too many plugs for your sponsorship. Too many mentions of your name and the tapes will not be used and you will also spoil your chances of getting other material used in future.

If your event involves competitors or participants from other regions or countries beyond the one in which you are staging the event don't forget to target the radio media in those areas. They will almost certainly be interested in a story on one of their local individuals provided the event is of sufficient interest, and you will get the benefit of widened exposure.

When setting up a media monitoring service don't forget to include national and local radio as well as television and the press. Radio is a medium that achieves very impressive audiences, especially during the daytime, and exposure through this medium can be extremely valuable.

TELEVISION   While radio is often a forgotten medium the same cannot be said of television! Although the majority of sponsorships do not get television coverage it is still the most valuable means available of achieving the wide exposure that is a requirement of many projects. If media exposure is a key requirement of your sponsorship you must plan your targeting of television very carefully.

There are several types of television exposure; the programme dedicated to an event, inclusion in a general sports, arts or other magazine programme, and news bulletins, all of which may be available on a local, national or international basis. The key to obtaining television coverage is to be aware that television needs quality story material but has very specific requirements and deadlines, and is often restricted in covering your event, not because it is unsuitable but because of the difficulty of allocating airtime or of rostering a limited number of camera crews to the coverage.

As we have already seen, the world of international television is changing rapidly. Budgets available to produce programme material are often shrinking in real terms while the number of hours that must be filled is increasing rapidly. In addition, television itself is becoming more global with broadcasters more and more ready to accept material of an international nature. While the situation is extremely complex you should not despair; the opportunities for sponsors are increasing rapidly, not only in the field of sponsored programming, but also in the ability to encourage coverage of sponsored events.

The first task is to identify *all* the programme editors who should be sent details of the event. For a large, perhaps international sponsorship this can be a major task that could require a dedicated press officer who is confident working with television journalists and understands their needs. Television journalists and editors receive more press releases and requests for coverage than any other type of journalist, reflecting the importance placed on television exposure, and you must find a way of attracting their attention and interest. Don't try to do this with stunts or other time-wasting activities. They have seen it all before and will not be impressed. Instead, it is best to take the time to visit or call as many as possible to establish a personal relationship and to find out what they need in order to make your event of interest.

If the event you are sponsoring is important and will attract television coverage as a matter of course your task is to find a way of interesting the editors in your sponsorship and to find ways to ensure that coverage includes your branding (the amount of which may be restricted by any regulations the broadcasters have to operate under).

The dedicated programme The ideal situation is to have your event covered for a complete programme or series. This may happen because the event, usually a long-established one, has inherent attributes that make it attractive to television, or if a new event can be used by broadcasters to provide programming to a large or important audience. One of the key considerations is likely to be the ease and cost of making the programme. An event that programme-makers are used to covering, and which does not cost a lot of money, has far more chance of getting on air than one which requires new techniques or equipment and which costs more per hour to produce.

Depending on the rules under which programme-makers have to operate you may be able to help reduce costs, either by the provision of funds or services directly to the broadcaster, or by paying for the independent production of the coverage which is then provided to broadcasters at low cost, or even on a cost-free basis.

There are many permutations that can work in such cases but you should start your investigations by talking to the broadcasters themselves to see which approach suits them best. Since you are unlikely to have enough experience of the television business you should consider hiring a consultant specifically to handle this side of the sponsorship.

Magazine programmes   Such programmes offer enormous potential for exposure since they are always on the lookout for short items of a varied nature. At the very least you can often get them to take material for possible use as fillers and it is surprising how often such material gets used. Magazine programmes exist that cover virtually every type of interest and activity and you should cast your net widely when targeting them. For instance, although your event may be a sporting one it could also provide a useful piece for a children's programme, or a technology programme. Or how about one for health and fitness addicts? The possibilities are many, you just have to use your imagination as in so many other areas of sponsorship.

Once again, though, you will be in a better position of having your sponsorship obtain airtime on this sort of progamme if you can produce material for supply to programme editors. This does not have to be in the form of an edited slot. Indeed, it is usually best if it isn't edited. Programme editors would normally prefer to receive rushes, or an over-length cut piece, from which they can edit the story they require.

If you are not in a position to provide material you will have to contact all the possible outlets and try to convince them that it is worth sending a crew to cover the story themselves. This will always be hard to achieve but you can make it easier by, for instance, laying on transport and ensuring that all the people and supporting material the crew will need are assembled in the right place at the right time.

News coverage   This is probably the most valuable sort of publicity a sponsor can receive yet it is often treated in a most hit-and-miss way. News crews attending a press conference often have to battle with the other media for space and for some interview time with the key people yet their deadlines are usually the most demanding. When inviting television news programmes to cover a press conference or other event try to arrange for them to get the material they need before the main event for the rest of the media. It will also help if you can supply background material that can be edited with the interviews in order to give a more complete report. Always ask in advance if programme editors can use supplied material — more and more can these days — and ask, too, what format they would prefer.

It may surprise you to learn that it is quite possible to increase your chances of obtaining news coverage across the whole range of international, national and regional outlets through a technique that has become known as the Video News Release (VNR). This works in a similar way to the press release except that instead of providing a simple written piece, you produce a complete edited story on video which is then distributed to all your target news, and magazine programme outlets.

When planning a VNR operation you should inform all the broadcasters in advance about the story they will be receiving, and issue a reminder just before distribution. On the day of the release you must ensure that the material reaches the programme editors well in advance of their bulletin deadlines and you should also include a written fact-sheet covering the story. In Europe it is normal practice to send out un-voiced cut stories with a suggested script plus a detailed dope sheet that will allow a journalist to write his own script; while in the US it is common for VNRs to be complete with a commentary. A typical length of a VNR in the US is about two and half minutes while in Europe you could extend the length to about four or five minutes depending on the strength of the story. On no account send a VNR that is significantly longer than this since its value to a news editor depends on the ease with which it can be incorporated into a bulletin with the minimum of editing.

If VNRs are to be used they must have a valid storyline that has real news interest and is not based solely on your need to publicize your sponsorship. They must also be consistent with the journalistic and technical standards of news programmes and should therefore be produced by experienced news journalists. Commercial services for the production and distribution of VNRs exist in the US and Europe with the widest reaching being those offered by the commercial divisions of the international television news agencies.

Such services can provide advance information to broadcasters worldwide, produce the coverage of your event, edit it into suitable formats for the various outlets, and distribute the stories, often on the same day, to outlets anywhere in the world. If your sponsorship activities are aimed at an international audience, as an increasing number are, you should seriously consider retaining such a service to publicize your activities to all your key markets. The use of VNRs can be monitored, and experience shows that they can often provide quite staggering results in terms of audience reach that are quite unachievable by many other forms of promotion.

Producing your own coverage

As we have seen above there are often a lot of advantages in producing your own coverage of your sponsorship. If quality material is available there are many opportunities for achieving broadcast time in a whole range of different programme types. The key to producing your own material is to retain a professional agency experienced in producing broadcast material *and* working with sponsors. The skills and resources required to handle this sort of work extend far beyond those of the average production company used to producing promotional videos or documentaries. The agency must be experienced in working with broadcasters and meeting their deadlines and requirements. And since a lot of the opportunities for exposure come from news programmes the agency producing and distributing your coverage must be used to dealing with news editors and must have a distribution ability that matches your requirements for exposure. If you are only interested in coverage within a single country the job is not that difficult. If, however, you are concerned with achieving the maximum coverage on an international basis you will require an agency that deals regularly with international broadcasters, including the news outlets, and is able to handle the complex requirements of international production and satellite distribution to meet short deadlines. The difference this ability makes when you have a topical sporting or news item to be distributed is amazing and you will achieve far more exposure if you work with an agency experienced in this area. Another benefit of this type of agency is that you should find that they can offer an international resource for covering your events wherever they may be in the world. This sort of facility really helps an international sponsor wishing to make use of national sponsorships in as many markets as possible.

Another advantage of producing your own coverage is that the agency you employ should be able to advise you on the staging of events to achieve the maximum acceptable level of branding and will help you avoid the pitfalls that regularly befall sponsors who do not have experience of the television medium available to them.

Producing your own coverage works best when your event is one that is marginal for normal TV coverage because it is either difficult or expensive to cover or has an unproven audience potential. In such cases one often finds that broadcasters are happy to receive programming, much of which gets used, although they will usually be reluctant to stage their own coverage. One mistake that is often made by companies who commission their own coverage is that they tend to expect to make money by selling the coverage. This is most definitely the wrong approach. For a start, as we have seen, the tendency now is for broadcasters to be increasingly reluctant or unable to pay large rights fees, and indeed most are becoming increasingly eager to receive free material in order to help reduce their programming costs. Secondly, the most important aspect of achieving television coverage is the requirement for maximum awareness. If broad awareness is not among your sponsorship requirements you don't need television at all; if it is then airtime is the most valuable commodity you can get and you shouldn't limit your chances by expecting the coverage to be a revenue source. If you do your job properly and achieve good coverage the increased exposure for the event can easily be marketed in many other areas such as merchandising, gate receipts, etc., that will offset, at least, the often surprisingly modest costs of coverage.

Controlling the coverage of your event has the advantage that you can use the raw footage in many different ways on broadcast television; for news bulletins, magazine programmes and documentary coverage. All that is needed is that you decide in advance what the end uses should be so that the coverage of the event can be designed correctly from the outset. Therefore, before you go ahead and commission your own coverage make sure that the agency you choose will undertake research among the outlets you hope to hit in order to determine their level of interest. Often their response will aid you in designing the coverage to get the maximum exposure possible. You will also be able to determine whether you can charge a modest fee for the material or whether it should be given away rights-free. This will vary from market to market. Some broadcasters won't accept free material but will always insist on paying a nominal sum at least — to ensure independence! In other markets material is bartered in exchange for advertising airtime. Thus a one-hour programme may be offered in exchange for 2½ minutes of advertising space which the sponsoring company can use or, sometimes, sell on. When bartering is permissible the sponsor can effectively recoup much of the cost of the production, albeit in an indirect way. When this sort of arrangement is considered in addition to the major levels of branding now allowed in some countries the benefits of controlling your own television material are obvious.

While talking about the opportunities that can be found for advertising in and around your own programme I should also mention one spoiling tactic that is increasingly used by rival companies. If your major rival wants to confuse the audience and to interfere with the exposure you receive he may try to book airtime within the programme covering your own event. While it may be impossible to prevent this if you have no control over the coverage of your event, you stand a better chance if you are providing a rights-free, completed programme or if you are bartering the material.

Another advantage of producing as much of your own coverage as possible is the opportunity it offers for using the material in non-broadcast outlets such as for in-flight showing by airlines, and the home video market. The latter is becoming of increasing significance with the high level of penetration of VCRs in homes in Europe and the US. The great advantage of this market is that it is usually one made up of the natural audience for the event — the enthusiasts who are presumably one of your main target audiences. The lack of restrictions on home video programming means that you can incorporate a higher level of branding than if the material were for normal broadcast showing. This advantage alone could make it worth commissioning the coverage of all stages of your event independently of whatever broadcasters may decide to provide. In addition you can often use material from your sponsorship activities in corporate videos, aimed perhaps at shareholders, and may be able to make use of it for advertising purposes.

While considering all the outlets for your own coverage don't forget the official film of the event. Often these are made for cinema use, usually as a short feature, and will be shot on film rather than video tape. If this is the case it usually requires a completely separate production from the video coverage you would use for television programmes. If an official film is your major reason for covering the event, however, you might as well shoot on film. It will still be fine for television documentary purposes but will not usually be used for news due to the longer time required to process the material. Usually, though, you will want to keep the film and video productions separate since both different techniques and concepts are likely to be involved.

A final point about handling your own production; consider very carefully before you refuse access to interested broadcasters who wish to produce their own coverage, however small, on the grounds that sole rights will help you sell material. Your goal should be maximum exposure first since this makes the overall property much more valuable and allows you to maximize revenues from all over areas including co-sponsorship deals. To this end welcome all broadcasters to produce their own material if they wish to. You may find that your initial approach offering material was sufficient to arouse their interest. The more quality coverage the better should be the motto.

WORKING WITH A HOST BROADCASTER   If your event is proven enough to warrant coverage by a host broadcaster you should find that you get satisfactory coverage on that channel. If you wish to exploit that coverage in other markets, however, you may run into a problem. Quite often title sponsors of events buy products with guaranteed television since this makes the events attractive. Yet this usually means that the TV rights to the event have already been assigned and you may have less freedom than you would like to exploit the coverage in the other markets and ways we have discussed above. If you are already locked into this sort of deal you may have little choice but there is usually some way of ensuring that you gain access to material and the rights to use it in other countries and the non-broadcast media. Don't rely on the broadcaster to help you with this. It is usually beyond their sphere of expertise — you need an agency that understands international television *and* the techniques for marketing sponsorships — and there is usually no incentive for the broadcaster to help you with any degree of urgency. 'Of course,' the producer may say, 'you can have a copy of the rushes as soon as we've finished with them.' The question is, 'When will that be?' You may well wish to feed a video news release on the same day to international news outlets, but if you can't get access to the material until days later your options are severely limited.

12

Research

The idea of using research in sponsorship evaluation is regularly dismissed by many practitioners from all sides of the industry on the grounds that the effects of sponsorship cannot be measured, or at the very least, not in the same sophisticated way as can the effects of the other marketing techniques. If this is true I, for one, would be asking why any commercial company is involved with sponsorship since to expend so much time and money on a medium you cannot justify by results seems unbusinesslike to say the least. The argument that says effects cannot be measured also makes a nonsense of the idea that you should start your sponsorship in support of specific objectives. If you can't measure results why bother with objectives? You won't have any idea of success or failure.

While it is true that few sponsors use rigorous research techniques to evaluate, select and monitor their sponsorships the number that do is growing and is certain to continue. And the fact is that research techniques can be brought to bear on questions concerning sponsorship; they can help you determine the right activity and event for you, and they can measure effects of the sponsorship on specific objectives. It is true, however, that sponsorship is less easy to monitor with research techniques than other marketing methods such as advertising, partly because many of the goals of sponsorship are either less rigorously defined or because they are to do with more subtle factors than a straightforward increase in sales — building goodwill, for instance, for long-term business benefit or targeting groups of potential future customers.

The other reason that sponsorship research lags behind that conducted for other media is simply to do with the fact that the sponsorship industry is a lot younger than the other disciplines and has yet to achieve the sort of structured approach practised by advertising. The techniques and expertise do, however, exist within the market research industry and can be applied to sponsorship as long as the reasons for research and the goals that are set are clearly defined.

One of the common arguments as to why sponsorship research won't work suggests that it is impossible to separate the effects of the sponsorship from the effects of advertising or sales promotions. It is certainly true that researching sponsorship does involve a lot of variables but it is no more impossible to measure the specific effects of sponsorship than it is to do the same for advertising. I have yet to hear the obvious corollary to the argument — it is impossible to separate the effects of advertising from the effects of the other techniques — and it is interesting to note that many of these suggestions originated in advertising agencies in the days when they viewed sponsorship with suspicion. When the advertising agencies were concerned that a generally increased sponsorship spend would damage their ad revenues, they used, as their major weapon, the argument that sponsorship could not be researched like advertising. Nowadays, when many of the larger agencies have expanded to include public relations and sponsorship departments and are fast becoming marketing services agencies, they have suddenly realized, it seems, that all the media can be researched; and of course they can offer you the services of their own research departments to do the job!

One point I must make, however, is that extensive research done properly is expensive and may not be justified by small sponsorship projects or those aimed at a small target group, like dealers, whom you can research yourself. A major sponsor who uses research for all large projects is likely to have a well-developed feel for the business and may easily get away without researching the small projects that he wishes to undertake, relying instead on a gut feeling, perhaps backed up by a small amount of research conducted in-house or as part of a larger survey. The first-time sponsor testing the water with a small project will not, however, have this experience at his disposal and should plan to include research in his budget despite the increased cost this will incur. If you are to give sponsorship a chance of working for you then it is essential to build knowledge and experience as quickly as possible and accept the cost of doing so. Researching your early projects thoroughly will teach you very quickly whether you are on the right track and could save you considerable expense by preventing costly mistakes. The knowledge you accumulate will also pay off when you increase your involvement in sponsorship and will allow you more readily to identify objectives and opportunities.

If, when considering whether or not you should undertake research, you find that your in-house sponsorship executive or your outside agencies are dismissive of the idea, beware. While projects are not researched you will have to rely on subjective impressions and these could be 'talked up' by executives or agencies with vested interests! With research techniques in place you have a way of assessing performance and those responsible for managing and exploiting projects have to be more concerned with their own performance.

While sponsors may have been able to get away without conducting research in the past the situation in the industry now virtually requires the use of these techniques. The clutter in some parts of the sponsorship industry, notably in sports, is now so great, and still increasing, and the number of sponsorship opportunities available has grown so much, that unless clear objectives are set and rigorous research undertaken it is likely that your activities will be lost in the crowd or golden opportunities will be missed.

Objectives
In Chapter 4 I insisted that sponsorship projects should be evaluated carefully using a tailor-made system based on your own

product or corporate objectives and I would like to extend that argument here.

The objectives you wish to meet will have been identified by market research initiated to identify the current position and the overall marketing aims for the future. This research will have been implemented, not on the basis of using any one medium, but to assist overall marketing information. From these research findings the marketing department will have set certain objectives; what remains is to set the strategy for achieving those objectives. If sponsorship is believed to have a part to play in this strategy specific objectives will be set for the sponsorship element. With these in place a sponsorship strategy will be determined, leading to implementation and, finally, an analysis of effects. Objectives have to be set before a strategy can be decided, first at the overall marketing level and then for the specific communications media used to achieve the overall objectives.

The point is that research is used to provide information that can be used for marketing decision-making. If research is to be successful at any level it has to reflect this marketing orientation and must address the issues that are essential to success. When we come to the sponsorship level the objectives must be stated in such a way as to allow effects of the sponsorship to be measurable. There is no such thing as a generally effective sponsorship in an abstract sense — any project must be evaluated against specific objectives and in this sponsorship is no different from advertising, PR or sales promotion.

If research is to be used it is essential that you express your objectives in a quantifiable way. It is not enough to state, for instance, that the aim of a sponsorship is to increase awareness of a product. This objective is far too broad to enable you accurately to select a sponsorship that will work for you to measure its results. It is far better to be more specific when you set your main objectives; thus you could say: 'The main aim is to increase product awareness by 10 per cent among young, non-professional males between 18 and 30 years.' This much more clearly defined objective allows you to select more easily projects that stand a chance of succeeding, forces a more critical questioning of the role and the ability of sponsorship to satisfy the marketing requirements, makes it possible to research effects of the sponsorship, and is likely to make sponsorship executives focus their attention on achieving definable goals.

Before setting objectives for sponsorship projects step back to your overall marketing objectives and try to find specific, clearly definable objectives that sponsorship has a chance of delivering. Don't allow yourself to start from a point where your objectives are too broad otherwise any apparently rigorous techniques you put in place to measure the viability of projects or their success may be unable to work effectively simply because the objectives have not been expressed in measurable terms.

Techniques

There are several research techniques that can be applied to sponsorship; the ones you choose will depend on the particular objectives and the importance, and budget, you give to research.

Among the types of research you could consider are attitude research amongst groups of consumers to check their attitude to sponsorship, and the various activities you may wish to sponsor; market research into the opportunities available within sponsorship; desk research using published material; exploratory research to test hunches before undertaking more comprehensive studies; qualitative research to give a broad feel for the effects of sponsorship; or quantitative research to provide detailed answers using larger, representative samples.

If you are a major advertiser you will probably use research regularly, perhaps using panels of consumers to measure changes in attitude or behaviour over time. You should consider whether it will be possible to incorporate your sponsorship research into the product work your agency is already doing. In such cases the extra cost of researching your sponsorship needs could be insignificant to your total research expenditure.

Do beware of putting any reliance in most of the general surveys published occasionally on the sponsorship business. Most of these rely on questionnaires mailed to sponsors, recipients and agencies without any follow-up by telephone or interview, and are often of doubtful value. In the first place the number of respondents is usually a very low percentage of the overall group; and secondly, those who do respond may well exaggerate or distort their answers for their own reasons, either to spread disinformation to confuse competitors, or to improve their status or simply out of a sense of mischief. Very few busy executives have the time or inclination to complete such questionnaires, especially in a developing industry that is quite secretive, and the task may be handed over to an office junior who has little idea of what is really going on.

You must also be extremely cautious about the techniques used to measure the value of media publicity generated by sponsorship activities. Since the central strategy of many sponsorships is to gain publicity it may seem sufficient simply to measure the column inches and minutes of television and radio airtime in order to come up with a measure of success. The first problem with this approach, however, is how you place a value on that publicity to determine cost-effectiveness compared with buying advertising space. Many agencies, especially PR or sponsorship consultancies, claim they can compare the value of editorial mentions or name exposure on television or in photographs with the cost of media buys. I have yet to see such a system that makes much sense. In the first place how do you measure the impact of a couple of name mentions buried within an article covering an event, or of a banner display in the background of a photograph, or one exposed for so many minutes during television coverage of an event?

Yet many agencies collect all these mentions, analyse them in some way (sometimes apparently associated with witchcraft or an inspired guess into how much the client is willing to believe) and then declare that the visibility was worth so many millions of dollars of media buys! Of course, they always take the maximum ratecard price for advertising purchases to increase the supposed value of the mentions. Do you know any major advertiser who pays full rates for advertising? And how, exactly, do you measure the amount of time or space that is to be compared? If an article covers ten column inches but only mentions the sponsor's name once, it is clearly unrealistic to value that mention on the cost of a similar sized advert.

A classic example is the one repeatedly given about Richard Branson's efforts to promote his Virgin Airways company in the US by way of a record-breaking attempt on the Blue Riband Trans-Atlantic record. According to one agency the enormous publicity Branson achieved when he sank close to the finishing line was worth $123 million at ratecard, against a sponsorship cost of only $½ million.

The problem is that these mentions in the media are often taken out of context when the material is analysed. True, a book of press cuttings with your name highlighted in every appearance looks very impressive when presented by your agency and will give you some nice warm feelings, but it represents something very different from the way the newspaper reader or television viewer notices your sponsorship. Of course, you will register your name every time it is mentioned in print or shown on TV (especially if it is highlighted for you), but will the consumer? And if he or she does notice, what impressions are received?

The second and associated point about analysing media coverage is that what you should be interested in is awareness and attitude. While you can certainly get a guide to the visibility of your sponsorship and the potential for awareness among your target audience, which is useful for adding to your knowledge, you certainly cannot tell, by measuring media mentions, how many of your *target audience* saw and registered the mentions, nor how the viewers' attitude to you or your product has been influenced by the sponsorship.

In order to research awareness and attitude you must conduct properly designed research within the specific target group, preferably using a control group not exposed to the sponsorship to help eliminate the effects of any other promotions you may be running at the same time. Analysing media coverage can be done if you have time and money to spare but do not treat it as definitive research. Rather, use it to check on overall, comparative visibility and to impress any critical shareholders who may be as naive as the consultants who seem to believe that such results are sufficient justification for sponsorship activities.

Selection
The subject of project selection and evaluation was covered in Chapter 4 but this is a good point to reinforce the point that a critical approach must be used if you are to identify those projects which can deliver the commercial terms you want.

Research must be drawn on when setting objectives for sponsorship and should be the basis for your evaluation system. Before you get down to evaluating specific sponsorship projects, research can be used to identify broad types of activities that may offer the audience you wish to reach. This is the key to selecting sponsorship projects since only those activities that reach your target group and are relevant to their lifestyles can deliver your message. Research can be used to discover the market segmentation of the various types of activity, thus allowing you to match more accurately the project to your requirements with maximum effectiveness and minimum waste.

In order to discover this information you can research your current and potential product consumers to discover which activity will reach the largest section of the total audience or the most important group. You can also research the product usage, the demographic and psychographic tendencies of participants and fans of particular activities to select the activity and the specific event that can offer the audience that most closely matches your target group. And you can even use research among actual or potential consumers to identify activities that, for them, reflect the image you wish to project.

Results
As sponsorship costs escalate so the importance of being able to

measure its strengths and weaknesses compared with those of the other marketing tools increases considerably. You also need to be able to identify the type of project most successful for you so that you can avoid future mistakes while identifying new opportunities. The best option is usually a three-part survey conducted before, during and after the event. A comparison of the results will show any changes in the parameters being measured and you can also break down the research to give information on particular groups who may be affected by the sponsorship in different ways.

If you are to measure the effectiveness of particular events it is imperative that you conduct research in advance in order to have a base from which to measure changes.

In order to assess results you could research the change in awareness and/or image in the target audiences and you could also measure the change in the likelihood of buying the product. Another measure that is a helpful guide is to research the recognition and recall of the sponsored event, together with similar measures of other events within the same activity or those sponsored by competitors.

Some people attempt to give a cost figure (CPT) (Cost Per Thousand) for the reach of events, either beforehand as a guide to the price to pay, or afterwards as an indication of cost-effectiveness compared with other media. While it is possible to estimate a CPT in terms of the numbers of on-site spectators and television viewers, plus other media mentions, provided a very realistic attitude is taken to valuing media coverage, this measurement gives you absolutely no guide to the impact of the event, or its ability to affect the attitudes of the target group. For this reason the measure of cost-effectiveness should be sponsorship's ability to meet its objectives (percentage increase in awareness within a target audience, for instance) compared with the cost of achieving the same result (if it could be achieved) using other communication tools.

Once you have begun to use research to set sponsorship objectives and to evaluate the effectiveness of particular strategies you will find that the medium begins to offer far more opportunities for success. In order to increase your understanding of the medium you should retain all the research information you obtain and feed it back into the system to refine further your approach, especially concerning prior evaluation of opportunities and ideas for new events.

13

Working with agencies

One decision you will have to make early in your sponsorship planning is whether you will use agencies to handle the selection, management and exploitation of your projects or choose to have as much as possible handled in-house. There are several types of agency that could be involved in any one event, including sponsorship agencies, agents and managers for events or individuals, public relations and advertising consultancies, plus agencies that offer specialist services such as design, hospitality, event production, media monitoring, research, or television production.

If you are completely new to sponsorship you may decide to hand over the running of the project to a specialist agency, with one of your executives appointed to keep an eye on things. At the other extreme you could choose to use an in-house team to handle all aspects of the sponsorship, perhaps bringing in your PR and advertising agencies to consult in specialist areas. It is difficult to give specific advice since much will depend on the skills your staff have, whether you are able or prepared to make the commitment to the medium by employing specialist staff, and the size of the projects you are planning. As a minimum I suggest that you insist on forming a project team that brings together your own marketing staff and the specialist skills you need from agencies. That way you can learn by watching others while at the same time retaining some control, and you avoid the problems sometimes associated with allowing an agency too free a hand with your budget.

Even at this early stage look to the long term. If you decide to continue to expand your use of sponsorship it will be much more effectively used and more cost-effective if you can bring as many of the skills required in-house. Your own staff should better understand your objectives and be more committed to meeting them than any outside agency and should also be in a better position to come up with new ways of using the medium, based on your needs and objectives.

It does, however, take time to build up experience with the medium and if you intend to make a substantial commitment to this marketing tool you should consider employing a specialist to head your sponsorship department and to lead project teams in the early stages while other staff are learning how to maximize the opportunities.

Agents and managers

Even if you have not yet been involved in sponsorship, agents, managers or agencies will probably already have approached you, attempting to sell you properties for sponsorship. Agents, whether individuals or companies, generally take on the task of selling projects to potential sponsors and earn their fee by taking a commission that typically ranges from 10 to 30 per cent. In some cases the agency that approaches you to sell a project is also a full-service agency that will be hoping to be retained by you to handle the project once they have made the sale. There is no reason why you should be led down this path, and I would suggest you treat the questions of whether the project is right for you, and who will run it if you proceed, entirely separately.

The experience and integrity of agents varies enormously and you should learn as much as possible about the relationship between the agent and the person or organization for whom he claims to be acting. In particular you need to know if the agent has exclusive rights to the property, preferably by asking the rights holder. If an agent tries to prevent your meeting the rights holder for direct discussions walk away from the deal. The only reason an agent would try to keep you apart is if he has something to hide. You will often find several agents all trying to sell you the same property. Do not get involved with negotiations with any that do not have exclusive rights. Ask to negotiate with the rights holder and the agent together. The agent should be quite happy with this since he can expect to receive a commission if an introduction and negotiations organized by him prove fruitful.

As your involvement with sponsorship increases you can expect to receive approaches from managers of individual celebrities, athletes or artists. Some will be offering advertising or endorsement opportunities and others may suggest full sponsorship deals. The manager's job is usually to maximize his client's earnings from previously agreed areas for which the manager will receive a percentage commission. Like all sellers of sponsorship deals, managers will usually attempt to convince you that their client has the image and ability to reach audiences that are just right for you. Whenever I hear an agent of any description say that, I always wonder how they know the client's requirements better than the client!

The worst mistake to make when approached by a manager or agent of one of the stars is to feel impressed simply because the product for sale is a celebrity you have always wanted to meet. As with all sponsorship projects, the only important question is 'Will an involvement with this property help us meet our objectives at a realistic price?' Put such proposals through the same evaluation procedure you would an event and be especially careful to ascertain exactly what is being offered, and whether the star has any other contracts that might conflict with yours. If part of the deal includes having the right, say, to ten days of the star's time each year for promotional activities ask yourself if you can actually use those days effectively. You might decide that half that number would be more appropriate. Negotiate a deal that suits your specific requirements, not what the agent wants to sell. Also be careful to check the star's previous performance for other sponsors. I'm afraid that some stars don't give value for money, 'forget' to mention their sponsor on public occasions, or cause image problems by becoming involved in controversy. Ask for references from previous companies the star has worked for and follow them up. You will usually be able to find out quite easily if there have been any previous problems which, if they are not sufficient to cause you to say no, can provide a useful way of negotiating a price reduction!

Sponsorship agencies

Agencies specializing in sponsorship vary tremendously in experience and the number and quality of the services they offer. One distinction to make is between agencies that either sell or run projects and those that sell projects on behalf of the recipient for a percentage commission *and* offer support services to the sponsor to help with the management of the project. Obviously the latter can involve working for two masters but the situation can work when the specialist skills of the agency (perhaps in a particular activity or sport) enables them to ensure a successful relationship between the sponsor and the event. If you decide to employ the agency that sold you the deal you should wait until after the sponsorship agreement has been finalized and would be well advised to accept presentations from other agencies to check the expertise that is available.

Some agencies do not attempt to sell projects, preferring instead to work only for sponsoring clients. The argument in favour of this approach is that the agency can get to know your specific requirements before analysing opportunities for recommendation. This type of agency becomes an extension of your marketing department; the sort of organization that, if you wished to do so, you would try to create in-house.

The number and type of services offered by agencies varies, but could include:

- Defining client's objectives
- Evaluation of proposals and opportunities
- Contract negotiations
- Project management

- Event organization
- Design
- Hospitality
- Film and video production
- Public relations and advertising
- Media relations
- Research and monitoring of results

Most agencies will not offer the full range of services but that should not necessarily put you off. The essential services you require are the first five; the rest can be obtained from other specialists offering services to the sponsorship industry or from your existing agencies.

Most agencies specialize to some degree; some concentrate on sports, others on the arts; some handle only one or two types of sports, or only represent individual artists, while a few claim to have sufficient expertise to cover all areas of the medium. The question of which type you need depends on the type of activities you are likely to be involved with. If sport is the area you expect to concentrate on you might choose an agency experienced across a range of several sports. Alternatively, if you are only interested in one activity, at least for a while, you may benefit by using an agency that specializes in that activity. This is especially so when the activity you intend sponsoring is not well known or has aspects that require specialist knowledge. Since it is quite important that the team handling any sponsorship understands the activity and knows the key people involved in its organization there is a lot to be said for retaining a specialist agency, even if they cannot offer the full range of services available from a larger agency. If you do decide to go for the non-specialist agency make sure that they have individuals on staff who are thoroughly conversant with the activity you wish to sponsor.

Finding agencies should not be a problem. Many will approach you and others can be found in the trade periodicals. The difficulty may be in selecting one to suit your needs. Treat this selection process just as you would for an advertising or PR agency, don't allow yourself to be seduced by promises of untold publicity or other benefits. Do some research into the agencies available and draw up a short-list. Before approaching them define the objectives you wish to achieve from sponsorship and take the time to think about the sort of activities that you feel would be appropriate. Contact the agencies on your short-list and have them visit you for an initial presentation. At this stage you want to know about their business, whom they have worked for, the events they have been involved in and their philosophy on sponsorship. Also, ask to see examples of promotional material they have produced for other clients and take up the references they provide. Then ask each to come up with some outline proposals based on a brief you have prepared. This should contain details of your objectives, the audience you wish to reach, the time-scale you anticipate for the promotion, and a guide to the total spend budget you wish to allocate.

Give the agencies sufficient time to work up outline proposals and arrange to visit each agency's offices for the presentations. At this stage you will already have ranked the agencies according to your initial impressions and the outcome will depend on the proposals and the impressions you gain when you have the chance to see their offices, the number of staff, their attitude to clients and all the other factors that indicate an efficient operation. Ask to meet the account executives that will handle your business and make certain that you will be able to work with them. Sponsorship requires a lot of 'people dealings', often in very sensitive situations, and personalities can be extremely important.

When making your final choice be less influenced by the specific details of the proposal — these can always be changed, and inevitably will be, by further consultations — than by the ability each agency demonstrates for analysing your requirements and building proposals based on them. Some agencies, even if they claim not to sell projects, will have an interest in seeing specific projects receive your money. If the agency seems to have bent your requirements to fit in with a particular project, or if they try to sell you too hard on a specific route to follow, be careful. The agency you want is the one which, after the initial brief, pesters your executives for more marketing information, talks to your PR department, visits your dealers and conducts its own research (in total confidence, of course) and does everything possible to learn more about your company's needs; that agency is the one that puts its clients' requirements first.

The next consideration is to get value for money. Once you decide on a particular agency agree the fee structure that will apply, how much you will be charged for each person who will work on the account and how bought-in services and out-of-pocket expenses will be charged.

Before agreeing to take all the sponsorship services from your agency check on the services they really offer and the costs of each compared with the same service bought from a specialist agency. For instance, the agency may call itself a full-service operation, but this often means that some departments, hospitality or TV productions, for instance, will be run by a single person who knows where to go to buy in specialists. You will get charged for this service which you may be able to get better and cheaper by going direct to the supplier. The latter approach also offers the opportunity of having the specialist's skills working directly for you where you can take advantage of their experience in the particular field.

The really good agency will actually point out to you where their strengths really lie, which services they can buy in on your behalf or which you may wish to provide through your existing agencies. Unfortunately, there are far too many jealousies in this business, and too many greedy people with insufficient in-depth knowledge. Few agencies, and clients for that matter, seem to realize that it is far better to take the realistic approach, to bring in the best talent available for every project, and to show the client how to get the best value out of sponsorship than it is to be so hysterical about protecting your account to the extent that you hide your use of specialists and do everything to keep them and the client apart. Of course, agencies earn extra revenue by marking up the services they buy in and pass on to the client, if only with a handling charge, and in fact they may be able to make cheaper purchases than you could, but the important point is that you should know what they are doing and approve the arrangements.

Agencies should be less afraid to allow specialists direct access to the client if that is beneficial; if they and the specialists they recommend or hire operate successfully you will be satisfied and will continue to use the agency. The better run and more successful sponsorship projects are the more likely clients are to increase their spend in the medium. This brings in more fee-paying business to agencies and more than makes up for any loss of earnings from allowing specialist suppliers to deal directly with the client if that is his preference.

One final point in selecting a sponsorship agency: check their approach to research and who they use to handle it . If they do not normally undertake detailed research other than measuring media mentions consider using another agency.

Other agencies

It is highly unlikely that a sponsorship agency, if you use one, will be able to offer all the services you will require and so you should expect to work with other suppliers offering specialist services. The obvious agencies who could be involved are your existing advertising and PR consultancies. Some advertising agencies offer full sponsorship services as part of their below-the-line services to clients but most have yet to enter this area, and some, fortunately a shrinking number, actively dislike marketing funds being allocated to sponsorship. You are likely to have some advertising requirements with the project but these need not be handled by your regular agency. Look for one that is prepared to get involved in what you are doing and work out a creative approach to linking advertising and the sponsorship.

In my experience it is the PR companies that cause the most problems of all agencies involved in sponsorship projects. I am not really sure why this is so, but certainly few of those I have dealt with have proved to be efficient or knowledgeable in the exploitation of the PR opportunities that exist within special events. My experience of the general level of media relations performance by many PR agencies has also, I'm afraid, proved to be less than outstanding. Far too many see media relations as the simple business of churning out uninteresting press releases to the largest number of media possible.

When considering how to handle the public relations side of your sponsorship you have the choice of using the services of your sponsorship agency, using any existing in-house facility you have, employing a PR agency, or bringing in specialists to work on the team for the duration of the project. I would recommend that you investigate all opportunities since the public relations exploitation of sponsorship is always essential and can often provide the major benefits of the sponsorship.

Once the outline plan of the sponsorship campaign is in place, i.e. whom or what you are going to sponsor and when, draw up a simple brief to give to potential agencies or specialists. What you are looking for are ideas; preferably some new and fresh ones, that can be used to reinforce your message to the target groups and the media. Your promotional activities have to attract attention and they have to be relevant to the activity you sponsor and the audience. Take a long hard look at the experience those on your short-list have of working on sponsored events, especially those in the same activity as yours, check on their references and, if possible, talk to a few specialist journalists to see which agency they take notice of.

In the end allow yourself to be sold on ideas, knowledge of the event and activity and enthusiasm for the project. If an individual publicist seems to have a track-record and better ideas than your large agency, hire him or her for the duration of the project. You can always provide the support facilities needed at a fraction of the cost of paying an agency; what you need is a skill that is quite hard to find.

For other services like the provision of design skills, hospitality planning, research and television production you can find agencies that specialize in each particular area. If you use the same approach to selecting your supplier as was recommended earlier, you should have no problem in selecting a service that will be useful for many future projects. Perhaps the most specialist area of all is the provision of video, film and television services. This is a relatively young area since it is only recently that companies have begun to realize the opportunities offered by the changing face of international television.

As I described in Chapter 11, there are now many ways of achieving television airtime for your sponsorship activities provided you have planned this exposure well in advance. The best way, by far, is to try to keep control of the television rights to the event, or if this is not possible, to create some new opportunities that can create exposure for your sponsorship. Even if a national broadcaster has the rights to live or recorded coverage of an event, it is often possible to gain the rights to documentary or magazine coverage for use outside the area covered by the broadcaster, or you may be able to negotiate a co-production deal that gives you use of the programming in key markets.

Even if feature coverage is barred to you, news coverage may not be, and you may be able to achieve coverage within news bulletins by producing VNR coverage as described in Chapter 11. There are far more opportunities than are generally realized but the only way you can exploit these is to produce your own coverage. There are a few agencies which are experienced in providing television services designed for sponsors and some can provide the added advantage by being able to produce and distribute material on an international basis. If you are serious about exploiting your sponsorship to the full please remember to investigate thoroughly the opportunities for television coverage.

This chapter brings to an end the material devoted to the sponsor's side of the business equation. The last section of the book concentrates on the problems facing the seeker of sponsorship and I hope that actual or potential sponsors will also dip into these areas so that they can discover that not all of the problems with sponsorship lie on the sponsor's side of the equation.

Part Four

How to find a sponsor

14

Know what you are selling

Finding a potential sponsor and then selling your project is one of the most difficult marketing jobs imaginable and can be the cause of tremendous frustration. First of all, it is definitely a buyer's market! The number of individuals and organizations all trying to do the same thing as you is huge. They're all after a share of a finite sponsorship cake and they are all approaching much the same companies as you will be doing.

Seekers of sponsorship come in many different forms. First are the professional agencies, agents and managers who make regular presentations to many companies, who get to know the types of projects different companies are interested in, and are known to the people to whom they are selling. Then come the sports, arts, charities or other organizations who control activities, to a greater or lesser degree, and who run events. Some of these organizations are extremely professional and experienced at marketing their activity or events. They will be used to dealing with sponsors and probably have a number with whom they regularly work and can approach with new projects. Many of this type of organization don't need to use agencies to sell for them since they have their own in-house department devoted to sponsorship marketing.

Other organizations are inexperienced in this area, may just be starting to exploit the sponsorship opportunities of their activity, and have little experience in the use of marketing skills. Finally come the individuals or small groups of enthusiasts trying to raise money for some particular project or event they wish to undertake.

Such individuals come from all walks of life, are keen to do something for which they need to raise money, and turn to sponsorship as the seemingly natural source of funds. This group rarely have any great understanding of the commercial nature of sponsorship or a sponsor's typical requirements and probably have few skills to help them market their proposal.

Whichever group you fall into I would suggest that you do not read the remaining chapters without reading the first part of the book. If you are to stand the best chance possible of obtaining sponsorship you should try to understand the complete equation; learn why sponsors put money into lifestyle marketing, what they expect to gain and how they will typically involve themselves in the exploitation of the opportunities. If you spend some time doing this you will be able to approach the potential sponsor from his point of view and should save much time and energy that can otherwise be wasted in the search for that elusive sponsor.

What's for sale?

Of course, you understand what you're trying to sell, don't you? The fact is that many people who approach possible sponsors know, roughly, what they want money for but have not put sufficient thought into the reasons why the sponsor might find the proposition worthy of investment. Indeed, many are surprised to be asked for a detailed financial breakdown and then find it difficult to produce the figures and to justify them in the light of hard commercial questioning.

The key fact is that unless you know your planned project inside out, and then understand its potential benefits from a sponsor's commercial viewpoint, you are unlikely to be able to sell the idea to a hard-nosed marketing director.

Although sponsorship is the fastest growing communications medium and is becoming more respectable and understood by the day, it is certain that the number of individuals and projects requiring sponsorship is far greater than the number of companies prepared or able to consider the use of the medium in their com-

INTEREST IN FOOTBALL %

Which age groups have the
most interest in football.

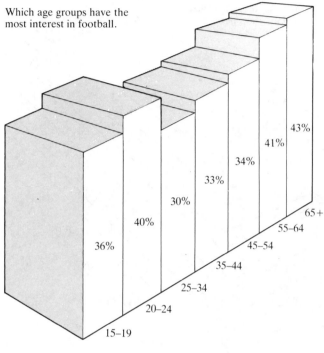

43%

41%

34%

33%

30%

40%

36%

65+

55–64

45–54

35–44

25–34

20–24

15–19

14.1a

Ages base – 1457 SOURCE: BMRB/MINTEL

Figure 14.1a, b, c, d Research such as this compiled by the English Football
League helps sell a sport to sponsors.

munications mix. This means that the individual or organization
seeking sponsorship has to face tough competition and must be
prepared for a long, and sometimes dispiriting, marketing
exercise.

In order to achieve success in this competitive marketplace a
sponsorship proposal must be actively marketed rather than
treated as a fund-raising exercise. And to be able to market your
proposal you must first understand your product, know it inside
out, to the point where you can detach your personal enthusiasm
for 'your baby' and still argue logically for its commercial value
while accepting any associated risks. The person or organization

1986 ATTENDANCE %

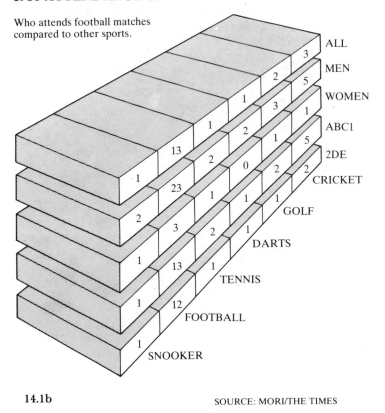

Who attends football matches
compared to other sports.

14.1b   SOURCE: MORI/THE TIMES

that hopes to sell a proposal based only on pure enthusiasm, hype
and perceived values, such as 'patriotism', 'adventure', 'personality-
building', etc., should concentrate on patronage and stay out of the
sponsorship business. Ninety-five per cent of such proposals fail;
they waste an enormous amount of executive time and simply add
to the confusion about sponsorship that is still all too
prevalent.

Don't assume from this that if your project has the ability to
excite people's emotions, smacks of nationalism, involves young
people and is extremely exciting for all involved, that you haven't

PAYING SPECTATORS %

Who attends football matches analysed by sex and
socio-economic groups. %

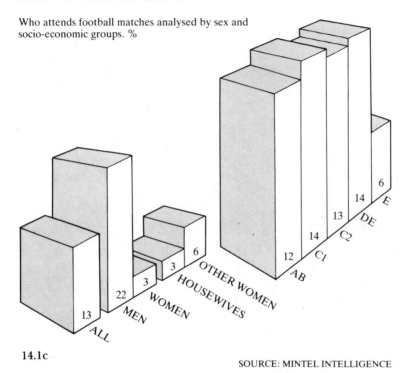

14.1c

SOURCE: MINTEL INTELLIGENCE

got a chance of success! Of course, you probably have a winning
project — but only if you can also sell it on the basis of what it can
do for the sponsor. If you can't you will find those desperately
needed funds heading the way of projects far less worthy but which
can demonstrate their commercial value.

It must be accepted, however, that sponsorship is not yet a
mature communications industry. Many managers and executives
do not fully appreciate the potential benefit of sponsorship or the
techniques for ensuring success and you will find that even the best
prepared proposal or the most professional pitch will not be sufficient to break down the prejudice or lack of understanding.

This lack of understanding is also responsible for the opposite

SPORT WATCHED ON TV %

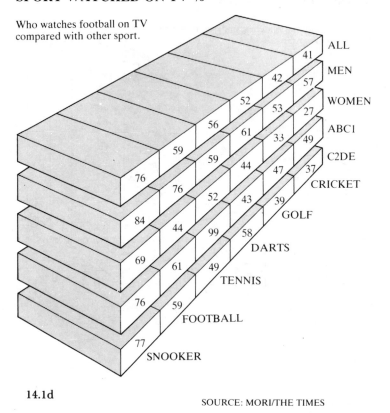

Who watches football on TV compared with other sport.

14.1d

SOURCE: MORI/THE TIMES

effect. Sometimes the worst prepared and presented proposals achieve success, usually because of a chief executive who buys the project for personal interest or charitable reasons rather than as part of a thought-through business strategy. Such executives often cause major problems for their staff who then have to implement the policy. As one sponsorship executive put it, 'We recommend projects based on marketing strategy and known aims. But it's not unusual for the CEO to take an interest in something — like underwater snooker perhaps — that is totally unsuitable from a company communications point of view, and then buy a proposal and tell us to make it work. When that happens we usually end up working out the reasons why it was right to buy the project in the first place!'

It's best not to rely on an executive's personal interest when preparing your project. It's great when it happens and it may tip the balance when a company is deciding between equally viable projects, but you should remember that only the best prepared, thought out and presented proposals stand a real chance of success.

But before you even get to putting together a marketing campaign for your sponsorship project, are you certain that sponsorship is what you're looking for?

Patronage or sponsorship

The key difference between the two is that a sponsor is, or should be, seeking a commercial return from his investment. The patron, on the other hand, does not usually require an overt return but may, unless the funds are provided anonymously, be keen to receive public approbation and image enhancement or to secure some other desired reward. Alternatively, the patron may just be in it for fun!

Patronage of the sports and arts has been, and remains, vital to the continuation and growth of both. Without the support of generous benefactors many fine works of art, sporting and adventurous achievements would not have been possible. But the situation today seems to be that patronage is less well regarded and not as highly valued as it should be for the good it does to our arts and sporting societies.

There is a strong case for rewarding patrons by allowing tax concessions on donations. Such encouragement costs the Inland Revenue very little and helps ensure a steady flow of patronage. Certainly, it is cheaper than using public funds to support artists and athletes who, if they have not a sufficiently high profile to attract commercial sponsorship, have few other opportunities for raising funds.

To the individual searching for funds the idea of finding a patron often appears faintly absurd. With connotations of the wealthy patron supporting a starving artist in a garret, the patron has become almost a mythical beast. After all, do you know anyone who has ever met one?

But there are patrons to be found and, in many cases, they offer at least as good an opportunity as commercial sponsorship. If your project could be described as 'worthwhile' or if you have a particular talent that cannot be nurtured without help, you may well find that others are prepared to give support. The methods of marketing yourself to a patron differ very little from targeting and approaching potential sponsors and are covered in the next chapter but the preparation to be done before any pitch remains exactly the same. Patronage or sponsorship, you must market your product.

Before leaving the subject of patronage you should be aware of the situation that sometimes occurs when a company sponsors a project for reasons that appear to be commercial but which, in reality, are pure patronage or a combination of the two. The chief executive who has the funds, and the power, within his company to provide 'sponsorship' because he likes you, the project or the idea of being a sponsor is really a patron for whom the act of helping and being involved is far more important than using the project to achieve commercial returns for his company. He will probably enjoy being personally involved and will generally act like a patron and should be treated as such.

Other sources of funds

Before deciding that sponsorship is the complete answer to your needs you should consider what other options are open to you for raising the necessary funds. If you are an individual sponsorship seeker try to raise as much money as possible from other sources so that you don't need to ask a sponsor to bear the full costs of your project — you are more likely to receive a favourable response if the sponsor recognizes that you are spending your own money as well as wanting to spend his! This is often a test of commitment that companies who take the risk of sponsoring individuals want to see.

Talk to your bank manager and check out loan arrangements, perhaps conditional on support being found. Involve as many friends as possible in what you want to do; organize local fund-raising events, talk to representatives of your town or city council — others before you have received support in this way — check out charitable funds for the activity you are involved in and keep an eye on the papers for any local patrons who appear to be active. Starting by involving your local community is often the best way to begin a fund-raising campaign. A surprising amount of support can often be raised in this way and if you can raise the level of local awareness enough to interest the media you will find this support can rapidly snowball. Once you are featured in the local media you have the chance of building on this interest and, if your campaign goes well, finding your story picked up by the national press. Publicity gained at an early stage of a fund-raising campaign is extremely valuable since it will help impress and attract sponsors and may also arouse the interest of a suitable patron.

If yours is an organization running an event or activity it is even more important that you find other sources of funds and reduce your reliance on sponsorship to a minimum. Sponsors are invariably more ready to become involved with an organization, especially one that is relatively new to sponsorship or is comparatively unknown, if they can see that the activity is taking a sensible approach to marketing itself and using all its sources of funds effectively.

Do you, for instance, make as much money as you could from ticket sales and the sale of merchandising to the fans of your activity? Many non-spectator sports, like my own sport of yachting for instance, assume that since their events do not attract on-site spectators that there is no way of making money out of an audience of fans. This idea may be, and probably is, wrong. Even with such sports there are often ways of attracting a direct audience and of selling to them. And even more importantly than on-site fans, these types of activities often have a large pool of participant and non-participant fans who can be sold to through specialist magazines and direct mail. If you feel unable to evaluate clearly the marketing opportunities surrounding your event or activity, employ a professional consultant to do the job; don't just sit back and assume that sponsorship is the only way to go.

Check the pros and cons

If you are looking for sponsorship, patronage or funds from public sources it is essential that you know all your project's strengths and weaknesses and the benefits you can use to sell the idea to the various sources of funds.

If commercial sponsorship is what you are looking for then you must accept that sponsorship is a two-way process, dependent for its success on the close workings and mutual understanding of partners who are unlikely to have common aims or requirements.

For the sponsor-seeker, the object is, of course, to raise the necessary budget to allow a particular project to succeed. What must be realized is that asking for sponsorship implies a readiness to support and work with your sponsor to help ensure that his commercial requirements are also met. This is time-consuming, often frustrating, and invariably requires careful forward planning to define the sponsorship objectives. You must be aware of the level these commitments could reach before you promise to deliver them.

Before setting out to write a proposal you must identify the marketable assets that can be used to sell the deal. The best way to do this is to analyse your project in detail. I can already hear the response to this from readers who say that they know their projects inside out. But do you really? Only by knowing every facet of the project can you hope to identify the opportunities it offers for commercial exploitation. It is simply not enough to describe your plan in outline to possible sponsors and leave it to the recipient to identify why he should buy what you want to sell. Neither is it good practice to include masses of detail in your initial approaches to a random selection of potential sources. By doing the homework you will be able to distil the project down to its essentials and will also end up with a very fair idea of the type of sponsor you are looking for.

The first stage is to write down your plans in a simple and straightforward way. Whether you want to climb a new route up Everest, win a round-the-world yacht race, stage a new performance of *Richard III* or take an orchestra on tour, you should begin your listing of the assets of the project by describing it as fully as possible.

As important as the immediate plans is the background. Why do you want to climb Everest or stage *Richard III*? What need, and whose, does it fulfil? Who gets the benefit, a small group of hardy adventurers or a wider audience? If there is an audience for the project, either on site, or via television, newspapers or specialist magazines, what are the details? Knowing the background to your project is one of the most important parts of preparation for finding a sponsor. You can expect to be questioned closely on all aspects of your plans, and the more homework you do now, the easier you will find things when you have to give a presentation to interested parties.

Of primary importance to most sponsors will be the type and size of the expected audience for the project. Who can be made aware of the undertaking and the sponsor? And who can be influenced by the sponsorship? One of the most common reasons given by companies making use of sponsorship is to increase public awareness of the company or a product.

Another sponsorship reason associated with audience type and size is the need to reinforce or alter public perception of a company or brand. In this case it is the 'image' of the company or product that is being changed. In an extreme example a name that is perceived by the public as having a poor image can sometimes be upgraded by actively associating the name with something prestigious. A similar use of sponsorship is the positioning of a new product for a certain target market using a sponsorship vehicle that appeals to the type of people who may buy the product.

Yet another use introduces a company to an audience who may, in the future, be potential customers. A good example of this is the sponsorship, by the Royal Bank of Scotland, of youth sailing in Britain. Like the other banks, Royal Scotland had determined that they should influence young people before they became established customers. A youth-oriented scheme proves a good vehicle for such targeted image-building.

Any research you can do on the subject of audience interest in your project will be well rewarded. If the project involves sport find out how many people take part, or watch. Check the demographic profile of the audience. The demographic or social grade system is a way of classifying people according to occupation and social background with the assumption that such groupings behave in certain, predictable ways. Since the type of audience will be of importance to most sponsors it makes sense to get as much information on your project's potential audience as you can. It also helps when you end up talking to people from the sponsor's advertising agency. Agency people are often not too fond of sponsorship since some believe that it detracts from the budgets available to them, and you stand some chance of convincing them that you have done your homework if you talk in their language.

Tracking down such details will not be easy. In Britain try the Sports or Arts Councils, whichever is appropriate to your project, or similar bodies in other countries; national sporting authorities, local education authorities, the general media and specialist magazines. The latter are often the best source since magazines that would cover your project should have fairly detailed information on their readership in order to sell advertising space.

While you're working on the question of audience type and size don't forget their geographical spread. Is this project only of local or regional interest or does it have national potential? Or perhaps it can even be used internationally. Don't get too carried away about the international bit. Simply because you see the scheme as creating interest everywhere in the civilized world doesn't mean the sponsor will. Few companies can make use of such large-scale sponsorships and, even if they can, such projects don't always travel well.

Along with the question of the potential audience for the project is how they are to be reached. After all, it doesn't help at all if the potential audience is just what your sponsor is looking for but you can't find a way of getting the message across. With this question comes the thorny one of publicity. Will the project interest the media and, in so doing, be passed on to the target audience? The best solution to this problem is to have the support of the media before you approach a sponsor. This doesn't mean that you have to have signed a world-wide television deal before you start fund-raising but do talk your ideas over with journalists and editors from the major media and see if you can get any letters of intent out of them.

Take a hard look at other similar projects. What sort and how much publicity did they achieve and in which media? What are the parallels with your project? Analyse the publicity; what type of story 'hooks' did the journalists use? Are there similar 'hooks' in your project?

Some sponsor-seekers have had examples of previous publicity for their own or other projects analysed by a friendly advertising agency. The object here is to measure the value of the column inches, radio and TV time in terms of what an advertiser would have to spend to achieve the same result. Personally I am not convinced by these arguments and neither are many sponsors. For one thing, the messages being delivered by advertising and editorial coverage of a sponsorship are totally different and, for another, the statistics used in the analysis are usually of the 'black magic' variety! Rather than go to such lengths it is best to assemble honest, accurate data on the audience you expect to be interested in your project and leave it to the companies you approach to analyse those data with reference to their own requirements.

The worst thing you can do is to present figures for audience size or expected media coverage that are obviously unrealistic. The most common error here involves the expectation of television time. If one believed every sponsorship proposal that spoke of 'guaranteed' television coverage you would expect to see non-stop, prime-time coverage of all sorts of wonderful ventures! Do remember that you are dealing with professional marketing people who know how difficult it is to get television coverage. And often, surprisingly to most fund-raisers, it is not always the most important objective the marketing department has in mind. But if you appear with wild and ridiculous claims you are likely to be shown the door. If you've done your homework and been honest in your assessment of the benefits available from your project, you will give yourself the best chance possible of raising the funds you require.

When listing the benefits your event offers include all aspects that can help a sponsor achieve awareness and image benefits. These could include:

- *Sponsor's name exposure*   Event or team title, banners, signage, competitors' clothing, printed matter, tickets, free programme advertising. Use of full title in media coverage, product display areas, branded merchandising and give-aways.
- *Details of the audience*   Size, demographics, product purchase profiles, competitors, participants and fans, geographical spread, media coverage, specialist press audience, image of the event and the activity.
- *Publicity*   Activities organized to publicize the event and the sponsor before, during and after the event, expected media attendance, budget for promotions and advertising.
- *Other benefits*   Free ticket availability, special prices for staff, facilities for hospitality, availability of stars for special events, product sampling, dealer tie-ins, co-sponsorship benefits, etc.

If you are running an activity and have several events to sell to sponsors you are sure to find that some events are more attractive than others. Some, most notably youth projects, or others for the benefit of less newsworthy groups, are important to the continued good health of an activity yet are difficult to finance. One way of dealing with this is to package less attractive events with the easy to sell ones. Sponsors often understand this approach and accept that they can gain a stronger link with the activity and enhance their efforts by accepting this type of arrangement.

While you're doing all this homework the next things to be sure of are the logistic details of the enterprise you hope to be undertaking. This includes all the details of the project from the time you get the 'Go' decision from a sponsor. Naturally some aspects, notably the sponsor's supporting promotions and publicity activities, will depend on the sponsor's needs but for these purposes you should treat the project as independent from any sponsor. Imagine you have just received a cheque for the amount you need and work out the details of everything that needs doing, who will do them, what can go wrong and solutions to the problems. Much of this information will not be needed by a prospective sponsor but you never know what will be asked for and anyway, it's very good homework that guarantees you will be capable of answering any question that may be thrown at you.

The budget

The budget demands particularly careful thought. This is a major area that a sponsor will, or should, want to know about in detail. The budget should include a full breakdown of costs plus an expenditure timetable so that a potential sponsor can incorporate it into his own budget planning.

Having gone through the process of identifying all sources of revenue, and costs, you will be able to identify any shortfall that you need to fill through sponsorship funds. (Don't, by the way, assume, that if you have a surplus you should not look for sponsorship. There is nothing wrong about making a profit and a sponsor can be very useful to aid publicity for the event.) But rather than measure a shortfall then go out to look for this amount from a sponsor, try to work out what the sponsorship is worth, in commercial terms, to the sponsor. The problem with this approach, which if you think about it should be a sensible commercial one, is that unless you have considerable experience at costing projects you will be able to do little more than guess at a price. One way around it is to use an experienced agent, or you could cost out an advertising campaign aimed at your audience and compare it with that. Alternatively, you could leave it to the companies you approach to place a value on the event. Since this value will vary between companies depending on their objectives and the price they can afford to achieve them, it will be difficult for you to judge, so allowing companies to make the first offer can work to your advantage.

Having worked out a possible price for the total package as you have conceived it, put that in the back of your mind and avoid quoting a fixed price package to any sponsor. It is far better, as we shall see in the next chapter, to work out what your project can offer and to approach companies with the intention of matching their budget with tailor-made packages.

It is sensible to ask an accountant to help you with the event budget, especially the cashflow forecast. If the figures are professionally presented it will give corporate financial directors warm feelings about your project. The finance people are usually the hardest to convince since they generally hate spending money. Provide them with a budget that they can at least see has been thought out and could even be accurate and they will be more inclined to take you seriously.

If, for some reason, you have to approach a company with a fixed price package don't make the mistake of thinking that the project budget is all the sponsor will have to spend if he takes on your project. A potential sponsor will be interested in the total spend, which includes the costs of all the aspects, such as publicity, entertainment and innumerable small details that will be required to ensure the project achieves his commercial objectives. The relationship between the cost of the sponsorship and the total spend varies greatly depending on the project and the amount built into the sponsorship budget for such items as publicity, but usual ratios are between 1:1 and 1:3, fee to support expenditure.

It is not possible or necessary to present a total-spend budget since this will depend on the sponsor's objectives and the level of in-house support that can be assigned to the project, but it is sensible to demonstrate that you realize that the sponsor's costs will be higher than the figure you require and to show that you have thought through the ways in which commercial benefits can be gained from an involvement in your project.

In particular you should build in a healthy budget for publicizing the sponsorship. This can be obtained by asking a number of public relations and publicity consultancies to suggest solutions to your problem and to provide budgets for a publicity campaign. Armed with these you should get a good idea of what can be achieved at what cost.

Although you will build this figure into the overall budget don't be surprised if the sponsor immediately deducts it on the grounds that the company will handle it in-house or through their own agency. If this occurs welcome the suggestion (but see Chapter 16). It implies serious interest on the part of the company and, more importantly, reduces the size of the budget — an important psychological factor that will encourage a decision in your favour.

15

Selling the proposal

Now that you have been through your project in considerable detail you should be ready for the job of selling. In order to make sure take a long, hard look at yourself. Have you got the right attitude, ambition, drive and ability to succeed?

The right attitude is essential, without it you won't even get your foot in the door. If you have followed my advice and taken the time to analyse your project from the sponsor's point of view you will already have at least the beginning of the marketing approach you require, but this must stand out in your presentation and reflect the attitude sponsors want to see.

Take a look at top athletes who earn considerable incomes from endorsements and other forms of sponsorship. The successful ones not only put a lot of effort into marketing themselves, they are also aware of what a sponsor requires and work hard to provide it. While looking at those athletes who have made it, make a note of the different types of image they present. Everyone is different and some do not have what you would classify as a 'good' image, yet each has some audience which sponsors wish to reach and most have a 'public personality' that for one reason or another attracts publicity. Whether you wish to reach this level or not, the study can be quite revealing!

The vital ingredient, though, is that business people must feel comfortable with your attitude towards the deal and to them as partners. You must present yourself as being ready and willing to work to fulfil your commitments and as having an understanding of the commercial needs of the sponsor.

Whether you are seeking sponsorship as an individual or are part of an organization you still have to convince a sponsor to back you and not one of the hundred other applicants all searching for a share of sponsorship funds. If you are an individual you need a large helping of ambition, drive and ability coupled with unquenchable optimism and an ability to take knocks and bounce back. Some people are accused of being 'lucky' in their search for a sponsor. While there is no doubt that fate does sometimes take a hand in this business I am a firm believer in making your own luck. If you have spent the time to approach the business in a professional manner and have a worthwhile project don't complain about others' luck or knock competitors to sponsors; get back in the marketplace and keep searching.

One thing that is probably out of your hands, although there are some things you can do to influence it, is whether you have the 'media factor'. Some individuals are just more attractive to the media than others and this has not just to do with their status as stars or the newsworthiness of the projects they are involved in. Some people have the ability to provide the media with stories or one-line quotes without seemingly thinking about it. Show them a television camera and they just perform. The media will happily cover these people because they know they are almost guaranteed a good human interest story. The amazing emergence of Eddie 'The Eagle' Edwards at the Calgary Winter Olympics is a good example of an individual with not much else to offer a sponsor who was 'created' by the media, in this case on an international scale.

You either are, or are not, this sort of person; lessons in how to handle the media will help enormously, but unless you have TV charisma you can't create it. If you've got it, or think you have, then work hard at convincing television to cover your story. If you can get this sort of coverage you stand a much better chance of interesting a sponsor.

Organizations trying to raise sponsorship need somewhat different abilities but very much the same attitude. If you are heading an organization's attempt to raise sponsorship you have to demonstrate that the organization has, or is learning, the ability to market the activity or event. Once again, and I cannot emphasize this enough, you have to learn how to see your activity through the eyes of a sponsor and to keep your undoubted enthusiasm subordinated to commercial persuasion. As we have already seen, you should have in place a marketing campaign to create awareness and interest in your 'product' with its natural audience of fans and participants, and should have identified all the ways of achieving income apart from sponsorship.

Despite all my entreaties for you to think commercially and to approach the fund-raising in a commercial way, I would also advise you to make sure that you never relinquish control of the activity or event, whatever the immediate financial temptations. You have a duty to participants and fans to deliver the best possible event for them; that is the bottom line for many sports and arts organizations. If you fail to do this you will probably kill the major rationale for the existence of the event. Some sponsors — but thankfully very few — do try to take control of an event and to alter it to suit their commercial ends. This can start in a very mild way, but if it is not controlled can escalate to the extent that competitors and spectators take second place to the media or the sponsor's guests. When this happens you may find the sponsor withdrawing when he has achieved his objectives leaving you with the difficulty of marketing an event that has lost its own identity or reason for existence.

This does not mean that you should not be prepared to discuss changes; very often the sponsor or agencies will have ideas that can benefit the event. You may also be in the position where you have raised funds for a new event and the sponsor has become a shareholder in the rights in return for providing the funds. In such cases you must be ready to listen to all ideas and to accept that the sponsor is likely to be more experienced than you in the so important marketing skills. But keep fixed in your mind the overriding importance of the activity's participants, spectators and fans.

Agents

If you are an individual or organization inexperienced in the sponsorship business you should give serious consideration to retaining the services of an agent to advise you on your fund-raising activities. A good agent will be able to spot all the benefits and weak points of your proposal, will have a good idea of which companies to approach, and can cut out a lot of the timewasting activity that often accompanies dealing with potential sponsors. The first problem then, is to find a good agent.

If you have a choice you should try to find an agent who understands your activity and, preferably, has raised sponsorship for similar events before. In order to draw up a short-list of agents you should study the trade advertising in specialist magazines, ask the national authorities of your activity for their advice, ask other organizations who have seemingly had successful experiences, and listen for any word-of-mouth information on the subject. Selecting an agency from a short-list requires the same approach as that described for a sponsor in Chapter 13, and will not be repeated here, but you should be aware that you may find that an agent you would like to represent you actually refuses the offer! The largest agencies — some of which combine sponsorship-raising and the supply of services to the sponsor — will not be interested in small projects, especially those that require considerable work to get off the ground.

When interviewing your short-listed agencies there are several points that must be clarified before you can decide which is the best deal on offer. The usual fee arrangement is for the agency to be paid a commission on any money raised. This commission typically ranges between 10 and 30 per cent although figures of 50 per cent or even more are not, I'm afraid, unknown. Unless there are exceptional reasons why you should accept an outrageous commission you should try to limit it to 25 per cent and, if the sum required is very large, impose a sliding scale to prevent the agent earning quite unrealistic profits from your project. Although fee payments are usually based solely on success, some agents try to charge a fee regardless of whether or not they succeed. If you can negotiate a small fee and the agency has a good track record — which you should check very carefully — it may be worth taking this arrangement, but usually you will employ an agent on a commission-only basis. Make it plain whether the agent is to receive his commission for an introduction, when a contract is signed, or when money is actually paid. Failure to do this could lead to some painful arguments just when you should be celebrating securing a deal.

Coupled with the question of fee are those of exclusivity, the timescale for the search, costs of presentation material and out-of-pocket expenses, all of which must be covered in a contract. If you believe you have found an effective agent give him an exclusive contract for a specific period. Exclusivity will allow the agent to operate more effectively since sponsors will not be confused by several agents all presenting the same proposal. It should also make the agent more committed to the project and more likely to dedicate resources to the search rather than keeping the project on file and relying on chance to throw up a company for whom it is suited. You would be advised, however, to put a realistic time-limit on the period of exclusivity — realistic in the sense that you must allow sufficient time for the agent to do his job, at least to get some serious interest, but you should also allow yourself enough time to find another agent if the first fails.

Find out if the agency expects you to pay for all its presentation material or whether it is prepared to risk that against its commission; this may provide you with a bargaining counter and should also indicate the agency's confidence. The same applies to out-of-pocket expenses. If you are not prepared to meet them expect to have to pay a higher commission. There is a lot to be said for producing your own selling material while using the agent's experience. First, you won't have to worry about having to veto something the agent produces for lack of accuracy or quality for instance; you will own the material should you sack the agent; and you may be able to produce it more cheaply, especially if you can get the assistance of a local printer. Take the agent's advice, though, on the style and detail of the material. If the agent is experienced several will have been produced before and the competition will be known.

Decide early on if a particular type of sponsor is unacceptable. Some activities just cannot accept sponsorship from the tobacco or the alcohol industries and there may be other areas with which you do not want to be associated. Surprisingly perhaps, you should be wary of accepting sponsorship from the media. Although you may think that such an arrangement will guarantee your event publicity, the opposite can be the case. Sponsorship by a newspaper or television station is likely to result in their competitors avoiding covering the event whenever possible. (Since most media outlets consider that they are providing you with valuable publicity they are always reluctant to pay the 'commercial' price for the sponsorship and you will have difficulty in securing sizeable funds from this type of source. The media can, however, be useful sometimes if you are trying to secure a number of co-sponsors, when their guarantee of publicity plus the various competitions and free prize draws that can be arranged, help attract the other sponsors.) Make sure your agent understands any limitations such as these before the selling starts!

Draw up a contract with the agency of your choice but resist any attempts to sign up a longer-term deal that gives the agency any other rights to market your event. Now is not the time to make such arrangements. If the agent secures sponsorship, if the sponsor doesn't insist on using his own agencies to promote the event, and if you feel that a longer-term marketing agreement could benefit your activity, then you can consider this sort of deal. Doing it too early simply ties you to one approach which may prove not to be the most suitable for you. Earlier I warned about the danger of allowing a sponsor to take over your activity. The argument applies, with perhaps even more urgency, to allowing an agent or agency to do the same.

A contract with an agent should spell out clearly all the above arrangements and should also cover the level of authority you are giving your representative. Can the agent negotiate on your behalf or must you be present in discussions with potential sponsors? The agent will have personal views but now is the time to agree the way you wish the arrangement to work.

Once you have appointed an agent keep in touch. Keep feeding information on the project, media publicity, or any other factor as is becomes available, and try to have regular meetings to allow you to be informed about all developments.

While an agent can be very useful and helpful to newcomers to the game (provided you manage to avoid the sharks of the business!), far more deals are done directly between sponsors and recipients than through agents. This fact should give you heart to do the marketing yourself and the rest of this chapter aims to give you some hints on how to do so.

Preparation

Before you are ready to begin selling you need to do a bit of preparation and organize a marketing campaign. We shall deal with producing selling material later; now is the time to get the organization and support activities in place. The first thing you need is time, because the whole business takes plenty of time, and because companies tend to make their sponsorship plans well ahead, often in the autumn for the following year. If you have a very short deadline you restrict your chances of finding sponsorship enormously.

The next thing is to ensure you have ownership of all the rights you wish to sell. The last thing you need is for squabbles over rights ownership developing when you are negotiating with a sponsor or after he has signed the deal.

You also have to ensure that your own organization is equipped to handle the marketing campaign. An individual may have to work alone or rely on volunteers for help but an organization, especially one responsible for an activity like a national sporting authority, needs competent individuals to handle the marketing of the project. An organization should also look towards the long term by ensuring that it is properly geared towards handling sponsorship projects. This may involve having specialist staff to manage sponsorship and to handle publicity and public relations for the activity.

The first selling step is to identify the market. Having gone through your project in detail and looking at it from a sponsor's point of view you may have formed impressions of the type of sponsor you are looking for, or the area of business that is most likely to produce a sponsor. You should also read the trade press for information on who is buying what, the sort of projects that are selling well, what your competition is doing, and names of decision-makers within sponsoring companies.

The strongest lead you can get towards the type of sponsors who may be appropriate is from the nature of the audience for your event. If it is an up-market audience look for a company or product that markets to this sector. If the audience is only a regional one consider approaching local sponsors, or regional offices or dealers of larger companies. If the audience is truly international and the project large don't waste time by approaching any companies that cannot market to an international audience.

While you may well add to your database by looking through reference books like *The Times 1000* try to avoid using a scatter-gun approach to accumulating leads. It's not the quantity of contracts you are interested in, it's the quality of the leads. Also, don't assume that big is always best. The large companies always receive nearly every proposal going but they, like everyone else, have limited funds and very specific objectives. Such companies often don't even use sponsorship on a corporate basis, they often market specific brands that make their own sponsorship decisions, or are the parent company of several others who also make their own decisions.

Identifying brand managements to approach can be difficult but again the trade marketing, advertising, public relations and sponsorship periodicals can often provide the leads.

The proposal

Although you should, by now, have the content of your proposal finalized you still have to decide how to present it to best advantage. Proposals vary from a simple, typed letter through to full-colour printed brochures and promotional videos. The type to go for depends very much on the size and type of your own event — using a full-colour brochure to sell a £10 000 sponsorship would be as inapproprite as trying to sell an Olympic sponsorship with a photocopied circular — and the competition in the marketplace. Obtain as many proposals from other seekers of funds as possible and study their approaches.

If your event or activity has a design theme with a logo, colour scheme, etc., try to use these to aid your visual presentation. The more you can create an 'identity' for the event in the eyes of potential sponsors the more they are likely to perceive you as a serious possibility now or in the future.

The most common advice for approaching a sponsor is to present him with a single sheet of paper. This is based on the fact that all company managers and executives do not have the time to waste reading a lengthy letter and proposal. This is quite true but it also has to be borne in mind that it is very difficult to pack important selling points into a single typed page. Even if this is possible you are still likely to require a more comprehensive selling document, unless your project is very simple, containing important background information, audience studies, etc. You may also decide that your project can be best illustrated through a video presentation in support, or instead of, a printed brochure. So the chances are that you will want to prepare two or three stages of proposal; an initial single-page outline, a bound or printed proposal, and maybe a short video.

Prepare all the information you want to include in each stage and, unless you have experience and talent in these areas, consider using a specialist writer and designer to prepare the package. The finished product should then be of a standard that can impress company executives with your professionalism and help to provide the 'warm feelings' that are essential if negotiations are to proceed. If you choose to use a video presentation, or even one using slides, you should certainly get professional advice. There is nothing worse than being asked to sit through an amateur-produced video, often made by enthusiasts of the activity on a home video camera. If you cannot afford the cost of professional production do not consider using video as a selling tool.

You may find that you can reduce your costs of designing and printing a brochure by asking a local printer for full or partial sponsorship in return for a credit. If you can show that the people who will receive the brochure are potential customers, or if the printer is an enthusiast for your activity, or just feeling generous, you may save yourself a considerable amount.

The approach

There are more ways of approaching companies than simply telephoning or writing to them, if you are prepared to invest some funds to do so. You could consider advertising your activity and/or the project in marketing magazines. If yours is an activity that companies have not thought of sponsoring before some attention-getting advertising should at least help to make them aware of you before you contact them directly. You may also decide to advertise the specific project for which you need funds and may receive direct approaches from interested companies.

Using a public relations strategy is another approach that is especially applicable to activities that need to increase awareness among sponsors. You should try to interest the media in, first, the activity and then the event and your search for sponsorship. Have a presence at sponsorship exhibitions and those covering your activity and have hand-outs available that outline your aims. You could also arrange for hospitality facilities at one of your events to entertain potential sponsors, to inform them of your activity, and to give them a presentation of specific opportunities.

All the above activities will help publicize your activity and will raise your profile in the market but it takes time to achieve. You may sell your project in this manner but you should also expect to make many direct approaches before you achieve success.

The most important point about the direct approach is to identify the key decision-makers *before* you submit a proposal to a company. The worst sort of approach is to send a letter or proposal to the 'The Marketing Manager' or 'The Managing Director'. You must always know whom you are writing to or phoning, what their title is and their area of responsibility. And before you contact a decision-maker you should do as much homework as possible on the company and its use of sponsorship. This is even more important when you need to contact brand management within a parent company that may own hundreds of brands. It is no use then to contact the company's senior management, unless you expect a corporate sponsorship; you need to identify brand decision-makers.

The best way to do this is to make a list of potential sponsors then work your way through it, one by one, and telephone each to ask them what you wish to know. Receptionists are one source of information — they can sometimes tell you the name of the executive responsible for sponsorship — but the best approach I have found is to call the public relations officer or the press officer. Explain your problem and what you wish to do and most will give you all the help you need. In many cases the press officer will be close to a company's sponsorship activities and may be a person who, if you get that far, will be involved in discussions and the eventual promoting of the project. If you can interest him or her in your project you may be recruiting a useful ally as well as a good source of information.

When telephoning for information there is no need to be defensive. You are offering the company a commercial opportunity and are seeking to discover the best way of doing so. Sometimes, however, you will run into suspicious staff who refuse to talk to you. If this happens try asking for the managing director or chairman's secretary or assistant. Say who you are, that you are trying to identify the correct executive to approach and you are more than likely to be given the information you need.

Keep all the information you obtain in a card index or computer database so that you build up a picture of the companies you are interested in. Every time you receive more information add it to the file immediately until you have sufficient knowledge to approach the company directly.

Once you have sufficient information to know who the main decision-makers are and whom you should first approach, you have to make the decision whether to telephone the executive or to make the first approach by letter. The advantage of phoning is that it is quick and will help you eliminate possibilities from your list since you are likely to receive several immediate refusals. A phone call will also confirm that you are talking to the right person, may provide you with useful background information on the company, and can result in a quick route to a meeting.

Making the first approach by phone is, however, difficult to do since you are calling 'cold' and because the executive may well be very defensive as soon as the question of sponsorship is raised. It can take a lot of fast talking to break down the barrier of suspicion and to demonstrate that you are not just another hopeful amateur in the sponsorship business and that you have something to offer this particular company. Unless you are a confident telephone seller you will find this method difficult. If, for some reason, it has to be done make sure that you list the important points you want to get across before you make the calls and that you are careful not to waste the target's time. Get straight to the point, try to give the impression that you have done your homework, that you are approaching this company because you believe you have something to offer, and that the purpose of this call is to ascertain interest and to arrange a meeting.

Unless you are a very good salesperson or have a very 'hot' property to offer the chances are that the target will ask you to send written details for consideration before you get to a meeting. This still leaves you in a better position than if you had sent the material without phoning first. You now know that there is some interest there, that you have identified the correct point of entry to the company, and that your package is likely to receive more attention when it arrives than if you had sent it without phoning first.

If you are not confident in your ability to sell on the telephone, or if you have a large list of targets, you will find it safer and easier to use a mailshot to distribute your sales package. As with phoning it is essential that you have identified the correct individual and you should ensure that every proposal you send out is personally addressed. The type and size of the package you send will depend on the type of project you are selling, how much information on the activity you need to supply to explain the proposal, and any information you have been able to obtain on how each company prefers to have proposals presented. If the full proposal and background information is quite extensive, more than three pages say, I recommend that you send only a personal letter and a single-page information sheet in the first mailshot.

The letter should be personal to the targeted executive, should explain why you are approaching that company (base this on possible marketing links with the project), and should explain who you are and the rights you have in the property on offer. The single-page information sheet must distil all the important, relevant information that a company needs in order to decide if there is enough potential to justify a meeting. This information includes:

- When and where the event is to be held
- Details of the event's on-site audience — size and demographics if known
- Details of the off-site audience — media coverage
- Details of the general audience for the activity
- Opportunities such as hospitality, signage, tickets, etc.

Keep the detailed proposal with all its background and supporting information for later, when you have received indications of interest. Waiting for replies can be a torment and whether you decide to follow up by phone or wait for replies is a difficult one. You may tell the recipient in your introductory letter that you will call him in a few days to arrange a meeting. This gives you a reason to call and prevents the problem of companies taking weeks to reply. It also means you get to hear 'no' more quickly and can concentrate on more likely prospects.

When you do get a promising reply you will be asked either to supply more details or to go for a meeting. In either case it is now that your detailed proposal and your promotional video (if you have one) can be used.

The meeting

When you are invited to a meeting with a potential sponsor increase your efforts to obtain marketing information on the company. Find out how experienced they are in the use of sponsorship, whether they have been involved in your activity before, who will have to take the final decision and what the hierarchy and in-house politics are within the marketing department. You should have approached a decision-maker with your first call or letter, but you may be passed down to more junior staff for a first meeting. Try to find out in advance whom you will be meeting, what their position and status are, and their known views on sponsorship in general and your activity in particular. It is surprising how much you can find out just by asking and explaining why you want to know. Don't be afraid to ask. If you can find out which organizations the company has sponsored before you could approach them for information on how good the company is to work with on sponsored projects. But don't base assumptions on criticisms that may be caused by jealousies or other personality conflicts. These sometimes arise in sponsorship and can generate a great deal of bad feeling.

Prepare yourself very thoroughly for the meeting. Decide how many people you will take with you — don't take any more than you really need — who will be the spokesperson and what the others will say. Have someone play devil's advocate in a rehearsal meeting to try to predict the most awkward questions that may be asked and to plan your responses. If you want to use visual aids inform your contact at the company. Ask if it will be possible and convenient, and say exactly what you will require in the way of facilities. If you want to use a video make sure that the correct player is available for the presentation.

Once in the meeting there are certain priorities that you should try to achieve:

- Explain the basics of your project and your credentials
- Explain the possible marketing benefits you have identified
- Discover what the sponsorship objectives of the company are
- Try to marry these objectives with the benefits your project can offer.

Try not to go into a meeting with a fixed price for your proposal. Be honest with what you believe you can do for the company and about what you can't do. Show that you understand that much will depend on the amount of promotional support the company can commit to the project.

The more you define the package you want to sell before you meet the company the less chance you have of securing some support. If you go in with a £250 000 proposal when the company has only £50 000 to spend you have left yourself no room for manoeuvre. That £50 000 could be very useful to you if you can put together a package to suit the budget and the requirements. Also, many companies may be able to supply goods or services, not only for the event, but also ones that you can pass on to other sponsors as low-cost promotions or for cross-sponsorship activities. Maybe the company has an advertising budget they could use to help you publicize the event in return for a hospitality package, or perhaps they have hundreds of retail outlets that you can use to sell merchandising. The possibilities are endless as long as you do not put too many restrictions on what you want going in.

Don't, however, try to force your project to fit the company's objectives if it is obvious that there is no possible match. Instead, accept the situation gracefully, ask for advice on your presentation, and make arrangements to keep in touch if future projects occur that could suit the company. Always try to stay on good terms with companies even when they reject you. Keep a file on all the knowledge you have accumulated because you never know when you may have a project you can sell to them, or when their objectives may change and they turn to you for help. In the long-term business of finding sponsors for an activity and keeping them involved with you there is no substitute for personal knowledge and contact with company executives. If you know someone to approach when you next have a project to sell the introduction procedure is avoided and you will have an easier time getting your foot in the door.

Sometimes, when you first approach a company you will end up meeting just one executive, one level below the decision-makers. When this happens you usually have only one chance at selling — you have to convince this one before you can get to the boss — and you also have the problem of getting involved with this executive's own career prospects and 'political' status within the company. If you've found a rising star who decides to champion your project the situation can be beneficial. The problem is, you never know when you go in unless you have a friendly source within the company. You have to find out as quickly as possible about the people you are dealing with — whether they are sympathetic to your proposal, whether they have the power to support it, and what political battles, if any, are being played out within the management structure.

Sponsorship runs into these sort of problems more than any other marketing medium because it is so diverse. A sponsorship project typically involves several people from different disciplines and departments in the decision-making process and so can become involved with internal rivalry. If this all sounds slightly machiavellian I'm afraid I have to agree, but I do know of more than one managing director or chairman of a sizeable company who has lost their position over sponsorship projects that went wrong and which provided ammunition for a corporate shake-up.

As a seller of sponsorship you need to be aware of these problems and to do your best to avoid them. Essentially, this means learning all you can about the people who will be involved in the decision-making and trying to get them all around a table together. Try to avoid having a series of meetings with individuals or small groups if the major decision-makers aren't present. You cannot afford to waste too much time on any one prospect because it is all too easy to find that two or three months have passed in meetings and re-written proposals only for the company to make the decision they could have made much earlier. It should go without saying that you must never relax your approaches to other companies until you have a written commitment from a sponsor. All too many deals fail to reach an agreement and you must get used to such disappointments.

It should also be obvious that you must be ready to tailor the deal to suit a particular company's objectives within the limits you have set yourself for making changes to your activity or event. The latter should have been decided before you sat down to a meeting but you should have plenty of scope to customize the package without altering your event significantly. The chances are that you will have found a company that is interested in your project, whose objectives overlap with the benefits you have identified but which are not a perfect match. This situation is the best you can hope for since the project was not designed, in the first place, to meet specific marketing requirements. What you have to do now is to identify ways that your project can provide the benefits the company requires. I'm afraid that I cannot give you any hard-and-fast rules as to how to do this since every situation will be different. If the company's staff are experienced in the use of sponsorship you will, however, find that they will probably provide the ideas you need. But, rather than rely on the company identifying the formula you should go away and look at your event and activity again in order to find a way to deliver the results the company is looking for. If you are prepared to work hard on the marketing benefits of your event you are more likely to succeed since only you know your event and activity well enough to identify all the opportunities.

If you are going to tailor the package to match the sponsor's objectives it is essential that you know exactly what the key objective is and the size of the budget the company is able to spend. Don't be afraid to ask for a budget — you can't design a package without it. If the sponsor's primary aim is to increase sales in a market you can reach concentrate on packaging a deal loaded with trade incentives that can be presented to dealers or retailers, franchises or wholesalers to secure co-op funds or in order to encourage them to sell more products. If awareness is the major goal look for ways to increase your audience reach, of gaining more publicity, or of securing a media co-sponsor or guaranteed, exclusive outlet.

One of the best ways to impress a potential sponsor is to carry out detailed research of your own, among the desired audience, and to design your package to cater for this audience. Do this and the sponsor will know that you understand the subject, are prepared to work for the objectives, and are ready to find ways to work within the framework of a limited budget. Finally, and most importantly, don't promise more than you can deliver. Always under-promise and then deliver more; that way the sponsor will be back for the next season.

Once a sponsor is ready to sign, you need to draw up a contract. This is as much for your protection as the company's and you should treat it in that way. Rather than let the company's lawyers draw up the first draft sit down with the responsible executive and agree the draft details together. The sort of things you will want to include in a contract have been covered in Chapter 9 but make sure that you include the name of the person from the company who will be the responsible decision-maker for all aspects of the deal and who will handle the day-to-day contacts.

If you are trying to get several sponsors involved, perhaps a title sponsor with subsidiary co-sponsors, try to bring them all together at the earliest opportunity and involve them as a group with the development of the project. Many organizers are nervous about bringing sponsors together and avoid it at all costs, but this route is fraught with dangers. Far better to get everybody to state their objectives in advance and to work together to satisfy them. Since the aims for each sponsor should be different there need be no conflict between them and there are many cross-sponsorship promotions that can be done when all parties cooperate.

16

Making it work

For those of you who are new to sponsorship this is the point at which the work really starts and when you begin to learn about the subject. Those of you who have done it before know that this point is also the one when you increase your duties. Before you signed a contract your duties were towards your event, its participants and fans. Now you have added the duty to your sponsors, to help satisfy their requirements.

Working with sponsors

If your relationship with your sponsors is to proceed smoothly you must continue to talk with them regularly throughout the sponsorship. This can best be achieved by having one person on your team responsible for day-to-day contact with the counterpart on the sponsor's team. If you have set up a project team to organize and run your event you should consider including the sponsor's representative in that group so that the sponsor is involved with all developments and has a forum for airing his point of view.

You will need to have a plan and timetable for each stage of the event together with a plan and timetable for all promotional activity that you and the sponsors expect to organize. Don't form your project plan and leave the sponsors to sort out their own promotional activities; link the two together whenever possible and work to identify new opportunities for promotion alongside your sponsor.

Make sure that you do not get carried away now that you have
found a sponsor. You still have to keep a tight control over your
budgets and especially your cash-flow. There is nothing worse than
over-spending and having to ask your sponsor for more money at a
late stage. Temper your enthusiasm with a strong dose of realism
and make sure that you deliver on every promise you make. This is
even more important in the early days of the sponsorship when
you should try to out-perform your sponsor's expectations in
order to dispel any last-minute doubts among the company's
executives or their advisors, some of whom may be ready
to criticize your activities if you provide them with the
opportunity.

It helps if you confirm all decisions taken at meetings with your
sponsor in writing immediately after the meeting while the facts
are still fresh in your mind, but, since there is no need to be too
formal in such communication, try to keep everything on a
friendly level.

Try to involve and inform your sponsors as much as possible. If
you see an opportunity for the sponsor's promotion suggest it to
them, don't wait for them to identify it themselves. Put all the key
decision-makers and managers involved in the sponsorship on
your mailing-list to receive all relevant information as it is
produced. Keep a media cuttings file even if the sponsor is paying
for a cuttings service — these often miss coverage in specialist
outlets — and send them copies regularly.

One thing that you must organize at an early stage is communication with the media. The approach depends on the size of
the event but you may wish to handle all media communications
concerning the event while letting the sponsors handle their own
media requirements. There should be, however, consultation
between you on everything you issue, to identify cross-publicity
opportunities and to ensure that the same messages are being presented. If yours is a relatively small event or you are new to event
promotions you should consider asking your sponsor to provide
press relations staff and to operate the press office. Have one of
your own people who knows the event and activity well work with

the PR team to ensure accuracy on event details and to learn the techniques for the future.

One thing that event organizers and the people who run activities often forget is to communicate with their own participants, fans and supporters. You may be feeling very satisfied with having found a sponsor for your activity and receive a nasty shock when you find that your delight is not shared by all those you are supposed to represent. This is of serious concern since your first duty is to the activity, the event, its participants and spectators. The problem arises when the activity's decision-makers seemingly become divorced from grass-roots opinion and are seen to be treading a path of questionable value. If you are to avoid these problems you should create lines of communication to the participants through which you can inform them of your plans and the benefits the sponsorship will bring to the wider activity. By getting participants on your sponsor's side you can add immense value to the event.

I have been to too many events where many of the participants actively disliked or criticized the event sponsorship for irrelevancy to the activity, lack of understanding of the event, and many other justifiable or unjustifiable complaints. This attitude shows itself in an unwillingness by competitors to support the sponsor, sometimes leading to outright rebellion to wear a sponsor's identification or appear at press conferences.

If, on the other hand, you can get competitors on the side of the sponsor you add tremendously to the number of people working in the company's interests. Find ways to involve competitors in the sponsor's promotions, at hospitality events, in photo-calls with the sponsor's staff and guests, in pro-am competitions around the event — there are many ways that the stars of your activity can be involved to great affect.

In the run-up to the event continue to develop all the promotional packages you can dream up. If you have run the same event before with other sponsors you should have saved previous event manuals that detailed all the promotional activities undertaken. Hand these over to your sponsor to provide ideas for promotions that he may wish to run. For every sponsored event you organize make up an event manual that includes the details of the organization and results of every promotion organized around the event. Such records will prove extremely valuable in future, both for selling projects to sponsors and in helping them support their sponsorship to the best effect.

Once the event begins make sure that the sponsor's key decision-makers and guests are made to feel involved as much as possible. This does not necessarily mean giving them the best seats in the house. It often means allowing them access to areas where normal spectators are not allowed, getting them involved in the real action, close to the stars and behind the scenes. Provide VIP tickets for the sponsor to use as incentives for his staff or trade clients. These do not all have to be given away; consider providing a number of free tickets plus a heavily discounted price on the face value of the tickets that the company can pass on to its staff.

On the day you must ensure that the practical organization and presentation is to a very high standard as this will leave an indelible impression on the sponsor, especially if a visiting VIP from head office comes to check out a company sponsorship. Make sure that all the sponsor's banners and signs are in place and look neat. Assign some volunteer helpers to stay by signs to ensure they are not stolen or defaced. Put the sponsor's signs, stickers or other identification in all the places that the company's management are likely to go and make sure that any ticket collectors or security staff know how to recognize the sponsor's representatives and how to give them a VIP reception. If travel to the event is likely to be difficult or parking could take hours, consider making alternative travel arrangements for the sponsor's party. Many uninformed competitors object to this sort of treatment for a sponsor but it is essential. Such criticism usually arises because you have failed to get the competitors on your side, but competitors who are used to being treated as stars may also get upset at this seeming upstaging of their status whatever explanations you give!

Make sure that you document every area of the sponsor's involvement so that at the end of the event you can present a folder containing each promotional activity undertaken, the ways in which the sponsor's name was presented to the audience, and the media results obtained. Present this to the sponsor as soon as possible after the end of the event to demonstrate that you have continued to involve yourself in ensuring the maximum benefits obtainable for your sponsor.

Achieving publicity

The primary objective for many sponsors is an increase in awareness and for this the media coverage of the event *and the sponsorship* is often of crucial importance. Achieving this publicity is one of the hardest of tasks for a new event or one that has not previously received much coverage. The importance of this objective should be known by the time you have signed a deal with your sponsors and you should have discussed who is going to be responsible for running the press relations side of the sponsorship. If you are new to the game it will be a great help if the sponsor takes on this task and sets up the facilities you require.

You must, however, ensure that the people responsible understand your activity and the specialist media who are the cornerstone for the event. It is very easy for press officers who do not have sufficient knowledge or interest in the activity to upset specialist journalists and it is your responsibility to ensure that this does not happen. If you have your own press facilities you must make sure that it works to publicize the sponsor's involvement as well as the event. Work with the sponsor to incorporate the sponsor's name in all material that you send out and remember to include the sponsor's own trade press and other possible outlets in your distribution list.

The advice in Chapter 11 on how to achieve publicity is as applicable to event organizers as to sponsors; but in particular you will wish to develop strong links with as many media outlets as you can, starting with the specialist press that covers your activity. Don't ignore the possibility of involving a media sponsor in the event if that can guarantee exposure to an audience that is important to the event sponsor. Work hard at creating publicity for not only will that help your sponsor it will also help the long-term interests of the event and the activity, not to mention your chances of ensuring future sponsorship contracts. Use whatever facilities and expertise the sponsor can provide to improve your approach and the publicity you receive.

Working with agencies

At some point you are likely to have to work with agencies, either those that you employ to handle the marketing, merchandising or publicity of your event, or the agencies working for the sponsor in the same fields. Your approach to these agencies can make an enormous difference to the success of the event. Many of the points made in Chapter 10 concerning working with an agency apply as much to event organizers or governing bodies of activities as it does to sponsors. If you are appointing your own agencies to handle any aspects of your event you will want to go through the selection procedure suggested in that chapter. In particular you should ensure that the agency has some understanding of your activity, that they are in sympathy with it and your aims for the event. If possible you should ensure that the executive responsible for your account is someone who has the necessary knowledge and experience and is someone you can work with.

Most of the problems you are likely to encounter stem from working with agencies employed by the sponsor and nowhere is this more common than in relationships with the sponsor's public relations consultancy or publicists. It is not unusual for a company to hand the public relations exploitation of an event over to its normal agency without considering the special requirements of sponsored events. In such situations you must keep a direct line of communication open with the sponsor. If you have a problem talk directly to your liaison at the company. Don't hide the problem in the hope that it will go away, it often gets worse and more difficult to solve. Explain the problems you are having and the difficulties it causes the event, suggest possible solutions and involve your sponsor in the solution. Don't allow yourself to be intimidated by agencies who hold big accounts with the client. To them your event may just be a tiny part of the business they do for the client. To you it is your total relationship with the company and you cannot afford to let an agency compromise it for you.

As the sponsorship develops you will come across many opportunities for providing the sponsor with benefits. You should pass these opportunities directly to the company and not through an agency. If you don't you may find that the idea or opportunity never reaches the client, or if it does the agency claims the credit. Talk directly to your sponsor; if the information is passed back to an agency for consideration or action so be it, the sponsor will still know where it originated.

Renewing contracts

As the end of the sponsorship approaches you must consider the options open to you for renewing the contract. If all has gone well for the sponsor and yourself with this event you have a good chance of renewing the sponsorship for the next event or for an expanded involvement. Wherever possible try to conduct your own research into whether you have achieved the sponsor's objectives. Compile as much supporting information as you can for presentation at the end of the sponsorship and make your plans for future events in enough time to be able to offer firm proposals for future activities.

The contract you signed at the beginning of the deal should have spelled out the timespan of the deal and any arrangements for renewing or cancelling future involvement. Try to start discussions about future projects well before the due date in order to give the sponsor time to absorb the opportunities and to conduct research into the present event but don't allow the sponsor to create a delay that could jeopardize your finding another sponsor if necessary.

If your sponsor is keen to renew for future events don't take this as a cue to increase the price of your package unreasonably. Although your price should reflect the value of the product it should also reflect the added value that an existing sponsor has brought to your event by his own publicity and promotional activities. If you choose to price a founding sponsor out of the market he has helped create you can expect a very angry sponsor and, quite possibly, some adverse publicity and a reluctance on the part of other companies to get involved with you.

As we said at the beginning of this book, sponsorship has to be a business relationship between the sponsor and recipient. At times this relationship will be very complicated, will involve countless agents and agencies but still the prime responsibilities are yours, as the recipient, and your sponsor's. The relationship is often a complicated one if you and your colleagues have little experience of the world of marketing and your sponsor has little experience with your activity. The only way through this potential minefield is by ensuring that you both start the relationship with objectives clearly stated. Since both parties will have very different objectives the strategy for success involves marrying these varying requirements together in a way that allows both to be satisfied. This can only be done with constant communication between the parties and a total commitment to the other's needs. There is no such thing as a successful sponsorship deal in which only one party walks away satisfied. You must accept that once you have taken the step towards sponsorship you have made a commitment to adding your sponsor's needs to the list of objectives for your event.

Sometimes this can become an onerous responsibility if you did not know what you were letting yourself in for, but if you have done your homework and planned carefully it can also be fun. Not only will sponsorship provide you with extra resources to help you run and develop your event or activity but you will also have the opportunity to learn about marketing, publicity and promotions, some of which can be applied to marketing your own activity.

Once you have become involved in raising sponsorship please remember that you have a responsibility to the people who will come after you. If your activities bring sponsorship into disrepute within your particular activity it may take some time to repair the damage. Never be tempted to put short-term sponsorship benefits ahead of the long-term strength of your activity, don't over-promise results in order to snare a sponsor, and build your approach to the subject on the basis of understanding and fulfilling a sponsor's objectives.

Bibliography

Sponsorship of sport, arts and leisure

Law, Tax and Business Relationships
Stephen Townley and Edward Grayson,
Sweet and Maxwell

The Economic Impact and Importance of Sport in the UK
The Sports Council
Prepared by The Henley Centre for Forecasting

Committee of Enquiry into Sports Sponsorship
The Howell Report
The Central Council of Physical Recreation

Sponsorship
Longman Intelligence Report
By Nick Tate of Deloitte Haskins & Sells

Sponsorship and Sport
A guide to the ins and outs of sports sponsorship
The Scottish Sports Council in association with The Scottish
Sports Association

Private Funding of the Arts
News Report from the Council of Europe
No. 5-6/87

Arts Council Reading Guide
A reading list on business sponsorship based on material held in
the Library of the Arts Council of Great Britain.

Banking on Leisure Transcripts and *Special Events Directory*
Both published by
International Events Group
213 West Institute Place
Suite 303
Chicago
IL 60610
USA

What They Don't Teach You At Harvard Business School
Mark H. McCormack
Fontana/Collins

Ogilvy on Advertising
David Ogilvy
Pan Books

In Search of Excellence
Thomas J. Peters and Robert H. Waterman Jr
Harper & Row

Periodicals

Special Events Report
The International Newsletter of Event Sponsorship
published biweekly by International Events Group
213 West Institute Place
Suite 303
Chicago
IL 60610
USA

Sponsorship News
published monthly by Charterhouse Business Publications
PO Box 66
Wokingham
Berkshire
RG11 4RO
England

Sports inc.
The Sports Business Weekly
3 Park Avenue
New York
NY 10016
USA

Sports Marketing News
published biweekly by Technical Marketing Corporation
1460 Post Road East
Westport
CT 06880
USA

Index